W9-BVX-680

THE COMPLETE GUIDE
TO BUYING AND SELLING
A BUSINESS

Small Business Management Series
Rick Stephan Hayes, Editor

Simplified Accounting for Non-Accountants
   by Rick Stephan Hayes and C. Richard Baker

Accounting for Small Manufacturers
   by C. Richard Baker and Rick Stephan Hayes

Simplified Accounting for Engineering and Technical Consultants
   by Rick Stephan Hayes and C. Richard Baker

Simplified Accounting for the Computer Industry
   by Rick Stephan Hayes and C. Richard Baker

The Complete Legal Guide for Your Small Business
   by Paul Adams

Running Your Own Show: Mastering Basics of Small Business
   by Richard T. Curtin

Up Front Financing
   by A. David Silver

*How to Finance Your Small Business with Government Money:
SBA Loans, Second Edition*
   by Rick Stephan Hayes and John Cotton Howell

The Entrepreneurial Life: How To Go For It and Get It
   by A. David Silver

The Complete Guide to Buying and Selling a Business
   by Arnold S. Goldstein

THE COMPLETE GUIDE TO BUYING AND SELLING A BUSINESS

Arnold S. Goldstein

A Ronald Press Publication

JOHN WILEY & SONS

New York   Chichester   Brisbane   Toronto   Singapore

Copyright © 1983 by Arnold S. Goldstein
Published by John Wiley & Sons, Inc.

All rights reserved. Published simultaneously in Canada.

Reproduction or translation of any part of this work
beyond that permitted by Section 107 or 108 of the
1976 United States Copyright Act without the permission
of the copyright owner is unlawful. Requests for
permission or further information should be addressed to
the Permissions Department, John Wiley & Sons, Inc.

This publication is designed to provide accurate and
authoritative information in regard to the subject
matter covered. It is sold with the understanding that
the publisher is not engaged in rendering legal, accounting,
or other professional service. If legal advice or other
expert assistance is required, the services of a competent
professional person should be sought. *From a Declaration
of Principles jointly adopted by a Committee of the
American Bar Association and a Committee of Publishers.*

Library of Congress Cataloging in Publication Data:

Goldstein, Arnold S.
    The complete guide to buying and selling a business.

    (Wiley series on small business management)
    "A Ronald Press publication."
    Includes index.
    1.Business enterprises, Sale of.   2.Business
enterprises—Purchasing.   I. Title,   II. Series.
HD1395.25.G64   1983   658.1′6   82-24769
ISBN 0-471-87091-9

Printed in the United States of America

10   9   8   7   6   5   4   3   2   1

To my wife Marlene,
with gratitude and affection
for her guidance
and encouragement

PREFACE

Imagine two poker players strolling into a gambling den, squaring off with a deck of cards between them and throwing all their wordly possessions on the table to be won or lost on one quick hand. Chancy business? You bet!

And what if I told you that neither of these gamblers had ever played poker before? Well, you'd say, that's not just chancy but downright crazy. Sure, it sounds crazy, but most people about to buy or sell a business are in just such a predicament.

If you are a prospective buyer, consider the stakes of your game. You're risking years of hard-earned savings, most of your personal assets, and your future earnings and life-style. Your "chips" are the sum of your financial past, present, and future.

If you're a prospective seller, your chips are your years of hard work, a sizable investment, and the chance to "cash out" for a leisurely retirement, a new career, or an even bigger business. And, like the two inexperienced poker players, you are probably an amateur.

Don't let that statement offend you. Buying or selling a business is one of those once-in-a-lifetime decisions that can shape your destiny. But if you're like most people, you're playing the game for the first time. And considering that 90% of all business buyers are entering the marketplace for the first time, it's little wonder that they are 'eaten up alive.'

The overwhelming majority of all businesses are "small." Unlike the large corporate conglomerates, the small-business buyer can't lean on the expertise of specialists. And the large corporations use entirely different concepts and priorities in seeking to expand their empires. That's why I've designed the book specifically for the small-business person.

With the help of this book you will avoid that disastrously expensive "on-the-job training." You will see the proven strategies to find, analyze, and negotiate any business. Sellers will find effective ways to sell their business quickly, and on the best terms. I define the dangers you should watch for and the techniques to overcome them. Everything from taking that all-important first step, to what to do once you have the keys is contained within these covers.

You may be a top-notch baker, chef, or merchandiser, but when it comes to landing the business in which you'll ply your skill, you take on another role—captain of the business acquisition team. Though your accountant can decipher the numbers, and your attorney can protect you from legal problems, the rest is up to you. After all, you're playing with your money and future.

As you go through this book you'll meet other people who have played the game before you. Some won, some lost, but each case will be useful in showing you the mistakes and successes of others. Although I've changed names to protect client confidentiality, I share with you their true experiences and techniques that can save or make money for you. Numerous checklists and forms will help you spot potentially troublesome spots and guide you in your step-by-step strategies.

When it comes time for you to pile your chips on the table and deal the cards, I want you to have all the know-how you'll need. The stakes may be high, but once the odds are on your side you'll find it's worth it. Owning your own business can be one of the most fulfilling and rewarding experiences of your life.

ARNOLD S. GOLDSTEIN

Chestnut Hill, Massachusetts
April 1983

≡ ACKNOWLEDGMENTS ≡

A book is seldom the work of one person. I am indebted to Barry Levine, my law associate for his candid critiques; to Helen Siegal for her faithful and always punctual clerical assistance; to H. Michael Snell, my literary mentor for his invaluable assistance on the manuscript and to my wife Marlene for her tireless production efforts. No author could have a better team.

Perhaps I am most indebted to my many clients who have ventured into their own business and in the process helped define the right way to make it happen.

A.S.G.

AUTHOR'S NOTE

Every case and example in this book is based on a true case history. However, the names of the individuals and organizations are fictional to preserve confidentiality and privacy. Therefore, any resemblance to actual persons or organizations is purely coincidental.

CONTENTS

1. WHAT IT TAKES   **1**

Some Dream—Some Do   1
The Financial Hurdle   4
The Security Hurdle   6
The Self-Confidence Hurdle   8
The Fear-of-Failure Hurdle   11
The Family Hurdle   13
Applying the Brakes   14
A Dose of Reality   15
Right Reasons—Wrong Reasons   16
When Will it Happen?   17
Test Your Commitment   18

2. MATCHING YOU TO THE RIGHT BUSINESS   **19**

Thousands of Wrong Choices   19
How the Matching Process Begins   20
Ask Five Essential Questions   23
What Can You Earn?   23
Measure Your Management Mentality   25
A Matter of Motivation   27
Can You Afford it?   30
But Will You Find it?   31
Should You Start From Scratch?   32

3. HUNTING YOUR PERFECT OPPORTUNITY   **35**

Develop an Experienced Eye   37
Digging for the Diamonds in the Coal   38

Cold Canvassing for Hot Leads   39
Suppliers Can Supply Leads   42
Turning a Broker Into a Bloodhound   43
Brokers From the Seller's Viewpoint   47
What Newspaper Ads Really Tell You   49
Ads That Pull Leads   51
Looking for a Franchise?   52
More Profitable, but Little-Known Sources   53
Don't Overlook Your Boss   54
Final Pointers   54
Key Points to Remember   55

4.   INVESTIGATE FOR ALL IT'S WORTH   **57**

Qualifying the Business   58
Put together Your Team   60
The Information You'll Need   62
Why You Check the Lease First   63
What the Income Statement Tells You   65
A Quick Look at the Balance Sheet   67
Analyzing the Product-Oriented Firm   69
A Ten Point Checklist   70
Checking Out the Competition   72
Five Pitfalls to Avoid   73
The One Best Way to Test a Business   74

5.   FRANCHISING: A UNIQUE GAME   **77**

How a Franchise Works   77
What Can a Franchise Offer You?   78
A Tale of Two Franchises   80
Selecting Your Franchise   81
The Quick Scan   82
Narrowing the Range   83
What the Franchisor Must Tell You   84
Who to Ask for What   86
Four More Sources to Check   89
Negotiating the Contract   89
Clauses You Want in the Contract   92
Franchises to Avoid   93
Divorce, Franchise Style   93
Your Ten Point Franchise Checklist   94

6.   PINPOINTING THE RIGHT PRICE   95

You Determine Value, but Negotiate Price   96
Four Costly Myths   97
Develop a New Perspective   100
Factors That Control Value   101
Navigating by the Numbers   104
Projecting Profits   104
Putting a Price Tag on Profits   108
Turning the Numbers Into Reality   110
Counting Those Bigger Dollars   112
What is Good Will Really Worth?   113
Five Questions You Must Answer   114

7.   FINDING THE MONEY   115

The Two Layers of Financing   115
The Advantages of Borrowing   116
Why Seller Financing is Your Best Bet   117
Pushing the Right Buttons   119
Turning Promises Into Payments   120
Before You Meet Your Banker   122
Knock on the Right Doors   124
Negotiate the Best Terms   125
Structuring Your Bank Loan   127
What to Do if the Bank Says "No"   128
The Real Story on SBA Loans   129
Do You Qualify for an SBA Loan?   130
Other Deals—Other Sources   132
Key Points to Remember   133

8.   COMING UP WITH YOUR DOWN PAYMENT   135

Who Needs Money?   136
Pyramiding the Seller Loan   137
Turning Liabilities Into an Asset   138
Sell Your Suppliers   140
The Helping Hand From Brokers   141
Tapping Inventory for Cash   142
Taking the Cash Out of Cash Flow   143
The Simultaneous Spin-Off   144
Do You Really Need a Partner?   145

The Paper Clip Net Worth Theory   147
It Makes Sense to sell for "Low Cash Down"   148
Building the Financial Pyramid   150
Key Points to Remember   151

9. NEGOTIATING YOUR BEST BUY   **153**

Put on Your Poker Face   154
Smokescreens: Every Seller's Ploy   155
The Bogey Offer   156
Setting Your Limits   157
Your First Offer   158
The Right Way to Propose Your Offer   159
How to Interpret the Counter-Offer   160
Applying the Three for One Rule   161
The Phantom Offer   161
Combatting the "I Changed My Mind" Seller   162
Handling the Hold-Out Seller   163
Bring in Your Team   163
Salvaging the Collapsed Negotiations   164
Be Prepared to Take a Walk   165
Beware the Stranger From Afar   166
How the Walk-Away Artist Works   167
Some Final Pointers   167

10. CLOSING THE SALE   **169**

Anatomy of an Acquisition   170
Contract Terms That Protect You   174
The Four Best Ways to Avoid Liability   182
Between Signing and Closing   183
Coping With Last-Minute Problems   184

11. UNDER NEW MANAGEMENT   **187**

Move Slowly—Very Slowly   187
What's in a Name? Plenty!   188
Experiment With Your Employees   189
Cultivate Your Suppliers Early   191
Credit: Do's and Don'ts   192
Lean and Mean   194

Customers: Who's More Important?   195
Looking Ahead   196

12. PROBLEM SOLVING   197

APPENDIX 1 LETTER OFFER   217

APPENDIX 2 AGREEMENT FOR SALE OF ASSETS   221

APPENDIX 3 STOCK SALE/REDEMPTION AGREEMENT   229

APPENDIX 4 FRANCHISE AGREEMENT   237

  GLOSSARY OF TERMS   257

INDEX   259

1

WHAT IT TAKES

SOME DREAM—SOME DO

If you visited my office, you'd see framed behind my desk an artist's self-portrait: an elderly man named Harold, a palette in one hand, a paintbrush in the other, an easel before him, and a smile on his face. Neither the artistry nor any deep personal relationship with the artist compelled me to buy the painting. It was his smile. It carried an important message, and I wanted that smile to be my continual warning that hopes can grow old.

As a patient in a nursing home, Harold spent his retirement painting. Since he occupied the room next to my grandfather, I came to know him well. One day he confided the reason for his ever-present smile. "You know," he said, "when I was a young art student just out of high school, I wanted to open an art gallery and do portrait painting. My father wanted me to become a dentist instead. Well, I spent six years getting through NYU Dental School, hating every minute of it and wishing I were painting. I wanted so much to devote my life to art rather than to cavities and pulling teeth. But life plays nasty tricks on people. First came the Depression. Drilling those damned teeth at least gave me a living. Then came the war. The Navy needed dentists, not artists. When I got back I had a wife and two kids to support. Their security came ahead of my dreams, so I resumed my dental practice. After all, my kids were on their own and I had money in the bank. My wife called it mid-life crisis. My friends questioned my sanity. My kids wanted to know why their dad would give up a lucrative dental practice to 'sell pictures'? To make them happy I let them talk me out of it. I spent the next twenty years dreaming of my art gallery while filling teeth. Well, now I'm 73 years old and finally doing what I want to do," he smiled. "Better late than never, I suppose." Harold sighed as a faraway look stole across his face.

Today, over 50 million Americans, people like Harold, harbor dreams of their own businesses. Real people, unhappy people, they remain chained to a desk or slave away at work they don't enjoy while their dreams and ambitions grow old.

Let's face facts. Some of you will never buy your own businesses because your dreams are nothing more than fantasies. You'll read this and countless other books; you'll think about it, plan for it, hope for it, even pray for it, but in the end you'll never do it. Nothing I can say will or should change that. After all, many people don't belong in business because they cannot bring to the business the commitment and enthusiasm it demands. They'll remain perennial dreamers.

On the other end of the spectrum, some of you will resolve your inner doubts and conflicts. You'll make up your mind to do it. Perhaps you've been in business before, or presently have a business and are looking to expand. Still others have the remarkable ability to glide into business with apparent ease and never seem to wonder whether or not it is the right decision.

But for most of us the idea of buying a business can be frightening. For most buyers it's a first time experience, a vast unknown. Your financial future and an entirely new life-style ride on the decision, and you face the realization that you're gambling everything on your own ability to succeed. And it's never an easy decision. With it come hopes, fears, desires, and self-doubts. You want the financial freedom, but worry yourself sick over the fear of failure. The challenge excites you, but you question your managerial ability. You want opportunity, but find yourself looking over your shoulder at the job security you're leaving behind. You have countless motives that compel you to seek your own business and a long list of reasons why perhaps you shouldn't. Victimized by your own psychological tug-of-war, you vacillate between two extremes—"I'm just dreaming" and "I'll do it"!

I know what it's like. I've been there. I recall my first entrepreneurial venture, a small retail drugstore that sparked my enthusiasm back in 1962. Why did I want it? I had the usual array of motives. Looking back, I confess it was part ego-trip. The old "hey, everyone, look I'm in my own business" syndrome. And who could overlook the $400 a day (big money then) piling up in the cash register? It seemed the perfect way to put me through law school. Thinking about it, planning for it, and visualizing myself standing beside the cash register in full entrepreneurial splendor drove me forward.

Then, as the lawyers were drafting the papers, the sleepless nights started. First came the reality that I'd be giving up my "soft" job. My weekly paycheck was almost an act of larceny. Did I really need my own business to put me through law school? The tug-of-war in my mind began.

The seller then informed me of 101 "little things" that needed immediate attention as soon as I took over. Nothing major: replacing two key employees about to leave, repairing an air conditioner on the blink, and a customer falling for a competitor's overtures headed the list. Could I handle it? Did I even want the headaches? My sleepless nights became full-fledged insomnia.

The *coup de grace*? It came when my attorney reminded me to draw a check of $10,000 to cover the down payment. Heck, that was my entire life's savings. Suddenly my insomnia turned into a nightmare.

The next day I called the seller and canceled the deal. Of course I used the lame excuse about that straying customer, and I probably believed it myself. But years later I forced myself to accept the real reason. I just wasn't ready for my own business. I didn't have sufficient commitment to buy. Unfortunately you never know whether you have that commitment until you're halfway there; the day you quit your job, fork over your life's savings, and accept the responsibility your own business entails.

I've bought 15 businesses since, some on my own and some with partners. However, I'm not ashamed to admit that I still have a churning stomach and some sleepless nights before I buy. It's never easy when you are gambling your money, future and security.

Whenever I conduct a business buyer's seminar, I tell my class about my first aborted business venture. Then I ask the class, "How about you?" "Are you ready to buy, or do you only *think* you want your own business?" I tried that question on my last group of 100 enthusiastic business buyers. With a flash of 100 raised hands they all assured me they were ready, willing, and able. No hesitation for them. Just offer them the right business and they'd jump for it. That was almost two years ago. Want to know what happened to my 100 bright-eyed business buyers? I circulated a questionnaire and discovered:

80—Never did buy. They never even looked for their own business.

10—Looked but never managed to find what they were looking for.

5—Did buy but still wonder whether they made the right decision as they languish somewhere between success and failure.

5—Are well-entrenched in a highly successful business and think it was the smartest move they ever made.

That's what this chapter is all about. You, too, may be like any one of the 90 prospective buyers who thought they wanted their own businesses but, for one reason or another, couldn't turn the dream into reality. I'm not going to give you any inspirational pep talk about the wonderful world of business. You know what a business can do for you. You also know about the hard work, headaches, and risks that come with it. Nevertheless, you think you want it. Indeed you should, for it can change your life for the better. But on the road between dreams and reality lie many hurdles that may stop you. Let's look at them.

THE FINANCIAL HURDLE

If you asked 100 would-be entrepreneurs why they're not already in business for themselves, 80 to 90 would quickly blame lack of money. It's the number one hurdle. It's also the least credible.

In fact, I always translate such a complaint into "I want it, but I don't want it badly enough to make it happen; or I have other reasons I won't admit to you or even to myself."

Later in this book we'll discuss practical financing, and I'll even show you how to buy a business with no capital of your own. But if you see money as an insurmountable hurdle, try answering these simple questions:

1.   How much capital do you *think* it will take to buy your business?
2.   How do you know? Have you tested the market?
3.   Could you raise the capital if you wanted to badly enough?
4.   If not, have you designed a program to save or raise the capital?

Let's carefully consider your answers.

The first question tests the reality of your perception. Most buyers overestimate capital needs. Inexperienced buyers may over-shoot the mark by 50% or more. Why? These buyers do not understand the many ways to finance a business that can reduce down payment requirements substantially. They tend to equate purchase price with needed capital. Knowledgeable buyers, of course, understand that they can acquire most businesses with as little as 10–20% down.

Recently we handled the purchase of a restaurant for a young man, Henry T., who confessed that he always wanted his own restaurant but was frustrated with the thought of scraping together $50,000–100,000 to buy it. I asked him how he arrived at that amount, and he said, "The kind of restaurant I want sells for $150,000–200,000, and I figure I'll need a 50% down payment in order to convince a bank to loan me the balance." Henry was able to find not one, but several good restaurants available between $150,000–200,000. His surprise came when we showed him how he could take his pick with less than a $15,000 down payment. Henry finally purchased a high-volume seafood restaurant grossing $470,000 annually for a purchase price of $185,000. Through a combination of loans and assumption of seller's liabilities, he got the keys in return for a $7,500 down payment. It was a far cry from what Henry thought he needed. What about you? How much money do you *think* you'll need?

The second question determines whether or not you have sufficient motivation. How else can you find out whether or not your perceptions (or misconceptions) are accurate unless you test the market? Failure to get out there and beat the bushes for a business indicates lack of commitment to buy.

Whenever a prospective buyer cites lack of capital at my business buyer's seminar I ask, "How many businesses have you looked at or tried to finance?" A pert young woman at my last seminar told me she wanted a clothing boutique, but didn't have the $15,000–20,000 to swing such an acquisition. "How many stores did you look at?" I asked. "Oh, I haven't looked at any," she confessed. Would you have answered the same? If so, bear one point in mind. Sellers aren't going to call you. You have to hustle out there, scout numerous businesses, and design ways to acquire one on your terms.

The third question implies trade-offs. What are you willing to sacrifice to get into business?

Recently our firm showed a gift shop to a young lady eager to get into that business. We put together a "creative financing" package, but the young lady still needed a $10,000 down payment, which she claimed she couldn't raise in a million years. However, when my associate looked out the window at the new Mercedes 450 SL sedan she'd parked in our lot, he asked if she had a mortgage on it. "No," she replied, "it's fully paid for." Voila! My young associate thought he could easily obtain a $10,000 car loan for her and use the proceeds to finance the gift shop. Backed into a corner she turned and fled. It wasn't really raising the money that held her back, she was just afraid to buy.

Many buyers own substantial personal assets they could tap for a down payment. You may not have lots of cash, but you probably have equity in a home, a cash value life insurance policy, stocks, bonds, or other investments you could convert into a down payment. Add up your net worth. Ask yourself the honest question—how much cash could you raise if you really had to?

The final question separates the "dreamers" from the "doers." Not having existing means to buy a business rarely stops a serious buyer who's willing to hustle, work two jobs, and scrimp and save to get it together.

For years a close friend has been telling me about the auto body shop he'd open if he could find the $10,000–15,000 it would take, but he stands no closer to buying it today than he did six years ago. Admittedly, he works hard all day as a machinist, but most nights he finds the strength to go bowling. If only he spent a few nights a month at a second job instead of bowling, he could have bought his own shop years ago.

Sellers respond to buyers willing to sacrifice and struggle for their own businesses; so will banks and other lenders. The ambitions of a cash-poor but striving buyer can easily replace ready money. Not long ago a divorced mother with two children approached our firm seeking a small coffee shop. She worked long days as a garment stitcher to support her family, and she spent three nights a week waiting tables to scrimp together a down payment. She proudly showed us her $5,000 bank balance, representing a year's savings. I was so impressed, I called a client who had been toying with selling his coffee shop and retiring to Florida. He admired the woman's ambition so much, he agreed to lower his $10,000 down payment demand because he was convinced the buyer would make the business a huge success. It wasn't charity, only good business sense. Many people will help you if you can show them you will work diligently to help yourself.

I worry more about the over-capitalized buyer than about the under-capitalized one. Buyers who inherit money or experience a windfall suffer the highest failure rate of all. In too many cases they have nothing to bring to the business but money.

The financial hurdle can stop you cold if you set your sights too high and refuse to start on a more reasonable plan. Lower your sights to a business you can afford initially, and use it as a stepping-stone to your ultimate goal. Starting small offers two advantages to the first-time buyer with limited cash. Not only does it allow entry into business, it provides ownership experience that can insure success in a larger business. My files are full of prospective buyers who aim too high for their first business venture. Consider the buyer who dreams of owning a business demanding a $100,000–150,000 down payment. Anything smaller doesn't fulfil that dream, so he never buys. Don't make that mistake.

The business world is full of successful owners who started their first business on a shoestring and built it into a money-making enterprise. I once heard the owner of a chain of 16 ice-cream and sandwich shops comment, "I started with $6,000; and most of that came from friends and relatives. Any idiot can do it with money, but it takes a genius to do it without money." He's *almost* right. It doesn't take genius. It only takes commitment.

THE SECURITY HURDLE

Since nobody can guarantee your success, nobody can object to your concern over security. Leaving a steady paycheck and a promising future for financial uncertainty and a risky outcome stops many buyers.

If security worries you, you should think twice about leaving your job for your own business. I say this not because I believe a full-time job offers more security than your own business, but because resting under a security blanket shows lack of motivation and self-confidence, which seldom lead to success. If you believe you have sufficient motivation, but can't quite break away from the warm nest, I offer these suggestions.

First, ask yourself. "How much security do I have now?" Less than you think. Consider the possibilities. Your employer can go down the drain, or he can merge with another firm leaving you in the cold with a pink slip. The boss may decide your job should go to his nephew with a fresh Harvard MBA, or perhaps you'll end up with a new boss who doesn't like the way you part your hair. Face it, unless you are on civil service or are a tenured professor, your security extends only to your next paycheck. At least with your own business your security rests in your own hands.

Second, plan for the worst case. Say to yourself, "Okay, suppose I do fail. Can I get another job as good as the one I'm leaving behind?" The answer should be obvious. If you're not worth as much as you're making now, you wouldn't have your present job. Why should't you be worth as much to a new employer?

If you're still not convinced, try these tips:

1.   Set aside a contingency fund or an "alternate security blanket." I often advise nervous clients to set aside enough money to support them over the time period necessary to get a new job, should the business fail. Be realistic. A failing business usually gives plenty of warning and even a failing business can stay alive and generate a paycheck for many months, even years, before it finally collapses. You'll have plenty of time to look for new employment. Think positively. Most people, once in business, don't look for another job. No, they look for another business. Once in business for themselves they have no desire to ring someone else's cash register. That proves they make the right decision in the first place.

2.   Start your business on a part-time basis. You can hold your job until you're satisfied the business will make it and that it justifies a full-time involvement. In many cases this is the preferable route.

Recently, Carl S., a journalist for a large newspaper, tinkered with the idea of acquiring a small trade magazine for the electronics industry. The magazine had potential but Carl wasn't prepared to leave his $36,000 salary for a struggling magazine that couldn't provide the same income, and perhaps never could. He handled it the right way. He built the magazine on a moonlighting basis. Two years later he tripled its sales and then was prepared to devote his full time to it. There are thousands of small businesses one can effectively manage part-time until it justifies a full-time involvement. A word of caution:

Never attempt to run a business part-time if it demands full-time attention. Otherwise you may fail at both your job and your business. That's precisely what happened to Nick, a 15-year veteran of the police force who purchased a small bar and grill. He thought he'd see how the business went for a year or two before resigning from the police force. While on duty, Nick would frequently drop in to check on his new business. He wasn't fooling his superiors at the police department. They knew he was shirking his job. Since Nick could give the business only token supervision, his employees took advantage of his absence and pilfered thousands of dollars. Within two years, Nick was terminated from the police department and lost his business as well.

3.   Consider tackling a full-time business with your spouse or another trustworthy friend or relative working at it full-time while you gain the success and confidence to join them. About 30% of all small business buyers clear their security hurdle just this way.

A recent example involved a chef at a large restaurant who bought a small restaurant of his own but couldn't force himself to leave his old job, so he gave most of the responsibility for the new venture to his wife. Although his wife managed the restaurant well, it wasn't generating the income or growth to justify his leaving his $28,000 position.

THE SELF-CONFIDENCE HURDLE

Remember *The Little Engine That Could*? It chugged along tooting, "I *think* I can, I *think* I can . . . I *know* I can, I *know* I can . . . I *knew* I could, I *knew* I could." But let's forget the flowery nonsense. You're not the little red engine. You're a human being dreaming about a business which will demand a lot of managerial competence. Maybe you can, maybe you can't, but since you won't know if you can until after you take the plunge, you should't let this dilemma thwart you. Rather you should concentrate on matching yourself to the right business, of the type and size you can manage effectively. Matching yourself to a manageable business is unquestionably the most important part of buying a business. That's why I devote the next chapter to it.

I'm reminded of Saul, a young fellow who had worked for several years as an electronics engineer. His uncle died leaving Saul the opportunity to buy his uncle's Chevrolet dealership from the estate at a good price. What held Saul back? Lack of confidence. He'd sit in my office and lament, "What do I know about the automobile business?" He was right. He knew nothing about it. His shaky confidence was justified, so Saul passed up the deal. It was a smart move. Two years later, however, Saul entered into a partnership to form his own small electronics firm. He never raised the question of self-confidence. He knew the business was right for him.

For the uninitiated, ownership appears to demand superhuman skill and managerial brilliance. If you were planning to assume the presidency of Chrysler, I'd agree. However, a small business can succeed beautifully with an owner possessing absolutely no business training, but who enjoys sufficient experience and burning ambition.

Since I have no easy success formula, I get a chuckle from those who do. One recently published business book designed for new business owners offered these essential qualifications:

good health
mental alertness
analytic ability
human relations skills
responsibility
resistance to stress
ability to organize
decisiveness
integrity
persistence

Based on this list only Eagle Scouts would qualify. Should such a person with all these admirable traits come along, he wouldn't be looking for a small business, he'd be elected President of the United States by acclamation! So don't worry about special qualifications. Take a stroll down any main street and talk to a few business owners. You'll find they're people much like yourself.

If lack of confidence troubles you, consider these pointers:

1. Stay with the type business you know. Lack of experience can rightly destroy confidence. Buyers suffer managerial self-doubt either because they have not had experience with a specific business or because they have never managed any business before. Obtain that experience—you'll need it.

2. Solo ownership can scare the first-time buyer. For people who need a psychological boost, a partner can be the answer. Whenever potential partners approach me, they explain that the union benefits them by pooling capital, experience, and responsibility. In most cases those are not the only reasons. Many won't admit it, even to them-

selves, but partnerships are oftentimes insecure people leaning on
each other for support. The team approach is worthwhile if it allows
buyers to attempt a venture they'd otherwise shun. Once they're in
business, the partners may feud (most partnerships dissolve), but
that's of secondary importance. By then each partner has developed
self-confidence and no longer needs a partner.

Take the case of Shirley K. and Mildred P. They joined forces to
buy a large furniture store. After two years, Shirley and Mildred split
up because they couldn't agree on how to manage the business.
However, in two short years, despite their squabbling, they both
became super-charged entrepreneurs. Mildred bought out Shirley
and Shirley opened her own furniture store. If you had met these
women before they teamed up, you'd have seen that partnership was
the right way for them to take their first business step.

3.   Franchising (discussed in detail in later chapters) may close
the confidence gap. With a franchise system, the self-doubting owner
has the franchisor to guide him every step of the way. The owner
makes few crucial decisions.

One of our clients, Jack R. struggled for years with his own waver-
ing confidence. He finally bought a Taylor Rental Center franchise.
The franchisor gave him a proven blueprint for success, constant
support and supervision, and even handled his bookkeeping. As Jack
will tell you, "Without a franchisor to ease me into the business
world, I doubt that I'd have ever taken the leap. Now that I know
what it takes, I'm starting a hospital supply rental firm all on my
own." Jack realized his limitations and found the right solution to
build the expertise and confidence to fly solo.

4.   Test-drive the business before you buy. Here's how it works.
Ask the seller if you can help run the business on a probationary
basis for two weeks or a month before you buy. If the seller is convinced
you're a sincere buyer and the terms are agreeable, he may allow you
to work within the business without pay to get the feel of it. Of
course, the seller can override any decisions you make because it's
still his business, so you won't make any disastrous mistakes. The
opportunity to work a business before you buy is an excellent way
to evaluate a business, which we'll discuss further in Chapter 4. In
addition, it can also cure a case of shaky confidence.

It worked for Harry P., who was interested in buying a kitchen
cabinet business. He and the owner agreed upon the terms of sale,
but still Harry hesitated. He confessed that he just didn't know whether
he had the experience or capability to run that type of business,
since he had worked primarily as a general carpenter. It was a legit-

imate question. I convinced the seller to allow Harry to work in the plant for a month. Harry involved himself in every phase of operations—production, selling, installation, and repair. The seller watched him, guided him, and gave him a crash course on running a profitable kitchen cabinet business. At the end of the month, Harry was ready to fly solo. Not only did he have confidence in the business itself, he had confidence in himself. Try it. You'll probably find that running a business is not so difficult once you're actually doing it.

THE FEAR-OF-FAILURE HURDLE

Every weekend my friend Paul packs his bags and heads for the gambling casinos of Atlantic City. Knowing he was frustrated in his job as a credit manager for a meat wholesaler, I asked why he didn't go into business for himself. Paul laughed, "Are you nuts? The slot machines give me a 45% chance of winning. Those are better odds than my own business!"

There are plenty of buyers like Paul who fear putting themselves to the ultimate test. Just the hint of defeat freezes them. Let's face reality. You may succeed, but a cursory glance at the auction pages will remind you that you also may fail. No doubt about it, business is a gamble. But I insist Paul is wrong about the odds. It's true that four out of five start-up businesses fail within the first five years, but buyers of established healthy businesses fare appreciably better, increasing the odds to four out of five successes. That's one big advantage to buying an established business. Still, you do face that one chance in five of failing. So ask yourself, "What will happen if I do fail?" Consider the possibilities:

1. You'll lose some money.
2. You'll end up with a bruised ego.
3. You'll learn from your errors and become a much better business person the next time around.

I speak from experience. I've had my share of successes, but I've suffered a few failures too. My winning companies provided more fun and profit, but my losing ventures taught me considerably more. One blunder was a movie theater. It might have worked had I known something about the movie business besides who won the Academy Award for Best Supporting Actress in 1963. As it turned out, knowing *about* something you like does not necessarily mean you can make money at it. Today my movie theater is a bowling alley and stands as a monument to how not to go into business. Tuition cost me a bundle.

Did I massage a bruised ego? You bet. Despite several successful past ventures, or perhaps because of them, I was not prepared to fail. Eventually, I grabbed a piece of paper and pencil and said, "Okay, Goldstein, what did you learn from your mistake?" I compiled an impressive list, from ignorance of the specific enterprise to inadequate preparation for failure. Since then, I carefully define and limit what I stand to lose on a business venture. Knowing what you stand to lose and being willing to gamble that amount for the benefits a business may give can be a great tranquilizer. Here's how to do it.

1. Divide your assets into two categories, Touch and Don't Touch. Among the Don't-Touch assets should be your home, auto, and approximately half your savings. That leaves you the other half of your savings to gamble on a business. You might prefer a different list, but don't avoid defining what you are willing to risk.

2. Limit your personal liability on loans and notes needed to buy the business. Assume the worst. Suppose the business does fail. How much liability would you incur? Does it exceed what you have defined as a maximum limit?

3. Look at the business from a risk/benefit viewpoint. Approach business with the idea that the prospective benefits must far outweigh the risk of monetary loss.

4. Consult an attorney to see how you can shield personal assets from potential business liabilities. You'll be surprised to find how many ways you can protect assets from creditor claims if you act before you incur the debt.

As you proceed through this book you'll see practical and proven ways to reduce your losses, but for now simply remember that realistically you can buy a good business with very little risk of loss.

I remember a middle-aged couple negotiating to buy a car wash for $100,000. The couple could raise the money, but it would require mortgaging everything they owned. "What if we go broke?" worried the wife. I could see the fear of failure in her eyes, and it was causing them second thoughts, as indeed it should. I negotiated with their fears in mind, beginning with a $10,000 down payment. The seller would finance the $90,000 balance on a five-year note which my buyers would guarantee only to the extent of $10,000. If the business failed the seller could take his car wash back, but the buyers' loss would not exceed the $20,000 represented by the down payment plus the note guarantee. Sure, the seller resisted. He'd rather have cash, but, convinced the couple could make the business succeed and easily repay his loan, he let the buyers clear their fear of failure. They could live with the idea of losing only $20,000 and could buy the car wash with all their enthusiasm intact.

Enthusiasm breeds success, but fear erodes enthusiasm and can quickly lead to failure.

THE FAMILY HURDLE

Suppose you've cleared the financial, security, self-confidence, and fear-of-failure hurdles. You know what you want and you're ready to go. But wait. Is your wife or father-in-law or Uncle Pete telling you to have your head examined?

Surprisingly, one out of two buyers are prevented from fulfilling their ambitions by spouses or relatives who fight the idea. If husband and wife don't share the same goals, failure practically becomes inevitable.

Perhaps the spouse faces hurdles different from yours. Your wife may fear financial loss more than you ever will, or your husband may never muster as much self-confidence as you already own.

Once you become your own boss, security, risk of loss, and the impact on your life-style becomes a family affair. If you decide to venture forth against the wishes of your spouse, it's bound to affect your business and your marriage as well. I can't advise you on the marital consequences, but I have seen the impact on business careers time and again.

Not long ago a young man, John T., purchased a motel through our office. I knew he was married, but during the two months of negotiation I had never met his wife. Finally at the closing, John's wife appeared, threatening to divorce John if he purchased the motel. John hurried her out of the office to avoid a scene, then returned to sign the papers. A year later, John confided that he'd have to sell the motel before it failed. To pacify his wife he had limited himself to 40 hours a week, because she wanted them to spend all their evenings and weekends together. Unfortunately the motel demanded at least 60 hours a week.

With women increasingly entering the business world, many husbands resent the idea of not being the sole breadwinner, while many women wish their husbands could stop being such workaholics.

One leading business broker specializing in counseling business buyers holds two-day seminars for both husbands and wives. He claims, "A business acquisition is too important to be decided by only one spouse. Success requires the enthusiasm of both."

I offer the following guidelines.

1. Explain to your spouse why you want the business. Help him or her see it through your eyes. Many spouses resist because they don't appreciate your commitment. I recall a husband who for several

years objected to his wife opening her own interior decorating firm. Finally she did it, but only after leaving her husband. Her husband's shocked response was, "I didn't think she was serious about it. I thought it was only a passing fancy." Unfortunately his wife didn't do a very good job convincing him otherwise.

2.   Pinpoint precisely why your spouse objects. Many spouses don't articulate their concerns or identify their own hurdles. Once you determine genuine problems, you can tackle them. Chances are your spouse faces one of the hurdles we discussed earlier.

3.   Be prepared to compromise. If your spouse is more financially cautious than you, consider lowering your financial expenditures. If he or she dislikes your long working hours, devise a schedule that will satisfy both your spouse and the business. As with most marital problems, communication and reason can solve your dilemma.

4.   Involve your spouse in the buying process. Invite your spouse to join you as you search and negotiate for your business. Try sharing not only the decision, but the experience as well. Many of your spouse's concerns will vanish, once he or she feels a part of the excitement.

5.   Offer your spouse an active role in the business. Discuss the possibilities. I think it's a good idea to have spouses actively participate in a family business, even if they limit themselves to specific or part-time functions like bookkeeping. Remember, most spouses resist because they believe a business will strain rather than help a marriage.

Business success never comes easy. But it will come easier once both spouses want it and work to make it happen. With some patience and understanding, you can transform this hurdle into a major asset.

APPLYING THE BRAKES

You may not be cowering in the corner waiting for a hefty push to get you onto the track. Instead you may be an eager beaver who can't wait to get into business. Before you jump too quickly, make certain:

1.   You're doing it with realistic expectations, and
2.   You're doing it for the right reasons.

The bankruptcy courts are bulging with buyers who started with plenty of enthusiasm only to find out they didn't understand what they were running into. These misguided buyers end up buying without adequate investigation, buy at the worst price and terms, and eventually become disillusioned with being their own boss. Apply your brakes for a moment while we test your expectations and motives.

A DOSE OF REALITY

Be an optimist, but be a realist too. Don't overestimate the rewards while ignoring what a business demands.

What you will earn, and how hard you'll have to work for it, depends on the nature, size, and profitability of the business, as well as on your own management proficiency. Keep these facts in mind.

1. You may earn considerably less from a business than you think.
2. To succeed, you'll find yourself working a lot harder, and for longer hours than you will on any job.

Clara had her rose-colored glasses on when she found a small cosmetic shop for sale. All she could talk about was the $50,000 salary she planned for herself, a new Datsun the business would lease for her, and a long list of fringe benefits. I was very familiar with the business, a solid small firm, but it couldn't safely provide its owner more than $25,000 in salary. Clara wouldn't listen. Every week she'd write out her paycheck for $1,000 and she kept writing it until she watched her business fall under the auctioneer's hammer.

Syd Parlow, a management consultant for small firms puts it this way. "For many buyers a business is a big cookie jar. All they see is the money coming in. They don't realize the lion's share of the income has to be paid out or reinvested to make the business grow. It's tempting after years of struggling on a paycheck. So they buy expecting an immediate windfall and never remain alive to reap the long-term benefits."

Ken T. wore a different shade of rose-colored glasses. He thought he could effectively manage his large toy shop by overseeing it 10–15 hours a week while he retained his job as a school teacher. Investing $50,000 to buy the business, he soon realized his full-time business demanded a full-time owner. But Ken learned too late, and had to sell out at a $30,000 loss.

Too many buyers underestimate the time or attention a small business requires. Running the business looks easy before you buy. But once you own the business you encounter the 1001 daily problems demanding the attention of a boss.

Does it sound discouraging? It shouldn't. The rewards are there, for a price. You don't get something for nothing. Realistic buyers understand that.

RIGHT REASONS—WRONG REASONS

You may want just what everyone else wants from a business: wealth, security, independence, or status. Or perhaps you relish the challenge and satisfaction of building something. Countless good reasons exist, but so do many *wrong* reasons.

Consider Kevin T. He bought his children's clothing store, not because he wanted it but out of *desperation*. When his employer, a large clothing manufacturer, relocated its plant to North Carolina, Kevin found himself out of his job as a salesman. Kevin never intended to go into business and never wanted to be his own boss. He's happiest working for someone else. But as Kevin will tell you, "I looked and looked but couldn't find a suitable position. With a wife and three kids to feed, I took the plunge, seeing my own business as the only alternative." Now, Kevin admits his mistake, but only after he filed for protection under Chapter 11 of the Bankruptcy Code.

A large number of buyers, like Kevin, seek out businesses as cures for unemployment woes. For most of these buyers such an act of desperation cannot replace a keen desire to own. Why go from the frying pan into the fire?

If you do buy out of desperation, choose a business that offers a short-term arrangement until you can find a position. Select a small business requiring little cash and financial commitment and one you can resell easily.

A close colleague of mine at Northeastern University, Elliot T., gave up his professorship to start his own chemical supply firm. Elliot was very content as a professor, but his wife wanted more money than Elliot's professorship provided. Day and night she hounded him to go into business, and Elliot, the easily swayed type, went along with it. His wife is happy, but Elliot's miserable. Don't go into business because *someone else wants you to*. You have to want it yourself.

Recently, a young lady, Phyllis P., consulted with us during her search for a small retail store. Phyllis worked as a buyer for a large department store but expressed to me her *job dissatisfaction*. Her boss was a tyrant, working conditions were poor, and raises came few and far between. I asked Phyllis why she wanted her own business. "I just told you," she said, "I don't like my job." I frowned. "So why don't you look for a new job instead of a business?" Phyllis didn't have the answer. She's still looking at a business of her own as an escape.

Donald? Even today he doesn't understand why he purchased a large truck dealership. But if you knew him you'd spot the reason. Donald's father was a successful textile manufacturer, and his older brother owned two prosperous car dealerships. Donald is a wonderful teacher but never measured up in his own mind to his family's expectations. So Donald no longer teaches math at the high school. Today he sells Peterbilt trucks to *prove* himself to others. Donald has a good business mind and he'll succeed, but he'll never sell trucks with the same enthusiasm as he has for throwing an algebraic equation on the blackboard.

Examine your motives. There's only one good reason for being in business. You must sincerely want it to achieve positive goals.

WHEN WILL IT HAPPEN?

For many buyers, procrastination indicates indecision and hurdles. They want their own businesses, but they'll do it tomorrow.

One restaurant buyer was ushered into my office recently by a young associate in my firm. The buyer told me he had searched for a restaurant since 1975. Every Sunday he'd scan the opportunity section of the newspaper and line up appointments for the following week. I politely told the buyer to stop looking and take up golf instead. "What are you talking about?" he stammered. I was blunt. "It cannot take a serious buyer seven years to find the right business. You're dreaming, so you might as well take your illusion to the golf course." Behind every never-ending search hides an uncommited buyer.

Are you "just waiting for the right time?" A major symptom of this problem is over-preparedness. "Today I have $10,000 but next year I'll have $15,000." Or, "Next year I'll have one more year of experience under my belt."

Charlie dreams of his own furniture store, and has been fine-tuning his business plan for five years. Just when he thinks he's got it perfect he finds another flaw. Back to the drawing board. A month ago he showed me his most recent plan in which he had replaced Serta Mattresses with Slumberland. "Charlie," I sighed, "this is your twelfth revision." I showed him the manuscript for this book. "Charlie, I could revise this manuscript twelve times and make it a little better each time. But I'd never get it published!"

Sure, you need capital, experience, and planning to succeed in business. But how much? Define what you think it takes—then *do it!*

Some blame the bad economy for their procrastination. It's a fashionable excuse for dreamers. Three years ago the economy was good but businesses were selling at too high a price. Today, you can point to skyrocketing interest rates and bankruptcies. There's never a "right time" if you're not ready to buy, but it's *always* the right time if you *are.* List your own reasons for delay. Do they make sense, or are they just excuses?

Do you think your reasons are sound? Perhaps you're waiting for retirement, for your children to finish college, or for an illness to be fully cured.

Bona fide? Certainly, but if it does make sense to wait, set a target date for action. A fine line separates reasonable delay from indecision and fear of hurdles.

Remember Harold the artist. Your own moment of truth will come. It may strike tomorrow or lie far in the future, but can you afford to sit back, put it off, and watch your hopes grow old?

TEST YOUR COMMITMENT

Before we leave this chapter, take a few moments and provide honest, objective answers to these basic questions:

1.   Are you *really* ready to buy?
2.   If not, what's holding you back?
3.   How do you plan to overcome your hurdles?
4.   Why do you want your own business?
5.   Have you been procrastinating?
6.   Have you set a target date to begin your search?

Regardless of your answers, one year from today you'll see how accurate they were.

2

MATCHING YOU TO THE RIGHT BUSINESS

Butcher, baker, candlestick maker. It didn't matter to Eric S., provided his business could earn him at least $40,000 a year.

First he got excited about a Volkswagen dealership, but the deal fell through at the last minute. Next he pondered a Chinese restaurant; then, displaying versatility, he considered buying a chain of pizza parlors. Unable to make up his mind, Eric pursued a beauty supply wholesaler, then a plastics engineering firm. Finally, he found his perfect opportunity and forked over $85,000 for Puppy Land, a large retail pet and pet supply store.

Three weeks later Eric limped back to our office. "Sell the business! And fast." I asked him what went wrong. "Oh, it's a profitable business," he admitted, "but it's not for me. I can't stand the endless stream of people who think Puppy Land is the mall's answer to the zoo, and the cats are the last straw." "The cats?" I asked. Peering through puffy eyes, he sighed, "Yeah, it turns out I'm allergic to cats."

THOUSANDS OF WRONG CHOICES

This year 500,000 people will buy or start a business. Burt Nicholas, a career consultant, estimates that 60–70% will select the wrong type of business, adding "Too many people don't ask the important question—what business am I best suited for? Instead they choose the business easiest to enter or in which they imagine they can make the most money."

Eric's story illustrates the point. It's an easy trap to fall into. Your boss offers to sell his hardware store on bargain terms. It's tempting. A friend tells you about a hot money-making opportunity with a quick print shop. Who doesn't like money? Your brother succeeded with his seafood restaurant and never seems to work. If he can do it, why can't you?

The answer should be obvious: You need the business that's right for you. But the question remains—what will that business be?

HOW THE MATCHING PROCESS BEGINS

If you strolled into our office, our receptionist would hand you a very simple form to complete. We call it the Buyers/Business Profile.

It never hurts to take a little test. Complete your own Buyers/Business Profile.

The Buyers Profile will answer the questions of what you can bring to a business. Your present job or prior experience will show your management ability and what you know about the type of business you're interested in. Income? It's not really a personal question. We'd like to know what you now earn to see if your business choice can match those earnings. Education and special training may disclose skills or areas of interest not readily disclosed by your work experience. Hobbies and outside interests have a different mission. It points out what you enjoy in life and may even point you in the direction of a business you have never considered, but with which you would be much happier and successful. Cash availability, of course, tells us whether you have any reasonable chance for buying the business you describe with your investment capital. The profile can provide valuable insight about you as a buyer. You're one part of the matching equation—a very important part.

The Business Profile helps determine the type of business you might want. Most buyers have a reasonably accurate idea of the business they're seeking. For example, most will simply define it as a "card and gift shop, with sales of at least $100,000, within 10 miles from home," or a "motel on Cape Cod with at least 30 rooms." So to some extent you probably have an approximate vision of the type, size, and location of your business choice. Perhaps you are the undecided type, and either have several totally different businesses in mind, or have absolutely no idea of what you want. Hopeless? Of course not. The Buyer Profile will provide the clues to narrow the logical choices.

For the buyer in the maze of indecision, we'll scan his prior background, hobbies, and training to define several alternatives. But a composite of logical business choices will emerge. The decided, certain buyer with a precise business in mind will be put to the same test. How does he know his business choice is right or his best alternative? To find the answer we look at the Buyer Profile and the Business Profile to see if it is the perfect match.

Idrit.

UNITED BUSINESS BROKERS

BURLINGTON, CHESTNUT HILL, MA 02167 (617) 277-5700

BUYERS/BUSINESS PROFILE

Buyer Profile: Date:_____

Name: Tel. No.

Address:

1. Present Employer:

2. Job Description and Title:

3. Income (list sources):

4. Prior Experience:

5. Prior Businesses Owned:

6. Education or Specialized Training:

7. List Hobbies and Outside Interests:

8. Cash Available for Investment:

2-3

BROKERAGE • APPRAISALS • FINANCING • LIQUIDATIONS

EXHIBIT 1.   Buyers/Business Profile

UNITED BUSINESS BROKERS

Business Profile:

1. Check business category interested in:

   Retailing

   Wholesaling

   Restaurant

   Service Business

   Manufacturing

   New Product or Service Idea

   Mail Order

   Motel - Lodging

2. If applicable, describe type product:
   (example - food, drug, hardware)

3. Approximate size of business:

   Minimum Annual Sales $_____

   Selling Space (if retail) _____ sq. ft.

4. Geographic Areas:

   a) Within a _____ mile radius of _____.
                                          (Town)

   b) Type areas excluded _____.

   c) Willing to relocate? _____.

2-4

BROKERAGE • APPRAISALS • FINANCING • LIQUIDATIONS

EXHIBIT 1. *(continued)*

ASK FIVE ESSENTIAL QUESTIONS

With your completed Buyers/Business Profile before me, I'd immediately ask these five essential questions:

1. Can you *earn* from the business?
2. Can you *manage* the business?
3. Can you *enjoy* the business?
4. Can you *afford* the business?
5. Can you *find* the business?

Let's examine each one.

WHAT CAN YOU EARN?

Many buyers define their target business carefully enough, but don't realistically assess the earnings potential.

Start by asking yourself about the earnings you require. You best know your income requirements, so is it $15,000 annually or closer to $40,000? You may have outside income or investments that will supplement what the business initially can earn for you, and they can be considered.

Will the business you've defined provide the necessary income? That's where most buyers go wrong, overestimating both earning capacity for the type and size of business and, particularly, earning potential during the earlier years when loans must be repaid. Not long ago a young woman with years of experience as a public relations specialist for a large firm approached us to acquire a small retail store, preferably in the card and gift line, with sales in the $100,000–150,000 range. What did she require in income to give up her job? $45,000–50,000! From experience I knew a typical card and gift shop in that sales range can't produce a salary and profit beyond $25,000–30,000. During the first few years she'd be fortunate to earn $250–300 a week, as profits would be gobbled up to pay down her loans. Her solution? She either had to "trade up" to a larger-sized shop or select a business with a greater earnings potential.

You can find out what your target business will generate in approximate income through several excellent sources. Write to *Small Business Reporter*, Bank of America, San Francisco, California 94137, and describe the type of business you're interested in. For a $2.00 postage charge they'll send you a profile for your type of business showing typical profit and loss statements. You'll quickly be able to determine the approximate income range for the owner of such a business. Banks are another good source of information, as they subscribe to several of the larger publication services providing financial profiles for virtually any business. Many trade associations publish financial data on their industry. For example, *Lilly Digest* is the financial bible for the retail drug industry, and with a glimpse you can see the average income statement for any type or size drugstore. As with any reference, it can only give you a range of expected earnings, as actual income will depend on the profitability of the business you finally buy. Talking to owners of comparable businesses can also be helpful, but I suggest you rely on the published reports.

Many buyers believe they can defy the odds by rapidly increasing the sales or profitability of a business to meet income needs. Sometimes they do. Usually it doesn't happen as rapidly or easily as they hoped, leaving them with the glaring income gap. I hear it constantly: "Yes, I know a restaurant grossing $200,000–250,000 will only give me $400–500 a week, but in no time I can build it to $400,000–500,000 a year and take out the $1,000 a week I need." Unless you have a track record to prove you can build the business, it's not a wise gamble. My files are loaded with sellers looking to sell out because they, too, bought a business they thought they could build to produce the desired income, only to find out they couldn't succeed.

Frequently, a partnership produces a greater strain on the question of earnings. The classic error is the case of two partners buying a business that can only support one owner. Even beyond personality and management disputes, I believe more partnerships collapse because the business can't generate sufficient income. Similarly, it may be a case of one partner demanding more from the business than the other. If you're going into business with a partner, ask the honest question—can the target business really support two owners?

Investment partners providing capital, while you provide management, create yet a further step in the evaluation of earnings.

Your first objective as the active partner is to earn a salary. Your partners' objectives are to generate sizable profits to provide them a return on investment and, hopefully, to see the business grow. The objectives may be the same but the priorities are different. Whenever I counsel buyers that include investment partners, I suggest they carefully consider:

1. What salary will be allowed the working partner.
2. How profits will be allocated between increases in salary to the working partner versus reinvestment in the company.

Once partners consider those two elementary points they may find considerable disagreement, which should surface before, not after, they buy.

It's not unusual for buyers to tell me that earnings are of secondary or no importance. Many buyers are retired, or are housewives whose primary objective is not to make money, but to keep busy. Others aren't quite ready to ignore the question of earnings, but want to "trade down" their present high volume, high pressure businesses for smaller, more relaxed versions. Even if you're in that category you should define the minimum income you'd expect for your time, effort, and investment.

Would the business you see on the Business Profile provide you the income you need?

MEASURE YOUR MANAGEMENT MENTALITY

Anyone can manage a business—provided it's the right business, and I believe it. The converse, of course, is that very few people can effectively manage any business. We each have our own management mentalities and you should measure yours if you expect to find the right business. As the bankruptcy statistics will tell you, buyers oftentimes don't use the correct yardstick.

Did you know that over 50% of all buyers look for a business they have absolutely no prior experience with? That shouldn't necessarily rule out the business, but it raises obvious questions about management. Possibly you're preparing to journey into unchartered waters.

How do you know you can manage that type of business? What I usually hear from the optimists is "What do you have to know to operate a coffee shop, motel, food store" or whatever captures their eye. That was the war cry from a retired fireman who was interested in a coffee shop located in a downtown office building. "What do you have to know about pouring coffee and making sandwiches?" After three months of overbuying, waste, overstaffing, and trying to make the specialties the customers expected, he found his answer. He finally learned the business, but he has an ulcer and a depleted bank acount rather than a diploma to show for the education. No business is as easy as it looks.

Even if you have some experience in the business, you may have only the narrow, limited experience your job demanded, and not the broad overall experience ownership requires. Elliot Galahow, a management consultant to small firms cites lack of broad managerial experience as a common weakness among employees turned employer. "As employees, people perform narrowly defined functions within organizations. As owners, they must master all the functions."

Your management ability must be measured not only against the type of business, but against its size as well. Suppose you have experience managing a six-employee superette grossing $400,000. Can you handle a supermarket with 60 employees ringing $4,000,000 in sales? How do you really know?

That's why I usually advise first-time buyers to start small with a business size they are confident with.

Conversely, experienced, proven buyers can underestimate their management abilities, and should upgrade what they're looking for. One timid buyer had some interesting information on his Buyer Profile. He started a shoe store on a literal "shoestring," and built it into a $400,000-a-year-money maker. When it came time to look for a second store he thought he wanted to add another store in the $400,000–600,000 range. But with some prodding he ended up buying a faltering shoe chain that he revived to gross $3,000,000 annually. However, his right choice probably would be a mistake for the first-time buyer.

When assessing your management capability, consider it also from the viewpoint of the financial health of your target business. For example, if you were to approach me for a liquor store, I could show you eight to ten possibilities. But three or four would be hovering between poor financial health and bankruptcy. Can you revive a sick business?

Bear in mind that the troubled business will demand considerably different talent and management skill than will a stable business. Even in turn-around situations you must define your terms. For example, you may find a business that can be revived readily with a transfusion of inventory and promotion. Another may require massive surgery to bring it back to health. Ask, "How sick is sick?" and "How good a doctor am I?"

Some buyers are only interested in sick companies, and that's their only criteria. They don't care if it's a stereo shop, a nursing home, or a clothing chain. As turnaround specialists they rehabilitate and quickly sell for a fat profit. But the first-time or lightly seasoned buyer should probably look for the business that's reasonably stable.

What practical steps can you take if you believe your management skills are shaky?

1. If you have no experience in the type of business you have selected then don't buy just yet. Defer it until you can obtain valuable "hands-on" experience as an employee. You may have to sacrifice some income for 3–6 months while you obtain the experience, but it will be a much smaller loss than what you will sustain by operating a business you know nothing about.

2. Weakness or lack of experience in certain phases of operation can be handled in much the same way. See if you can expand your duties in your present job to give you increased exposure and responsibility in areas you are unfamiliar with.

3. Many buyers complain that they don't know enough about finance, accounting, or even basic management principles. Lack of knowledge

in these areas seldom makes the difference between failure and common sense, but they are important. Why not take some night courses at a local college to sharpen your theoretical skills.

4.   What about a partner? I have seen many cases where a partner provided the experience and management knowhow. A partnership also can be ideal for the larger business requiring either a broader span of management, or a division of responsibility. You may be excellent in production, but you may require a partner who excels in sales and administration.

Ask Floyd P. if it's important to measure your management mentality. A grounded pilot on the lookout for a boat marina, Floyd could flash a $50,000 bankroll and was the ready and willing but far from able buyer. I asked Floyd, "Suppose you approached the marina owner for a job. How much do you suppose he'd pay someone with absolutely no experience in the business?" Floyd stammered, "Well, I guess I'd be working for the minimum wage until I learned the business." That didn't discourage Floyd from buying; however, it certainly helped him to fail.

Don't be a minimum-wage owner. Be candid—can you effectively manage the business you have in mind?

A MATTER OF MOTIVATION

The third question—Would you enjoy the business?—may seem strange as a business criteria, but it's not at all. I consider it the essential ingredient of every successful business. You'll work hardest and happiest operating a company about which you're most enthusiastic. Why settle for any business, when a little thought can help you find one that will bring a gleam to your eye.

One of my most satisfying transactions involved Victor J., who responded to an ad for an auto repair shop we had for sale. Vic had worked as a mechanic for 12 years. Over coffee I asked him about the photographic hobby he had listed on his Buyers Profile questionnaire. "Why not open a camera shop?" I asked. "I wish I could," he confessed. "I have a complete darkroom at home, but I know more about cars then cameras." We talked it over for awhile, then a gleam came to his eye. "Could I start small to get my feet wet?" We found Vic a part-time job in a local camera shop where he was able to pick up all the tricks. Six months later he had his own camera shop and loves every minute of it. To top it off, he's making almost twice as much money as we'd projected for an auto repair shop.

Buyers look for the wrong type of business for a variety of reasons. Vic was looking for an auto repair shop because it was the type of business he had always worked in. Even as a teenager he worked part-time pumping gas. He never knew any other business and therefore never thought of any other business. Many buyers have their blinders on.

An associate in a friend's law firm, Peter S., hated the practice of law and wanted to go into business instead. So we had a long chat about what might interest him. He confessed, with some deep probing, that he enjoys baking. On weekends he'd bake cakes for the entire neighborhood. Why not open a bakery? I suggested. "My folks would have a heart attack," he screamed, "if they found their son the lawyer working as a baker with a dirty apron!" So Peter never did open his bakery, instead buying a small legal research firm. I'm still convinced he'd be more successful and certainly happier if he could forget his professional image and do what he most enjoyed.

Peter's story isn't unique. Many buyers walk around as though they have labels stamped on their foreheads: Auto Dealer, Haberdasher, Sales rep. Certainly, that may be what they have been, but it's not necessarily what they should be. Perhaps your business choice will be that brand-new field, or maybe you'll look for another type of business that can use existing skills. Many skills do cut across industry lines. A good merchandiser can sell anything, and an experienced auto dealer can sell boats, motorcycles, or motor homes. The skills are the same; only the product changes.

A friend once asked me how I could be a professor, lawyer, business acquisition consultant, and author at the same time. "Why didn't I simply stick to the one field I most enjoyed?" "It's easy," I replied, "for I enjoy them equally. You see I'm only in one business. I sell information." In defining your criteria you should expand your horizons and ask what alternative business choices could fascinate you.

If you are thinking of a business you've never tried before, keep in mind the grass may only look greener. The reality can be quite different than the illusion.

Remember my bankrupt movie-theater-turned-bowling-alley? I leaped before I looked. Perhaps I was thinking about partying with movie stars at grand openings or wearing a tuxedo to the Cannes Film Festival, but running a theater turned out to be nothing like that. No, I only remember hassling with film distributors, fixing tempermental popcorn machines, and chasing rowdy kids out of the balcony. Would I have purchased the theater if I knew what it really involved? Of course not. But I had to find out the wrong way. Since you don't know whether or not you'd enjoy a business until after you leap, the advice is to look first. Involve yourself in the type of business you're thinking of before you buy, even if it's only a part-time job.

Enjoyment in a business depends on many factors. Structure and relationships with the organization must be considered. Would you enjoy having a partner? It's a more important question than whether you need a partner to bolster management or provide capital.

Two years ago our law firm represented an embattled franchised donut shop owner embroiled in a bitter court case with her franchisor, who was trying to terminate the franchise. Our client, Sandy V. was what franchisors call a maverick. She refused to operate the donut shop the way the franchisor wanted. Three days after she opened it she wondered, "Why not sell sandwiches too?" Of course, the franchise contract prohibited the sale of anything not approved by the franchisor. The franchise manual decreed the shop remain open on Sundays, but Sandy didn't want to open on Sundays. The end came after she started promoting one dozen free with each dozen purchased. Sandy had a "better" way to run the franchise, but the franchisor didn't approve of those ways. Sandy was unhappy and the franchisor was equally frustrated. We finally convinced Sandy to give up the franchise, open her own independent donut shop 'and show them the right way to sell donuts. Flapping her own entrepreneurial wings she's outselling any franchised donut shop. But what's truly important is that she enjoys the business more without the shackles of a franchisor's rule book.

Define your criteria considering the relationships you'd enjoy, so you know whether a franchise or a partner should be in your future.

You might be comfortable operating a business only in certain areas. Business people, particularly retailers, oftentimes decide to sell not because they can't operate a profitable business in their location, but because they don't enjoy working in certain areas. If you were to ask me for a convenience store, for example, I could find you convenience stores in the high-transient "hustle-bustle" downtown areas, or in the quiet suburbs. Perhaps you'd be happiest in a small village in Maine? We have hundreds of convenience stores in low-income–high-crime areas listed by sellers who tell us, "We make an excellent living but can't put up with endless broken windows, holdups, or vandalism." If they're afraid to go to work in the morning how can you enjoy it?

Charlie T. enjoys it. Strapped to his 320-pound frame is a highly visible .38 caliber Colt pistol. And he knows how to handle the people in the neighborhood. He never has a problem. Then Charlie made a mistake. He found a business in a wealthy suburb. It was beautiful! Standing there in his dirty T-shirt, menacing revolver, and jiggling a Churchillian cigar in his mouth, he'd tell me in his throaty tone, "I don't understand dese people. Dey all wear green pants and pink shirts with funny lizards on 'em." Good old Charlie was a fish out of water, hating every minute of it.

Frank Kirkpatrick of Kirkpatrick Associates, Inc., a Vermont business brokerage firm handling country businesses, recently wrote an excellent book, *How to buy a Country Business* (Contemporary Books). If you're interested in relocating to the rural areas for an entrepreneurial life of quiet and solitude,

I highly recommend it. It insists that you assess your ability to adjust to a rural market, its way of life, and its unique manner of doing business.

Don't overlook business hours or travel requirements. Switching from a 9-to-5 job to a business that demands evening or weekend work is never easy, and can cause serious disruption of your life-style. Travel opportunity attracts many buyers to a business, or at least hardly appears as an obstacle; however, eight to nine nights a month in a distant city, away from family and friends can quickly turn enjoyment into frustration. They are very real factors to consider.

Before you decide you'll be happiest with your business choice, look carefully at the work you'll be doing, with whom you'll be working, and where! Since you're the one who'll wake up early each morning to open up the shop, why not do it with a smile on your face?

Assuming you have completed your questionnaire and satisfactorily answered the three crucial questions of earnings, management, and enjoyment, you're ready to leap into business. Or are you?

CAN YOU AFFORD IT?

What you want and what you can afford can prove to be two different things.

In Chapter 1, I gave you some pointers on how to overcome your financial hurdles to scrape together a down payment. In Chapter 8, I'll show you ways to buy a business with less investment than you dreamed possible. Still, a realistic assessment of the cash you have against the business you expect to buy is needed.

What you can afford will depend on many variables: available financing, negotiating ability, and plain luck are only three. But I try to qualify a buyer before the search to see if there's a reasonable probability he will be able to locate and buy the business that matches his criteria..

My guideline calls for available cash equal to at least 10% of the projected purchase price. If you described, for example, a family-style restaurant that earns $300,000–400,000 annually, I then would estimate that such a business would sell in the $100,000–150,000 range. Therefore, I would encourage the buyer to have at least $10,000–15,000.

How do you determine what you can expect to pay for the type and size business you're interested in? There's only one way. You have to ask, look, read ads, talk to brokers, and test the market.

How foolproof is my 10%-down formula? It's not foolproof at all. It's only a very tentative approximation of what it may take if you expect to find a business you can afford within a reasonable time and with reasonable luck financing creatively. Many buyers have trouble landing their business with a

25–35% down payment. Others know how to do it with absolutely no down payment. I, and many of my clients, have been able to do just that and, convinced that it can work, I recently uncovered the successful techniques in my book *Own Your Own/The No Cash Down Business Guide* (Prentice Hall). You'll see many of the strategies in Chapter 8, and these same techniques can work for you. But, as I say in my book, it doesn't work for every buyer or for every deal. That's why I suggest you follow the 10% rule.

Forget brokers who tell you a 10% down payment on a target business won't work. They just don't know how to finance a deal creatively.

Many buyers approach me and dolefully say they only have $20,000–25,000, so they're prepared to settle for a business that they estimate will cost $50,000–75,000. If that's the limit on the size business they can manage effectively, then that's where they should draw the line. But many of these buyers can properly operate considerably larger and better businesses; lack of money is the only reason they don't go after the more worthwhile company. It's a foolish mistake.

BUT WILL YOU FIND IT?

Do you now have a precise business in mind? Perhaps it differs somewhat from your first thought. You may have expanded or narrowed your scope, and you may have even changed the very nature of the business. Regardless, let's assume you've successfully completed and evaluated the Buyers/Business Profile. What happens next?

First, you probably won't find a business that precisely matches your criteria. Don't expect to. But do draw boundaries. If you find a business that falls short of your earnings goal, how low are you willing to go? Management? If you're looking for a tavern without food service, would you accept one with half its sales from food, even though you have absolutely no experience or desire to handle food? Maybe you've set your sights on a hobby shop. Could a toy shop satisfy you instead? Expect and plan for trade-offs.

To complicate matters, if you can't find a business even close to fulfilling your criteria, you may be working with unrealistic criteria and may have to begin measuring your criteria against what the market has to offer.

Many buyers are too rigid in their requirements, and it's their lack of reasonable flexibility that prevents them from buying a business. I'm presently hunting for an Italian-style restaurant for a couple with very fixed demands: the restaurant must gross between $400–600,000 annually, have a seating capacity of 200–250, and must have a separate lounge and waiting area. To add to the problem they insist that the business be in one of four towns. They'll probably never find it.

Don was an example of a buyer who successfully modified his criteria to match the market and himself. With 15 years experience as a merchandising manager for a Connecticut supermarket chain he wanted his own supermarket. He had it all worked out. Sales of $2–4 million, located in a middle- or high-income area within 30 minutes of Hartford, his home town. By every test the business would be perfect for Don, and Don would be perfect for it. The only problem was that the one available food store in the area closest to his criteria only had sales of $800,000. "Too low," said Don. He rightfully waited six months, but still no supermarket came on the market. Shifting his sights he found a general merchandise discount store with $2,000,000 sales in a nearby town. He intelligently reasoned it would satisfy him, knowing it could generate the income he wanted, and that he could manage and enjoy a discount operation as well as a supermarket.

Many buyers don't follow Don's approach, impatiently discard what they believe to be their right business, and instead reach for any business that becomes available. Eric, who you met at the beginning of this chapter, made that mistake. He looked first at the Volkswagen dealership because it made sense for him, considering his background as a service manager for a Ford dealer. But when the Volkswagen deal fell through he didn't say "What's my next best alternative?" Instead he mistakenly pursued every business on the sole criteria of income. You see how he made out.

Try this approach:

1. Define the broadest criteria acceptable to you. Use outside limits, provided the range realistically represents what you're suited for.
2. Now pinpoint the specific criteria that represent your ideal business.
3. With both the broad range and your ideal business defined, you can begin at the top and work down, in descending order of preference.
4. Stay flexible and patient, for I know you'll be tempted to consider one more alternative.

SHOULD YOU START FROM SCRATCH?

The idea of starting your business from the ground floor instead of buying an existing business has probably crossed your mind already. Why buy someone else's headaches?

I have started five businesses and purchased ten, and I know now that I should have bought some of the former and started some of the latter. Usually you won't know the right answer until long after you've already been in business.

However, study the advantages and disadvantages of each.

The Advantages of Buying

1. The business has a track record. You know its sales and profits, so you can reasonably predict what the business will do for you. With a start-up you can only guess about sales and profits.

2. An established business probably sits at, or beyond its break-even point. It should be making money the day you buy it. Even a smart start-up takes time to reach the profit stage. You may incur sizable losses before wringing profits from your created business.

3. The takeover of a solvent, established business is free of start-up problems. You have customers, employees, suppliers, and physical plant in place. It takes a strong manager to put a start-up together and get it off the ground.

4. You'll usually win better financing with an existing business. Banks and other lenders will have more confidence lending to the established business with a track-record. Besides, the seller may help with the financing, or you might assume liabilities and other built-in sources of existing enterprise financing. I consider financing one of the most important advantages of buying.

5. You may be able to buy an existing business for even less than it would cost to duplicate the tangible assets with a start-up.

The Advantages of a Start-Up

1. You'll be able to create the business that matches your precise criteria by controlling size, layout, merchandising, image, and location that a seller might not be able to provide.

2. You won't have to pay a seller for "good will." All it will cost is money for licenses and tangible assets.

3. With a fresh image, free of an existing reputation, you may build your business faster.

Considering the advantages and disadvantages of each, I would recommend a start-up over buying in only two instances.

1. When you have a unique or very different business format in mind. Why pay for inventory, fixtures, or good will when you will completely change the business? One of my first start-ups was a discount prescription shop. The only available opportunities were for full-scale drug stores. If we purchased, we'd have to tear out the fixtures, discard

BUYERS/BUSINESS PROFILE

CHECKLIST

	Yes	No

1. Can the business provide adequate buyer income?

2. Can the business provide adequate income for investment partners? (if applicable)

3. Have income capabilities of business been verified?

4. Does the buyer have sufficient prior experience in this type business?

5. Does the buyer have all the necessary special skills for this business?

6. Does the buyer have the requisite educational requirements or licensure needed for this business?

7. Did the buyer express this type business to be of greatest interest?

8. Are business hours satisfactory to buyer?

9. Are travel requirements satisfactory to buyer?

10. Has the buyer decided whether partners may be accepted?

11. Has the buyer decided whether a franchise would be acceptable?

12. Has the buyer defined specific geographic areas.

13. Does the buyer have adequate capital for this business?

BROKERAGE • APPRAISALS • FINANCING • LIQUIDATIONS

EXHIBIT 2. Buyer/Business Profile: Checklist

most of the inventory and renovate to our own specifications. Obviously, it was better to start with a clean slate.

2. If you have an excellent new location available to you. Remember, when you buy a retail business, you primarily pay for its lease and location. If you can find your own high-traffic location, you may do considerably better than buying. That's how I decided on my second start-up. For months I scouted for a greeting card and gift shop in an enclosed mall. They're difficult to find, and when you do find one the seller wants an exorbitant price for good will, which, of course, means location. When a client developer offered me a lease in a new mall, it was an easy decision, considering the $50–60,000 I'd be saving over buying someone else's lease.

But these are only two situations where I think start-ups have a decided advantage. In most cases you'll probably do better looking for that right business to buy.

Will you be able to find it? The next chapter will show you how.

3

HUNTING YOUR PERFECT OPPORTUNITY

Whenever a potential business buyer says, "I've looked everywhere, but I can't find a really good business for sale," I say, "Nonsense!" Plenty of solid opportunities exist if you know where and how to look.

Lace up your hunting boots and turn your bloodhound loose. In this chapter you'll learn how to sniff out so many business opportunities, you'll be able to choose the one that suits you best.

DEVELOP AN EXPERIENCED EYE

When you begin your search you should be less occupied with finding a particular business than with gaining the valuable experience that will help you determine:

1. The full range of business opportunities meeting your criteria.
2. Differences among numerous businesses.
3. What you need to know to thoroughly investigate businesses and to negotiate with brokers and sellers.

Time, patience, and effort are the keys. You'll need plenty of each if you are to develop the experienced eye necessary to land prime opportunities instead of the tired, shopworn, and overpriced leftovers shrewd buyers have already by-passed.

Bill Von Buskirk, an acquisition consultant and entrepreneur with a string of successful businesses reports, "The trouble with most buyers is that they buy too soon. They don't realize the substantial spread in values and don't know how to dig out and investigate sufficient opportunities to provide an adequate feel for the market: they end up with the least for their money." I agree.

Buying too soon and rushing in too fast spelled trouble for Craig H., whose goal was to buy a liquor store south of Boston. After scanning the ads in the Boston Globe and placing a phone call to one local business broker, Craig uncovered five leads. "That's plenty," he thought. After three days of superficial investigation, Craig eagerly settled for a run-down liquor and wine shop with a hefty $80,000 price tag. "Don't buy just yet," I cautioned Craig. Flipping through the telephone directory yellow pages I counted 600 liquor stores in Craig's area. "How many of these stores are for sale right now?" I asked. "I don't know. At least five," he replied. Knowing that 15–20% of all businesses in a given industry are for sale at any given time. I told Craig he could have his pick of 100 liquor stores. Why settle for five? Craig, the overanxious buyer would not listen. Two weeks after he purchased his overpriced business he came across another liquor store with double the sales and profits and a bargain $60,000 price tag.

Several months ago a bank retained our firm to foreclose on a 20-room motel. Its hapless owner, Brian T., summed up his failure this way. "I managed the motel for someone else for twelve years before I bought it. My boss quoted an initial price of $400,000, so I thought I was doing well when he agreed to reduce the price to $360,000. I didn't realize comparable motels in the area were selling for about $12,000 a room and that a fair price would be closer to $240,000. Overpaying $120,000 was an expensive lesson."

You're not buying a pair of shoes you can easily replace if they're too tight; you are buying a business that demands a substantial investment. If you're a shrewd buyer you'll scan 20, 30, or even 100 businesses before you buy. You will if you want the business that fits.

DIGGING FOR THE DIAMONDS IN THE COAL

As a business acquisition consultant I demand a sizable fee for digging up the best opportunities—the diamonds in the coal-pile. Clients consider the fee a good investment, for they know the best opportunity will save them many times more than they pay me. But there's really no magic to locating worthwhile opportunities. You can do it yourself if you only:

1.   Uncover every business that's for sale in your line, and even the few that aren't for sale but could be with the right approach.
2.   Stand first in line when the right business does come along.

When I look for a business I use what I call the total scan. Face facts—

you're not only the buyer hunting for solid opportunities. You have plenty of competition. The trick is to go beyond conventional sources (newspaper ads and business brokers) to outdistance other buyers by tapping every conceivable source of leads. Contact sellers, talk to suppliers, advertise as a buyer, inquire at trade associations, and follow other commonly overlooked sources you'll learn about in this chapter. You never know who wants to sell or where or when you'll come across that important lead. But with a total scan you'll grow confident that if a business is for sale, you'll know about it.

Don't expect to find diamonds after everyone else has sifted the coal. You must be first in line to latch onto the best deals. Here's why. When a good business goes up for sale, an informal network springs into action. It only takes a phone call from the seller to a competitor to locate a logical buyer. Perhaps the seller has kept a list of buyers who previously have expressed interest. Even if the seller places the business with a broker, the broker probably has several long-standing clients who will snap up the business before you even know about it. You can't stand outside looking in; you must contact sellers *before* they decide to sell, and maintain contact so they come to you when they're ready.

COLD CANVASSING FOR HOT LEADS

No other source of leads beats going directly to the source itself. Direct-seller solicitation not only pulls the greatest number of leads—it pulls the best ones.

The majority of strong businesses aren't officially or actively for sale. Many sellers debate whether or not to sell, perhaps feeling they should wait for "the right buyer," or "the right offer." In other instances, the seller may have tried several ads or even a few brokers in the past, but stopped actively pursuing a sale because he changed his mind. Through direct contact, a buyer can open negotiations even when the seller never really considered selling.

I found an excellent coffee shop for a relative by being in the right place at the right time. The shop was owned by two quarreling partners who decided to sell on a Wednesday night following a bitter argument. Coincidentally, the next morning they received my letter advising them I had a client interested in buying a coffee shop. Anxious to rid themselves of the business, they snapped up my client's $20,000 offer. If the sellers had actively marketed the business they could have received substantially more. You have to let sellers know you want to buy.

Cold canvassing includes:

1.   Direct mail inquiry.

2. Telephone or personal visits.

3. Newspaper or trade journal ads.

Use all three to constantly bring your name to the attention of sellers. A seller may not respond to a letter, but may readily discuss his business over the phone. Newspaper or trade journal ads solve the problem of timing. A seller who is not ready to sell in March may spot your ad in a newspaper or trade journal in July when he is prepared.

The direct mail approach takes some effort, but it's worth it. A simple, personal inquiry letter can strike a responsive chord in the seller who might be put off by an impersonal newspaper ad. Follow the format successfully used by a young entrepreneur seeking his fifth greeting card and gift shop.

That simple letter mailed to 300 gift shops in the Chicago area pulled an amazing 60 inquiries from sellers. Only seven of these potential sellers had ever advertised their businesses for sale.

Some buyers offer a simple questionnaire on which sellers can provide details of their businesses. This is particularly common with large chains seeking to expand by acquiring independently owned businesses, because they can use the information to screen candidates. For first-time buyers the questionnaire approach may strike sellers as too formal. Remember, sellers

---

Arcade Gifts, Inc.
1000 Commonwealth Street
Chicago, Illinois 60666

Royal Card & Gift
14 Manchester Mall
Chicago, Illinois 60066

Gentlemen:

Our firm presently owns several card and gift shops and is looking to expand through further acquisition. We are most interested in shopping center, mall, and downtown locations between 1500–2500 sq ft.
If you are interested in selling now or at any time in the future, please contact us.

Very truly,

Arcade Gifts, Inc.
Ronald Henderson, Pres.
Tel. No. 888-1555

are cautious and often reluctant to share even basic information to other than a large or recognized buyer. Your inquiry letter can establish contact. Keep it simple, and:

1. Personalize the letter. You'll get a better response. Word-processing firms can create personalized letters at low cost, and the few extra pennies can be an excellent investment.

2. Send the letter to every business within the industry that interests you. The card and gift shop buyer simply consulted the yellow pages for names and addresses.

3. Identify yourself as a principal and not a broker. Many sellers refuse to respond to brokers because they'd like to save the commission.

4. Include a business card. A seller may disregard your letter because he's not ready to sell, but he can save your card for future reference.

5. Avoid using a fictitious name or a third party. It only makes sense when you have to protect your identity to protect your job.

6. Perfect your timing. If your target business experiences peak seasonal cycles, avoid business seasons. Sellers are less willing to part with their businesses when their cash registers are ringing.

Many sellers won't reply to a written inquiry at any time of the year. That's when the telephone becomes useful. After mailing letters I usually wait several weeks before resorting to the phone. Don't be timid. You only have one harmless question—"Is your business for sale?" As an ice-breaker, you can tell the seller you have heard his business is for sale and you're inquiring about it. He'll probably ask who told you it was for sale. Simply say you heard it from a friend who knows people in the trade. Oftentimes an interested seller will hesitate to discuss his intentions over the phone. After all, he doesn't know you and may not want to talk candidly in the presence of employees or customers. If you detect a willingness to talk, but some hesitancy, either offer to meet personally with the seller or let him return the call when it's convenient for him.

If you call 20 owners a day for 5 days, you'll find 15–20 potential candidates by the end of the week.

Sellers advertise, so why shouldn't buyers? I picked up my most recent acquisition through an $18 ad in the business opportunity section of the local newspaper.

For weeks my telephone kept ringing. One reason, of course, was the general nature of my ad. I was looking for any retail business with turnaround potential, and the mention of ready cash brings troubled owners out of hiding. If I had wanted a clothing store, I could have advertised for that specific type

---

BUYER WANTS SMALL
RETAIL BUSINESS
Cash available for any retail business
within 20 miles of Boston. Phone
principal at [tel. no.]

---

business. Run the ads every two or three weeks. Since telephone responses outpull written replies three to one, use a phone number rather than a post office box, even if you have to hire an answering service.

Don't overlook trade newsletters or journals as advertising media. Most trade publications accept classified ads and enjoy the interest of your targeted audience.

Our consulting firm has played a role in acquiring over 1500 businesses over the past 20 years, and our three-pronged cold canvass accounts for over 70% of them.

SUPPLIERS CAN SUPPLY LEADS

Next to the cold canvass, suppliers can offer your best source of leads. Make a list of all suppliers to your target industry. For example, if you wanted a tavern, you'd scout every liquor and beer distributor. But don't stop with the obvious suppliers, because you can get excellent leads from smaller or secondary suppliers, such as the paper supply distributors who stock the taverns with napkins and paper goods.

When contacting suppliers, get in touch with the right person within the organization, the people who frequently see their customers and are likely to have developed a relationship with them. Your best bets are credit managers and salespeople.

Unfortunately, suppliers tend to give their best leads to other valued customers, which not only creates good will, but assures the supplier customer continuity after the sale. Unless you happen to be an existing account, you're at a disadvantage. For that reason you should promise the supplier your own business should you buy through one of his leads. One client turned an entire crew of eight potato chip salespeople into his personal sales force when he told them he'd give a color TV to the one who steered him in the direction of an acquired superette. He knew the salespeople delivered potato chips twice a week to over 2000 food stores, and personally knew many owners. Over a period of months they put the buyer in touch with over 100 owners who were considering selling their superettes. My client laughs, "I don't know which business I'll end up with, but it'll certainly be worth a $300 television set." Remember, you compete with other buyers. Consider motivating people to bring you the leads first.

Be creative. There are many ways to reach sellers through suppliers. In one instance, a potential buyer for a bakery simply asked a wholesale flour company if they would insert a small mimeographed ad with their monthly billings. The bills and the bakery buyer's ad reached over 400 bakeries, and pulled 26 replies.

Don't forget to follow up. Out of sight is out of mind. Make it a point to call once a month to remind them you're still looking. But suppliers aren't likely to forget you; you may become a valuable customer.

TURNING A BROKER INTO A BLOODHOUND

Many buyers wonder whether brokers can help them find good opportunities. Though I own a large business brokerage firm myself, I rate brokers low on the list of valuable sources. Unlike many brokers, we specialize in acquisition consulting to buyers rather than to sellers. Most sellers turn to brokers after all other efforts to sell have failed. For every 100 listings, the typical broker ends up with 90 unsalable businesses, but that fact shouldn't stop you from calling brokers. The odds may not favor their listings, but that 1 out of 10 good listing may be your perfect business.

What about the 9 out of 10 unsalable businesses? Actually, if you go beyond the information contained on the broker's listing form, you may find a very good buy.

Consider these cases:

1.   We recently arranged a partnership for a large drug store we found in a local business broker's "morgue" file. The listing showed sales of $400,000 and an asking price of $200,000, but careful analysis proved it worth only $100,000. The broker insisted the seller was firm on his price and had recently refused a $160,000 offer. Nevertheless, I asked the broker to introduce me to the seller. It was perfect timing, because the seller's wife had recently left him, and he wanted to move to Florida. He was finally anxious to sell, so we accommodated him with $80,000. Never accept a broker's information at face value; circumstances change. What a seller tells his broker he wants and what he may accept can be two different things.

2.   In another case we represented a client looking to buy either

a stereo or appliance store. Contacting several brokers we finally found a stereo and record business for sale at $90,000. The broker had unsuccessfully listed the company for eight months because the seller demanded all cash and refused to help with the financing. A little investigation revealed that the seller thought he needed all cash because he had run up $86,000 in liabilities. Knowing the seller would end up with nothing after paying his debts and the broker's commission, my client offered to pay the seller $5,000 for his shares in the corporation and to pay the broker a $4,000 commission. For $9,000, my client took over the business, reduced the $86,000 debt to $25,000 through a Chapter 11 bankruptcy reorganization, and ended up with a highly profitable and solvent business. Many brokers and sellers don't understand creative financing, which I will discuss in detail in Chapter 8

3.   Arthur L. was a born detective. A broker told Arthur about a supermarket for sale for $120,000, which the broker confessed was overpriced, considering its anemic sales of $450,000. Arthur decided to look at the business and soon discovered that the seller intended to include as part of the $120,000 price the 5000 sq ft supermarket building, which was worth close to $200,000. The amazed broker now confesses he would have snapped up the deal himself had he known the facts.

Follow these guidelines when checking out a broker's listing:

1.   *Don't* pay any attention to what a broker lists as a sales price. No one knows what's acceptable until an offer lies on the table.

2.   *Don't* be discouraged by a broker's stated sales or financing terms. As with price, you don't know what will work until you actually structure a deal, and you may know more about creative financing than either the broker or seller.

3.   *Don't* pay any attention to how long a business has been on the market. An old listing may simply mean other buyers haven't probed deeply enough to get all the facts.

4.   *Do* check out every listing that could conceivably interest you. All a broker can tell you for certain is the name and location of the business. To find out more you must play Sherlock Holmes yourself.

5.   *Do* remember that a broker represents the seller, not you, the buyer. He's obligated to list the seller's terms and to do his best to bring the seller the best offer. But he's also obligated to show you the business

and introduce you to the seller so you can investigate and negotiate adequately.

Many buyers hope to buy businesses at lower prices by avoiding brokers whose commissions inflate prices. It's false economy. In very few cases does the broker's commission materially affect what you will pay for the business. In fact, the existence of a middleman in the negotiations can offer a buyer considerable benefit. Most brokers perform that valuable service quite well, and can mediate deals that wouldn't come to pass through direct confrontation between buyer and seller. Don't look at the broker as a needless expense. He plays a role far more important than merely showing you a business.

Approach all the brokers in your area. Don't limit yourself to the largest or the most responsive. You don't know which broker may have the right listing hiding in his or her files until you inquire. Bear in mind that brokers advertise fewer than 10% of their listings. Generally, newspaper ads promote easily salable businesses or those that have the widest appeal.

A few simple rules will help you deal effectively with brokers:

1. Start with ones that specialize in your type of business. Firms specializing in specific businesses such as restaurants, liquor stores, taverns, motels, food stores, drugstores, and greeting card shops are common in most major cities. For example, *Restaurant Brokers of America* handles only restaurants and related businesses. Interested in a country business in New England? You'd be wise to choose a firm such as *Country Business Brokers* in Vermont. If you want farm property anywhere in the United States, consult *United Farm Agency.* Though you'll find a list of specialty brokers in Appendix A, glance at your own metropolitan newspaper or yellow pages to find the specialists in your area. Specialty brokers know their industry and can help you establish values, arrange financing, and enjoy a wide selection.

2. Franchised, or networked, business brokers have multiple offices within your area or throughout the country. Like multiple listings in real estate, each office benefits from the listings of every other office, giving you a broad selection. For example, *VR Business Brokers* has offices throughout Massachusetts and in other parts of the country as well. If you visit any VR office, you can consider listings from all their offices. Like specialty brokers, they can offer you valuable assistance because their size permits them to employ specialists in all phases of business acquisition.

3. Smaller independent business brokers offer certain advan-

tages, too. You'll find wide variation in their abilities and approaches, so start with brokerage firms that advertise the most in your area. What results you obtain from business brokers may depend more on the specific broker within the organization than on the agency itself. Business brokers are like anyone else. There are the active and the lazy. The active broker may not have what you want but he'll actively look for it. If you contact a multiple broker office try to spot the most aggressive broker.

4. Occasionally real estate firms offer business brokerage as a sideline. In rural areas, which usually can't support a full-time business broker, all brokered businesses go through real estate offices. I don't suggest you spend time with real estate firms that only occasionally handle businesses unless you're looking for a motel, car wash, nursing home, or other business frequently considered a real estate investment, or unless you spot an ad by a real estate agent who happens to have a business closely matching your criteria.

Pretend you're fishing. The more lines you drop in the water, the better the chances that you'll land your ideal fish. If you can't visit every broker in your area, send out detailed letters outlining your specific needs. Periodic follow-up letters will let them know you are still interested.

Can you turn a broker into your bloodhound? That will depend on whether or not he sees you as a serious buyer. Nothing irritates brokers more than the perennial shopper who wastes their time. You must convince them that you are serious, you know what you want, and you are ready to buy.

You'll stand out among other buyers if you:

1. Call for an appointment. Don't walk in cold. Brokers are professionals and enjoy dealing with buyers who treat them as professionals.

2. Look like a business person. Appearance and dress count. Strive for a good first impression. The broker will size you up quickly and put you into a slot, and you want him to place you in the serious-buyer category.

3. Prepare a portfolio to give the broker. A brief resume demonstrating your experience and reliability will help establish you as a serious buyer. Your portfolio should contain a description of the type of business you want, including location and other requirements. Virtually all small business buyers simply come in to the broker's office and verbalize what they're looking for. There's nothing wrong with that, but when you show up with a well prepared package, they really stand up and take notice.

4. *Don't tell the broker you have limited cash.* Let him think you have

or can obtain required funds for the right opportunity. When a broker discovers your limited cash he may fail to show you some good listings requiring higher down payments. But as you'll learn in Chapter 8, creative financing can greatly reduce that obstacle.

5. Create the impression that you're relying on that particular broker. Brokers work harder if they think they have the inside track. Nevertheless, you should shop with every broker in town.

6. Make yourself available to inspect a lot of businesses with the broker. By visiting many firms, you'll learn to become a master investigator, and you'll convince the broker that you're an earnest buyer. Of course, the more businesses you inspect, the more likely you'll eventually find the ideal one for you.

7. When you decline a business, tell the broker why, so he can narrow his focus to the right business.

8. *Don't* lose contact with the broker. New listings arrive every day, and the broker may no longer consider you an active buyer. A phone call every two to three weeks is appropriate.

9. *Don't* try to by-pass the broker hoping to save a seller the commission and yourself part of the purchase price. Stay honest and you'll avoid what may be some very expensive legal problems.

10. *Don't* confide to a broker any information which may hurt you later in negotiations. One buyer foolishly told a broker he was recently fired and was desperate to find a business. That type of statement can come back to haunt you later. Remember, the broker works for the seller not the buyer.

BROKERS FROM THE SELLER'S VIEWPOINT

A buyer can benefit from looking at brokers from the seller's side of the table, which will not only help him negotiate more effectively, but will come in handy years later when the buyer himself becomes a seller.

A seller in search of a buyer can't rely on any one foolproof way to quickly and inexpensively locate that right buyer. But I offer the following useful tips to sellers:

1. Hire a broker as soon as you decide to sell. Many sellers unsuccessfully attempt to sell on their own for months, and by the time they turn to a broker the business has the reputation of being shopworn or stale.

2. Never give a broker an exclusive right to sell. Most brokers bargain for

such an appointment so they can get a commission no matter who finds the buyer within a certain period. Brokers argue that this protecton will motivate them to advertise and promote the sale more extensively than otherwise. In many cases their argument is logical, but you might suggest a compromise: an exclusive *agency*. That means you reserve the right to compete with the broker yourself to find a buyer, but that you will not appoint another broker during the contract period. Stand firm. Many brokers will try to talk you into the exclusive right to sell, and may even bluff that they won't accept your listing on other terms. Except for some of the very large or specialized brokers, most will agree to an exclusive agency.

3. Sensibly limit the time period for any exclusive agency. Most brokers will want the appointment to run from six months to a year. That's not unreasonable if you own a large or specialized business. However, typical businesses and virtually all retailers should bargain for a three-month exclusive agency, which is adequate for a broker to show you how actively he can sell. If you're satisfied, you can extend the contract another three to six months. If not, you can switch brokers without having wasted too much time.

4. Only grant an exclusive agency when you're convinced the broker can outperform any other broker or all other brokers combined under an "open" or "non-exclusive" appointment. Sellers should rank the various kinds of brokers the same way buyers do. Interview several brokers before you appoint one. Ask how they intend to promote your business and how many businesses like yours they have sold. Check the newspapers to see how actively they advertise other businesses.

5. Some sellers prefer to avoid any type of exclusive arrangement in favor of giving the listing to as many brokers as possible. That's generally a mistake. Under an exclusive a broker will work for you. If other brokers have a buyer for your business they'll work through your broker on a co-broker arrangement, sharing the commission.

6. Let's talk frankly about commissions. Prevailing brokers' commissions run about 10%. Larger businesses with high price tags may involve a sliding commission (10% of the first 200,000, 6% of the next 200,000, etc.). However, commissions are not regulated and may be open to negotiations. Again, large or very successful firms don't need to dicker over commissions, but many small firms do. You may agree initially on a 10% commission, but when it comes time to cement a deal where the financing is tight, the broker may agree to settle for 6–8% to insure the sale. So you really have two chances to negotiate the commission. In other cases a broker may accept your listing on a reduced commis-

sion if he's confident he will find a buyer with very little effort. Perhaps he already has a buyer in the wings. However, as your listing competes with other listings for the broker's time and advertising dollars, you should make it worth his while to spend time and dollars on your business.

7. Brokers work less hard for sellers who practice dual pricing, offering the business at $100,000 if the seller finds his own buyer, but at $110,000 if the broker finds one. Such "net price" listings usually end up in the broker's dead file. Why run an ad with a $110,000 price alongside the seller's own ad at $100,000?

8. Consult with the broker about your price and proposed terms of sale. Though brokers should know the market, you should never rely solely on their judgment. A broker may suggest a low sales price to achieve a quick sale and commission. After all, he sees little difference between $10,000 today and $12,000 six months from now.

9. If your business fails to sell after many buyers have looked at it, review the reasons with the broker. The broker hears buyer's comments and frequently can spot one major correctable reason a business isn't selling.

WHAT NEWSPAPER ADS REALLY TELL YOU

Experienced buyers seem to share the opinion that newspaper ads offer the least desirable businesses. I don't agree. Here's why:

1. Very small businesses with price tags under $35,000–40,000 can't afford the $5,000–7,500 minimum commission that many brokers charge, so newspaper ads provide a practical alternative for reaching buyers.

2. Many seller first try to sell on their own to avoid a broker's commission and only turn to brokers after they fail to obtain results through newspaper ads. For this reason you may discover the first announcement that a business is for sale in a newspaper ad.

3. Plenty of insolvent, unprofitable businesses haunt the opportunity sections, but some buyers want exactly those kinds of businesses, hoping to buy low and turn the business around. If you're a turn-around buyer, newspaper ads may be your best source of leads.

However, with these few exceptions in mind, you'll find few solid opportunities in newspaper ads. If you do, you'll have to move fast, for they won't be there long.

Of course, you'll notice that brokers place many of the ads. In a broker's ad you'll only see the best or most salable businesses. Brokers don't spend advertising dollars on losers, but they aren't above advertising "too-good-to-be-true" businesses or basically fictitious ones to lure naïve buyers. Here's how it works. A broker may have an inventory of 20 deadbeat food stores for which he needs buyers, but he'll advertise a high sales, high profit, low-priced low-cash-down superette. The next morning he hears from 50–100 buyers whom he sadly informs that the advertised business is "sold" but he luckily has 20 other "excellent" buys. It's the brokerage industry's own "bait and switch" trick. Not all brokers do it, of course, but you should read ads with skepticism.

Now for a quick course on how to find some winners among the many losers in your local newspaper:

1. Don't start with the current newspaper. Visit the newspaper office and pull the Sunday classifieds for the past year, where you'll find many ads for businesses that didn't sell, are no longer advertised, but may still be on the market. For example, a client hired our firm to find a large flower shop because current ads disclosed only six florists for sale. Scanning the ads for the past year, we found 30 others. Of these 30, 18 were still for sale. Our client eventually purchased one that had been advertised nine months earlier. A "stale" business isn't necessarily a bad business.

2. Be analytical. Today's ads include businesses advertised last week, last month, and the month before that. But notice how the terms change as the seller becomes increasingly desperate. Prior ads allow you to track that desperation and can provide a valuable negotiating tool.

Not long ago a client showed me an ad for a discount store for which the seller wanted $100,000 with $40,000 down. It looked familiar to me. Pulling last month's classifieds I found the same business advertised for $140,000, and two months earlier I spotted it for $160,000. My client, assured of the seller's anxiety, picked up the business for $78,000 with $18,000 down.

3. Read between the lines. How a seller words the ad can give you valuable clues. Here's how I translate:

    a) *"Established Business"*: It's either a business started in 1888 that should have closed in 1943 or a business started four months ago that bombed.

    b) *"Owner Must Sell"* or *"Illness Forces Sale"*: The owner either must sell before he goes bankrupt or he's sick of the business.

c) *"Financing Available"* or *"Low Cash Down"*: Either the business is grossly overpriced or the seller is desperate to bail out.

d) *"Terms Negotiable"*: Another subtle sign of desperation.

e) *"Call Owner's Attorney"*: It's probably either an insolvent business or an estate sale. Few attorneys handle such responses under normal circumstances.

f) *"New Store"* or *"New Fixtures"*: Such words signal a recent opening. Why do you suppose the seller wants to sell so quickly?

4. Some ads use a box number instead of a telephone number. Written responses should only say that you read the ad and you're interested in more information. Don't volunteer anything more.

5. Notice whether the ads appear only on Sunday or during the week as well. Anxious owners usually advertise several times a week. Brokers seldom do.

6. If you should ignore what a broker tells you about price and terms, you should also ignore what a newspaper ad tells you. One seller consistently advertised his auto body shop at a $60,000 cash price, which undoubtedly discouraged many buyers who swallowed it, but one young chap, who never accepts ads at face value, picked up the business for $38,000 with only $12,000 down. It's worth repeating: sources provide leads, not reliable facts. You never know about any lead until you investigate it yourself.

ADS THAT PULL LEADS

Now let's switch gears and consider effective newspaper advertising from a seller's viewpoint. The well-designed ad will attract the greatest number of qualified buyers and will screen out those who wouldn't be qualified.

The ideal ad will provide the reader three points of information:

1. General nature of the business.
2. Approximate size or sales.
3. Approximate area.

Look familiar? These are the criteria a buyer has in mind when he searches out a business.

Here are two effective ads as models:

Hardware Store Full lines including building supplies. $700,000 sales. Medford area. Owner. Tel. No.	**Motel For Sale** Modern 30-room motel and adjoining coffee shop. $1,500,000 income. Profitable. Excel. Financing. 10 miles south of Detroit. Tel. No.

Notice how these ads really tell the reader what he has to know to decide if he's interested.

But consider these points also:

1. You may not want to define your business or its location so precisely that employees and suppliers can identify it. So eliminate distinguishing characteristics. In the first ad it said the business was located in the Medford area in order not to alarm employees by giving the actual location (a town adjoining Medford). But it wouldn't matter to buyers.

2. Obviously, you don't want to use the business telephone number if secrecy is a factor. Don't use a known home phone number either. I recommend either an answering service or a new unlisted phone line to your home. Remember, box numbers don't pull.

3. Don't put price, cash requirements, or reason for sale in the ads. Knowledgeable buyers can estimate these terms, and it's best left to the stage of initial contact and negotiations.

4. I recommend a bold heading ad. It's slightly more expensive, but worth the cost.

5. If you have a large business, consider advertising in *The Wall Street Journal*. Buyers for larger, specialized businesses are willing to relocate.

LOOKING FOR A FRANCHISE?

Franchises involve following a different path, because most franchises are sold directly by the franchisor. When a franchisee wants to sell his franchise, the franchisor usually will reacquire the business or oversee its sale.

Whether you want to open a new franchise location or purchase an existing franchise, you'll save time if you simply contact the franchisor directly. Write to any of the following for comprehensive listings of franchise offerings.

International Franchise Association
7315 Wisconsin Avenue
Washington, D.C. 20014

U.S. Superintendent of Documents
Washington, D.C.
(ask for the Commerce Department's
Franchising Opportunities Handbook)

Pilot Books
347 Fifth Avenue
New York, New York 10016
(ask for *Directory of Franchising
Organizations*)

It's worth a phone call to obtain current prices of each.

You can also find some descriptive display ads, particularly for newer franchise offerings in both *The Wall Street Journal* and Sunday's *New York Times*. Other metropolitan newspapers may also feature such ads.

Three magazines that include franchise ads are *Entrepreneur, Venture,* and *Inc.*, which you can find at most newsstands.

You may notice that once or twice a year Franchise Opportunity shows are held in major cities. It's an enjoyable way to spend an afternoon, but you won't find many of the better, well-established franchisors at the exhibits. Most exhibitors are selling highly speculative distributorships.

Don't look for *McDonalds, Burger King,* or other "blue-chip" franchises in any ads or shows. Because they enjoy a long backlist of ready buyers, they don't have to advertise. If you think you meet their rigid qualifications and are willing to wait, you might fill out an application. However, if you can't afford to wait, you should probably start on a smaller scale. Consider the 1000 lesser-known franchises, that encompass virtually every type of business.

MORE PROFITABLE, BUT LITTLE-KNOWN, SOURCES

Have you laced your hunting boots tightly? Consider these frequently over-looked sources:

Trade or professional associations may not carry classified ads in their newsletters or publications, but many do maintain a buyer-seller file as a membership benefit. Call both local and state associations representing your target industry.

Check the bulletin board or talk to the placement director at local *schools* or *colleges* turning out people headed for your industry. Pharmacists, beauticians, barbers, embalmers, and even physicians and dentists attempting to sell their professional practices often inquire at their alma maters, hoping to attract recent graduates as buyers.

In the market for a troubled company? Excellent sources include *auctioneers, court-appointed receivers,* and *bankruptcy trustees,* as well as *public records,* which list recent tax liens and business attachments. A network of *insolvency lawyers* and *turnaround consultants* can constantly feed you leads.

DON'T OVERLOOK YOUR BOSS

Almost 20% of all buyers end up buying their employers' businesses. So your business may be right under your feet.

First, consider whether or not the business meets your criteria. As you recall from the prior chapter, it can be a mistake to buy a business simply because it's available or easy to find. Judge the business by the same standards as any other prospective acquisition.

Then, if the business does satisfy your criteria, keep your ear close to the ground for telltale signs that the business may become available. Employer's age, health, or business conditions are clues. If you think he may be interested, don't be too shy to inquire.

I can tell you about one sales manager who worked for a wholesale meat firm owned by a larger corporation. He considered it the business he'd most like to own, but of course his employers never knew of his interest. Anxious to sell for tax reasons, the company was sold to an outsider, to the surprise of the sales manager who had no idea it was on the market. Storming into his boss' office he stammered, "Why didn't you tell me the damn business was for sale? I would have bought it in a minute!" Peering over his glasses, his boss quietly answered, "Why didn't you ask?"

That's what the hunt is all about. Asking!

FINAL POINTERS

1. Be a systematic hunter. Set up a schedule and an itinerary. How many leads will you seek out each week? How many businesses can you visit each week? You'll probably want to visit only one out of every five leads, so plan accordingly.

2. Keep a notebook, and record the preliminary information on each lead. After you've looked at 20–30 businesses, you may feel lost in a maze unless you have the information for each business at your fingertips.

3. Spread the word. You never know who might give you a good lead. I know a barber in Chicago who has put many businesspeople in touch with each other.

4. Most sellers try to keep the fact that their business is for sale a secret from their employees, customers, and suppliers for much the same reason you don't want your employer to know your intentions. That's why you must honor confidentiality and arrange clandestine inspections and negotiations. Don't enter the seller's business, talk in front of employees or customers, or call suppliers for a reference without the seller's permission.

5. How long will the hunt take? It depends on your energy and available time, the nature and scarcity of the business you seek, your flexibility, and a little luck. I have purchased businesses a few days after I began the search, while in other instances it has taken me as long as a year to find what I wanted. In one case I wasn't even in the market for a business, but it presented too good an opportunity to pass up. That can easily happen to you too, once you're in business and people begin to approach you with additional opportunities. As one buyer confesses, "If you know what you're looking for, and if realistic, you won't have to wait long to find your right opportunity, if you look."

KEY POINTS TO REMEMBER

Before buying, you must investigate enough opportunities to recognize your best bet.

A proper search depends on considering every available source of leads.

Direct seller contact provides the best leads.

Motivate suppliers to scout for you.

Brokers work hardest for serious buyers.

Newspapers contain good opportunities if you know how to spot them.

Spread the word. As one broker insists, "Every business is for sale under the right conditions.

4

INVESTIGATE FOR ALL IT'S WORTH

Legend tells of an enterprising swindler who bilked a fortune from gullible people through a simple ad in a local newspaper: "Send $5.00 and I'll put you in a profitable business overnight." The $5.00 checks poured in followed by a quick response—"Do what I'm doing."

You'll be spending considerably more than $5.00 to buy your business. Investigate for all it's worth.

Investigating the business has several objectives. It will help you:

1. *Verify* the seller's representations about the business.
2. *Determine* the business' value.
3. *Detect* pitfalls and problems with the business.
4. *Forecast* the future of the business.
5. *Negotiate* by pinpointing problems the seller may have with the business.
6. *Finance* the acquisition through disclosures on its financial statement.

Sound like a complicated process? It can be. In this chapter we'll walk through a typical investigation of a small business to remove some of the mystery and to guide you in analyzing your own acquisition.

Let's assume you're interested in a hardware store with sales in the $300,000-$500,000 range. You're flexible, as overhead, profits, price, and financing are of equal importance.

One morning you see an ad in the newspaper announcing the sale of a hardware store. You know nothing else about the business. Where do you start?

QUALIFYING THE BUSINESS

Every investigation is a two-step process, and answers two broad questions:

1. It is a "do-able" deal?
2. It is the "deal to do"?

The first question requires you to qualify the business and quickly determine whether or not it meets your minimum criteria. It filters out the unworkable or undesirable opportunities that don't justify an intensive investigation.

Let's start with the hardware store ad. How can you put it through the filter to see if it qualifies for further investigation? Of course, you'll need substantially more information, so you call the number on the ad. What do you ask? Location is all you want to know by telephone. If it's in a town or area you don't want, why pursue it further? An on-site inspection won't change the fact that it doesn't match your location criteria. The only other purpose of the call is to set up an appointment. Ask nothing further by phone. The seller may not want to provide more information without meeting you, and even if he does, it's inconclusive without an on-site inspection.

Upon meeting with the seller at the business, you'll be able to scan the situation. Now the business is coming to life. You can see how it's run, how effective the merchandising is, and whether or not the business has potential. If the business still appears to interest you, it's time for your follow-up questions:

Sales
Asking Price (and how based)
Financing
Lease

Let's take a closer look at the importance and purpose of each question.

1. *Sales:* Perhaps the seller tells you the hardware store grosses only $200,000, but you're experienced in the hardware business and you need a store grossing $300,000–500,000 to produce the income you want. Did you waste your time checking out the business? Absolutely not. You see the business and how it's operated so you can quickly assess whether the $200,000 volume can be increased. Maybe it can, so it still qualifies. And it may even be a better buy than the business with the existing $500,000 sales if you can build the sales yourself. That's why you should never ask sales without inspecting the business. You're interested in what the sales can become, not what they are.

I know a buyer who refuses to inspect a business unless sales are at a certain level. He called on a supermarket and was told its sales were $1,500,000. "Sorry, not interested," he said replying he wanted one with sales of at least $3,000,000. He never bothered to find out how rundown the business was or measure its potential. Another buyer picked it up at a bargain price and within a year the registers were ringing up over $6,000,000.

Can that hardware store produce the sales you want?

2. *Asking Price:* You want the answer, but it's hardly a "qualifier." The seller tells you he's looking for $125,000 based on a $60,000 inventory, and the remaining $65,000 for fixtures and good will. You figure the business is worth about $70,000. Should you walk out? No, stay with it. The business shouldn't be eliminated because price is out of line. You don't know what the seller will really sell for. You'll find out later when you negotiate.

It's amazing how many buyers quickly disqualify a business based on asking price. If they stayed with it, they may have found they could have picked up the business for considerably less than what they think it's worth. If it's unimportant, why ask? You only want an idea of the asking price as a prelude to future negotiations.

3. *Financing:* Once you know the asking price, the logical follow-up question is about financing. Come right out with it. Ask "How much of a down payment do you expect and how will you finance the balance?" Of course, your question implies you expect seller financing. The seller will probably tell you "Sorry, no financing. I want cash." As with asking price, the answer means very little. The seller may end up financing 90% on a $70,000 sales price. He just doesn't know it yet, or *want* to know. You'll tell him about it later. However, the business still qualifies. Don't let high down payment or other excessive financing terms scare you away.

4. *Lease:* This is the important question. Ask the seller what lease terms are available. Since he's probably not the landlord he may not know what your lease will look like, but he does tell you he's paying $600 a month and has two years left on a 10-year lease. He hazards a guess that the landlord will give you 10 years, but increase rent to $1,000. Focus on the two essential terms, rent and term. An unfavorable lease can quickly disqualify a business.

Many businesses can't be sold because rents are unreasonably excessive. You can't work for the landlord. If the seller told you the landlord won't give a lease but will allow only a month-to-month tenancy, then you shouldn't continue.

Richard Tamer, with over 12 small business acquisitions behind him, puts the qualifying process in perspective. "When I look at a business I'm interested in, I quickly scan to see whether it has or can develop adequate sales to produce reasonable profits. I'm looking for the 'ballpark' estimate. The lease and rent terms is the only other essential point. I won't be saddled with excessive rents or a short-term lease. If those two points satisfy me I move forward, the reasons for sale, asking price, financing, and history of the business are of secondary importance."

You should qualify a business the same way.

1. Can it provide the sales you want?
2. Can you obtain an adequate lease?
3. Does the location satisfy you?

PUT TOGETHER YOUR TEAM

The time to retain an accountant and attorney is when you find a business that qualifies. You can't intelligently probe the business further without professional assistance.

I offer these guidelines in selecting your advisors.

Finding Accountants Who Know the Store

A small business doesn't require a certified public accountant, since your financial statements probably won't require certification for financing.

You do want to select the accountant who will remain as your permanent accountant once you buy a business. Your best bet is unquestionably an accountant with heavy experience in your type of business. There's a good reason for this advice: every business has its own characteristics. An accountant familiar with the hardware business is also familiar with its operating ratios. He can even help you with managerial decisions on handling creditors and suppliers, as he has worked with these suppliers through other clients. Needless to say, an accountant who knows the industry can best investigate the business.

Many accountants fall short in providing the financial guidance a business needs, and this need is even more acute with a newly acquired or start-up business. You want more than tax returns. When interviewing prospective accountants, inquire about the specific services he'll provide.

Where can you find the accountant who knows your type of business? Many accountants have a large client roster within an industry. I know accountants who specialize in nursing homes, motels, food stores, liquor stores, pharmacies, and virtually any other common business. Check around.

You Need a "Creative" Attorney

Your attorney's role in the investigation process may come later, as his primary responsibility is to see that you're protected from legal pitfalls. The financial investigation will help you decide whether or not to buy. The legal investigation starts once a tentative agreement is reached.

That shouldn't forestall the decision to retain counsel early. The right attorney can spot ways to structure the transaction, obtain financing, and help you negotiate.

The most important points to look for in hiring an attorney to represent you on an acquisition is his financing knowledge and negotiating ability.

Surprisingly, in most transactions it's the attorney, not the accountant, who designs the financing arrangement, although it certainly may be a team effort. Negotiations are almost always handled by the attorney. The mechancs of drafting the documents, checking title, the other routine matters can be handled by most attorneys, although you want one with experience in representing business buyers. But you want more than a technician. You want a creative attorney; the lawyer who can show you better ways to reach your goals, find the money and bargain the seller down. So forget your brother-in-law who only handles criminal cases. It's false economy.

When a Consultant Makes Sense

For first-time buyers, a third member of the team should be added. Bring abroad someone experienced within the industry to help you analyze operations. The investigation must go far beyond your accountant checking out the numbers or your attorney approving the legal documents.

In one of our recent transactions, a buyer for a large clothing store hired a New York clothing merchandiser to review the business, which featured an imported line of women's wear. The consultant immediately pointed out that the manufacturer intended to discontinue operations. With the foreseeable loss of the major supplier, the buyer wisely turned the business down.

Unless you're thoroughly familiar with the industry, you'll need someone who is. Inquire within the industry for someone who'll spend two or three days helping you check out the business. It's the best investment you can make.

THE INFORMATION YOU'LL NEED

Serious investigation of a business depends on sifting through a mass of information. But you'll have your team to help.

In large measure, the scope and priorities of your investigation will depend on the nature of the business, your objectives in buying it, and how it will be acquired.

> A mail-order firm for example, would require emphasis on investigating product lines, sales analysis, and competition.
>
> A hardware chain interested in acquiring our hypothetical hardware store may be interested primarily in its location, and may pay little attention to the seller's financial statements, confident that its operational approach will produce entirely different sales and profitability.
>
> If a buyer is planning to acquire the seller's shares of stock and take over his existing corporation, he must thoroughly check for hidden liabilities within the corporation. A purchase of assets creates much less concern over the liabilities of the seller's corporation.

Your accountant and attorney will decide what must be investigated based on these factors, however, the operational investigation is your responsibility.

What information do you need from the seller to start? Use this checklist:

1. Tax returns for prior three years
2. Financial statements for prior three years
3. List of accounts payable and liabilities
4. Financial books and records of the business
5. Copies of any notes or mortgages owed
6. Existing contracts
7. Present lease
8. Corporate books (if incorporated) or partnership agreement (if a partnership)

Don't hesitate to add to this list if a particular business justifies further information, however, for most businesses this list will suffice.

Once you ask the seller for this information, you may find that either he'll refuse to give you part or all of the documents or they won't be available. It's a common problem with small businesses.

If he refuses to give you the documents it may mean he doesn't consider you a serious buyer. Look at it from the seller's perspective. He doesn't know you. You only recently glided in off the street and now want him to bare his financial soul to you. Be patient, build confidence, and show him you're serious. It's the best cure. He may be afraid the information won't be held confidential. It's a legitimate concern. Offer to have your accountant review the records with his accountant. The seller's reluctance may be due to the fact that he's been skimming to beat taxes. He doesn't want to put together books that make financial sense.

Perhaps the seller hasn't the books to show you. Small business people are notorious for not keeping adequate books. At the least he should have tax returns.

Faced with the inevitable dilemma of getting your hands on adequate information, you and your team will have to make a value judgment on whether to continue or call it quits. With most small businesses you can restructure sufficient information without the seller's books, provided you at least have his cooperation.

WHY YOU CHECK THE LEASE FIRST

Qualifying the business was based on the seller's representations about the lease. The serious investigation should start with verification of the available lease. Often a good sale breaks down right there.

There are many cases of a buyer spending considerable time and money checking out a business, negotiating, and even committing to financing, only to approach the landlord for a new lease, and find out an acceptable lease can't be negotiated.

You can't realistically determine the value of a business, or negotiate price, or even decide whether or not you want the business until you know your lease terms. So starting with the landlord is a must.

Some sellers resist introducing you to the landlord at this early point. They may still question your sincerity as a buyer, or not want the landlord to know they plan to sell until a deal is finalized. Other sellers, with only a short-term remaining on their lease, fear the buyer will go around them by signing a lease to commence when their lease terminates. The buyer, of course, can then play the waiting game and pick up the location without paying for good will, while the seller is forced to liquidate instead of sell.

If you run into this problem, offer the seller a written acknowledgment that you will only sign a lease "pursuant to an agreed" sale. He's entitled to that protection.

For most businesses the lease is the most important asset and requires as much evaluation as the business itself.

Follow this checklist in evaluating the lease:

1. **Rent:** Is it for a flat rent, percentage of sales, or both? How does the proposed rent measure as a percentage of sales? Is the rent within industry averages as a percentage of sales?

2. *What does the rent include?* Does it include utilities, air conditioning, and heat, or are these your responsibilities. Are you required to pay real estate taxes or insurance? What other occupancy costs are you expected to pay?

3. **Term:** How long a lease can you obtain? Will you have an option to extend or renew? What are the option terms and rent?

Many buyers overlook the importance of the lease either by paying too high a rent or by settling for too short a lease term.

Follow these guidelines:

Rent and other occupancy costs in excess of industry averages can only be justified if you obtain a corresponding decrease in the price of the business, or if the location allows for higher price mark-ups. For example, hardware stores pay average rentals of 4% of sales. If you're confident you can generate $300,000 in sales, an appropriate rent would be about $12,000. Beyond that you're cutting into profits. However, gross profits within this industry are 33%. You may be in a noncompetitive area and work on a 40% gross profit. An extra percentage point or two for rent is justified.

Many bankruptcies are due to excess rent. We recently liquidated a pharmacy paying $30,000 rent on $300,000 sales. To say within industry averages and produce a profit his rent shouldn't exceed $9,000. The owner told us what so many owners say "I knew the rent was high, but I believed I could build the sales to cover it."

Don't accept a lease for a shorter time period than necessary to recoup your investment from profits. If a business is available for $100,000 and can generate only $10,000 in profits, a 10-year lease is an absolute minimum. Bargain for as long a lease as you can. If you can get a 10-year lease, try for one or two 5-year options. Many landlords resist by saying they don't know what a fair rent would be so far into the future. This can be resolved by basing rent on a cost-of-living index. If the landlord is looking for a high increase for a new lease, see if you can assume the seller's present lease. It may require you to take over the shares in his corporation to accomplish it. For example, the seller's corporation may have 10 years remaining on his lease, with an annual rent of $10,000. Under a new lease the landlord may want $15,000. Acquiring the seller's corporation and lease would save you $50,000 in the next 10 years.

Don't play blindman's bluff. Check out the lease. It may serve you wasted conversation.

WHAT THE INCOME STATEMENT TELLS YOU

The income statement is a summary of the income and expenses of the business for the period covered. It shows the profitability (or loss) for the period.

Let's analyze the income statement for the hardware store:

XYZ HARDWARE, INC.
INCOME STATEMENT
January 1, 1981–December 31, 1981

Sales:		$220,000
Cost of goods sold		140,000
Gross profit		80,000
Expenses:		
Owner's salary	$18,000	
Other payroll	35,000	
Payroll taxes	5,000	
Rent	10,000	
Utilities	4,000	
Depreciation	2,000	
Insurance	1,500	
Accounting & legal	1,000	
Miscellaneous expenses	3,000	
Total expenses		79,500
Net profit (before taxes)		500

In Chapter 6, you'll see how to use the seller's financial statements as a basis for calculating your own. However, for the purposes of investigating you'll focus only on several points in the seller's statement. Adopt this checklist.

1. *Sales:*

   a) What are the year-to-year changes in sales? compare sales for the past 3 years. Are sales increasing? decreasing? by how much?

   b) What growth in sales (if any) can be attributed to inflation? to growth within the industry? Define the real sales increases.

   c) Why are sales increasing or decreasing? This is the critical question. If sales are decreasing or stagnating due to location, it will be difficult to increase. If it's due to poor merchandising or internal reasons, isolate the reasons.

   d) How secure are the sales? Are a large percentage of sales generated from one or two sources or accounts? Can you retain these accounts?

   e) How accurate are the sales? This is for your accountant to verify. He should conduct an audit based on purchases, bank deposits, tax return comparisons, and daily sales records.

   f) Are sales seasonal? This may be important in deciding when to close the sale, and the resultant price.

2. *Gross Profit:*

   a) Are profit margins in line with industry averages? Why or why not?

   b) Has gross profit been based on actual inventory tabulations, or is it estimated?

   c) What is the gross profit trend? How has it changed over the prior three years? Be on the lookout for declining gross profits. It may signify increased price competition.

   d) Are prices in line? Does the pricing appear to be too low? too high? Consider both area and competition.

   e) Does the business buy on favorable terms? Check invoices for prices and terms. Are these same prices and terms available to you?

3. *Expenses:*

   a) What expenses are increasing or decreasing in relation to sales?

   b) What is the ratio of operating expenses to sales? How does it compare to prior statements?

   c) Are selling costs (salaries, advertising and delivery) increasing, decreasing or remaining the same in relation to sales?

   d) How accurate are the expenses? Each expense item should be audited by your accountant.

Calculate each item on the income statement as a percentage of sales. Measure it against averages within the industry using comparative statistics found in trade publications or obtainable from your bank or the Bank of America *Business Reports* (see Chapter 3).

The profitability of the business should not be the important question, as its profitability will change under your management and you'll be in a better position to project that profitability using the techniques in Chapter 6.

A QUICK LOOK AT THE BALANCE SHEET

The seller's balance sheet will show you:

1. The value of the assets
2. The amount of liabilities
3. The owner's net worth (assets less liabilities)

The balance sheet is an important document to investigate with a larger business, as the acquisition of the firm is usually structured with the buyer acquiring the shares in the seller's corporation. Since most small companies are sold by transferring assets, the buyer has considerably less concern about the seller's liabilities. However, the balance sheet analysis can quickly pinpoint the financial solvency of the business. This is important for two reasons:

1. A poor financial condition can define your bargaining position when it comes time to negotiate.
2. Assuming liabilities can be an effective way to finance the business, as you'll see in Chapter 8. The balance sheet will show whether those liabilities exist.

Here's what XYZ Hardware's balance sheet looked like:

XYZ HARDWARE, INC.
BALANCE SHEET
December 31, 1981

Assets

Current:	
Cash	$ 4,000
Accounts receivable	2,000
Inventory	60,000
Total current assets:	$66,000

Fixed:

Furniture, fixtures		
& equipment (cost)	$30,000	
Less depreciation	18,000	
Total fixed assets (book value)		12,000
Total assets		$78,000

Liabilities

Short-term

Accounts payable		$30,000
Taxes payable		3,000
Accrued expenses		2,000
Short-term notes (due within one year)		7,000
		$42,000

Long-term

Notes payable (due beyond one year)		30,000
Total liabilities		$72,000

Stockholders' Equity

Capital stock	$10,000	
Retained earnings	(4,000)	
Total stockholders' equity		$ 6,000
Total liabilities & equity		$78,000

The assets in this balance sheet have little significance, as the seller proposes to sell only three assets: inventory, fixtures and equipment, and good will.

The inventory is on the books for $60,000, however it may be more or less. Nevertheless, you'll only be paying their actual wholesale cost value at the time of closing. The seller may say he wants $25,000 for the furniture and fixtures, whereas his balance sheet shows they only have a $12,000 book value. So why pay $25,000? Because book value seldom represents its fair market or replacement value. When a business is sold, physical assets are based on replacement value, not book value.

This same seller told you he wants $40,000 for good will (the benefits of an ongoing business). Let's not concern ourselves here with the value of good will (we'll cover it in Chapter 6), but it's not even listed as an asset. Good will, as an intangible asset, seldom is listed, yet it may be the most valuable asset of a business.

Turn to the liabilities. If you were to pay $125,000 for the business as the seller asked, he would be required to pay his own liabilities totaling $72,000 and therefore, they would be of no consequence to you.

However, the balance sheet does point out that the debt is relatively high in relation to assets. You can confirm it with one widely used operating ratio called the current ratio.

$$\text{Current ratio} = \frac{\text{Current assets}}{\text{Current liabilities}}$$

$$\text{Current ratio} = \frac{\$66,000}{\$42,000}$$

$$\text{Current ratio} = 1.5:1$$

A company with a current ratio of less than 2:1 may be having financial difficulty. The low owner's equity and high long-term debt, coupled with low profits from the profit-and-loss statement also confirm the business is in a weak financial position. It may not even have sufficient profitability and cash flow to pay its long-term notes.

With these facts before you, you can detect the "value" of the business to the seller and the anxiety to sell. That's why you should investigate the balance sheet as a *negotiating* tool.

Returning to our second purpose, the existence of the $78,000 in liabilities can be an effective *financing* tool.

As you'll see in Chapter 11, you may decide to buy the business by acquiring the seller's shares in the corporation rather than by acquiring the assets. If that's how the transaction is structured your accountant's role is to audit the assets and liabilities, to make certain that the assets exist and that liabilities are not in excess of their stated amounts. The decision to acquire the corporation instead of assets may largely be based on your accountant's and attorney's confidence that the seller's corporation is "clean," subject to accurate audit, and free of contingent claims. The investigation would include the possibility of tax audits, lawsuits, and other nondisclosed claims and liabilities.

When acquiring corporate stock, the end result of your accountant's investigation should be an opinion letter regarding the accuracy of the financial conditions of the corporation. The accountant may have to qualify his opinion based on the adequacy of the records, but he will give you a reasonably good idea of whether the corporation should be acquired.

ANALYZING THE PRODUCT-ORIENTED FIRM

Product- or marketing-oriented businesses require investigation that goes well beyond location and internal operating data. Emphasis is on the product, distribution, and competition.

Product analysis can be critical. Ask a buyer who purchased a firm manufacturing an infant pacifier as the mainstay of its product line. Two months after he paid over $2,000,000 for the business, the Food and Drug Administration banned the pacifier.

Another buyer stumbled into acquiring a firm that was manufacturing radar components for the Air Force. It appears the Air Force changed its specifications shortly thereafter and switched to a competitive supplier. Product analysis is particularly acute when it's sold to a limited market, for it then requires an investigation of its customers as well.

One marketing executive for a Fortune 500 firm uses this checklist when investigating a product-marketing-oriented acquisition:

A TEN POINT CHECKLIST

1. What are the products?
   a) What are the sales by product line?
   b) What is the sales by product within each line?
   c) What are the sales trends for each product line? for each product?
   d) Are sales cyclical or seasonal?
2. Why do the products sell?
   a) What is the quality of the product?
   b) How important is credit, sales effort, delivery, service, or price?
   c) How long has each product been on the market?
3. How do the products compare with competitors' products?
   a) What competitive advantages are held by competitors?
   b) What competitive advantages are held by the company?
   c) What change in market share occurred within the past three years?
   d) What new or competitive products are planned by competitors? by the company?
4. What is the "return" history?
   a) What percentage of sales are returned?
   b) Why? Is the trend increasing?
   c) How will returns be handled under an acquisition?
5. What is the product trend within the industry?
   a) Is demand increasing or decreasing?
   b) What is the long-term forecast?
   c) Are new technological developments underway?
6. What is the pricing policy?
   a) Are prices competitive?
   b) What are the profits for each product line? for each product?

7. What is the method of distribution?

    a) How stable is it?

    b) Are distributors on contract? What are the terms?

    c) What are the costs of distribution?

8. Who are the customers?

    a) Who are the major customers?

    b) What percentage of sales does each buy?

    c) How long have they been customers?

    d) What is the customer growth or attrition rate?

    e) What is the marketing area?

9. What are the long-term marketing prospects?

    a) Is the population in this market increasing?

    b) Will consumption rate increase?

    c) What are the demographics or characteristics of the market?

10. Who are the sources of supply?

    a) Are they stable?

    b) Do they plan price increases or changes in terms?

    c) How long have they been doing business with the firm?

    d) Are there any disputes?

Unlike retail, service, or the more common businesses; product-oriented firms (manufacturing, wholesaling, mail order) are commonly acquired by existing firms. The investigation of the acquired firm should be considered from the viewpoint of fit, or matching, with the acquiring firm. Can the acquired product lines be handled effectively, can sales organizations be meshed, or can physical plant be combined?

With manufacturing firms, the investigation would extend to an inspection of the equipment and machinery. With a retail business, the equipment condition can be appraised with little effort and generally doesn't constitute as significant an asset. Equipment efficiency is another inspection point. Many buyers acquire plants with outdated or obsolete equipment, only to find that they can't produce product at competitive prices or afford the cost of new equipment.

One broker specializing in the printing industry states: "Unwary buyers are blinded by past profits, but fail to consider what it will cost to replace the fast-fading machinery. And that's precisely why the business is for sale. The sellers know the cost."

CHECKING OUT THE COMPETITION

More than one business has been sold because the company couldn't stand the onslaught of competition. The seller's books may not even reflect the impact.

Not long ago a small liquor store was sold in our area. The seller handed the buyer tax returns for the prior year showing sales of $380,000. Around the corner from this liquor store stood a very large discount liquor warehouse. The buyer knew of its existence but didn't realize it only opened two months earlier. Believing the competitor had done its damage and sales were now stabilized at the $380,000 mark he bought the business. Only then did he discover that sales were down to $130,000 annually.

This story points out two cautionary steps to take.

1. Always find out how long competitors have been in business.
2. Never rely on old sales figures alone. Check the most current daily sales to see if there's been a sudden drop.

Shrewd sellers may not wait for a competitor to move in before he sells. Many sell on the anticipation of a new competitor. It's not surprising that a large number of buyers acquire a business only to find a formidable competitor opening shortly thereafter. Chains, discounters, and franchises pop up unexpectedly and can devastate a small independent business. The seller has the advantage. He knows his area and knows who is planning to open up in competition with him. The buyer may know very little about the area.

There are some steps you can take to investigate and protect yourself.

1. Don't buy too quickly. It takes longer to check out competitive possibilities than the business itself. Inquire within the neighborhood. Be a good listener.
2. Check with the building and zoning boards within the town. Oftentimes a chain or franchisor will build rather than occupy an existing building. They may apply for permits long before they build.
3. Does your industry require special licenses? Drug stores, liquor stores, and nursing homes do. Call the licensing agency to see whether application was made for a new license in your area.
4. Talk to suppliers. They know what's happening within your industry.
5. Have the seller represent in the contract that "he knows of no new businesses" (competitive to yours) planning to open within a certain radius. It saved one buyer of a pharmacy a small fortune. I was representing the seller in this transaction. His pharmacy, grossing $500,000,

was on the market for only one reason. A giant chain drug store was planning to build a store directly across the street. At a price of $140,000 the buyer was anxious, but his clever attorney presented us with that warranty in the contract. My client, of course, wouldn't sign because he knew of the new competition, and the buyer would be able to prove it. So the buyer, detecting a reason for the refusal, turned the business down. Sales have since dropped to $190,000.

6. Look around for new shopping centers. Do you know whether or not they'll contain a sales-draining competitor?

FIVE PITFALLS TO AVOID

No matter how careful you are in investigating a business, you can still step on a booby trap.

One study suggests that buyers are most likely to make these fatal errors when investigating a new acquisition.

1. *Losing key customers.* A business may have sales of $300,000; however, one or more customers may represent a large percentage of the sales. When the seller leaves the customer leaves. I have seen this many times. In one case a brick manufacturer with 12 key accounts was sold, and two months later the business was left with only five accounts. Remember, good will is oftentimes tied to a seller as an individual rather than to the business. Check out the key customers before you buy and convince yourself they'll stay with you.

2. *Losing needed suppliers.* If you're in an industry with multiple sources of supply you don't have this concern. However, if your business does depend on a particular supplier, how solid is that source? Frequently, a business will be sold because the seller knows the supplier will soon terminate supply, increase prices, or terminate his exclusive sales rights. Do you recall the story of the buyer of the clothing store who dropped out upon learning his manufacturer was going out of business? He was fortunate. Walter P. wasn't as lucky. He acquired a shop featuring a line of bedding quilts only to have the manufacturer switch the line to a nearby department store. One phone call and he could have saved himself $45,000.

3. *Problems in doing business with the government.* I didn't need a study to tell me about this booby trap. Did you know that businesses relying on government (any governmental body) have the highest mortality rate of all. The problems are endless and the sellers either

know of a disaster in the making or believe it's only a matter of time. Bureaucratic buyers love to switch suppliers. They enjoy post-audits to collect overpayments. They deal with enough red tape to strangle any business. When they're through, they make you wait to collect. If you're looking at a business that deals with government, bring along a bevy of accountants and a platoon of lawyers. You'll need them.

4. *Declining neighborhoods.* Unlike the problems with government, the declining neighborhood is certainly not a well-concealed booby trap. It's right out there in the open. It may take several years before the declining neighborhood takes its toll, but it is still faulty investigation. It may not be the neighborhood itself, but the traffic patterns. There's a short strip of commercial roadway leading to Cape Cod from Boston. One of its many businesses was recently sold for a high price. I wonder if the buyer realizes that the state intends to build a super-highway to by-pass this commercial strip? I'm sure the seller knew it.

5. *Faulty sales forecasts.* This problem relates more to the perceptions of the buyer rather than to the business itself. The business presently grosses $400,000 but, through some magical wave of a wand, the buyer will quickly build it to $800,000. Financing and expenses based on the higher, but never realized, sales collapse the company. In Chapter 6 you'll go through the detailed process of projecting profits, but its accuracy will be based on your investigation of the business, its market and its true potential.

The investigative process should be retrospective to examine the business past. Realistically, however, few businesses fail because a seller overstated a few dollars in income or understated several expenses. But that's where most buyers focus endlessly. The proper investigation should consider the more important question of the business future.

THE ONE BEST WAY TO TEST A BUSINESS

Would you ever buy a car without driving it? Why should you buy a business without working in it? That's when you really know what's going on. Surprisingly, I have never read a business book recommending this as a method for checking out a business, but it's one of the best.

Face facts, books and records are sterile. They don't show you the personality, idiosyncrasies, or peculiarities of a business. Working in a business will. You'll see how loyal the customers are, what employee morale is like, the efficiency of operations, and the 101 games, tricks, and gambits that are part and parcel of every business.

An enlightening experience? Ask:

Carl L., who worked in a surgical supply firm that he had under serious consideration. He discovered that 30% of the sales were referrals from the owner's physician brother-in-law.

Irving T., who spent two days in a bakery before he realized the owner was shipping in supplies from his other bakery. No wonder cost of goods was so low.

Marilyn C., who discovered that three top decorators in the interior decorating studio under consideration were about to leave and go after the best accounts.

Every business has its stories, and you can't read the entire story on financial statements.

Will a seller go along with you working in the business for several weeks before you commit yourself to buying? Many won't. Some have stories to hide. Most say "no" because they don't want to let employees know the business is about to be sold. Offer to work incognito as just another employee or under some other pretense, if you must. Investigating is more than window shopping.

5

FRANCHISING: A UNIQUE GAME

See those two long lines of people waiting to pass through McDonald's golden arches? People hungry for hamburgers stand in the line to your left, while people hungry for franchises form the one to your right.

All along the highway other familiar signs flash and blink, beckoning customers and businesspeople alike. Holiday Inn, Midas, Hertz, Western Auto, and over 1200 others dot Main Street, 500,000 franchised businesses ringing up over $300 billion annually. Should you get in line for one of them? This chapter will help you decide.

Since franchising involves a rather unique relationship between the parent company (the franchisor) and you (the franchisee), you'll need to learn techniques that have little or no application to other business acquisitions. For many reasons a franchise may demand even greater investigation and considerably different analysis than will a nonfranchised counterpart. You must move carefully.

HOW A FRANCHISE WORKS

No two franchises are identical. In fact, franchising is so loosely defined that many businesses have adopted the term even though it does not really apply to them.

Franchising occurs when an independent businessperson markets an accepted or recognized product or service developed by the franchisor under a specific license to do so. The franchisee pays a fee to operate under the franchisor's tradename and established operational procedures, as well as paying a continuing royalty percentage of sales.

McDonald's owns its distinctive trademarks, its name, and its unique trade secrets. But the individual McDonald's outlets are owned by independent businesspeople who agree to conform their business operations to the standardized format designed by McDonald's. In return for the license, the owners agree to pay McDonald's a franchise fee. That's generally how most established, accepted, and better know franchises operate, though you will find a host of exceptions.

WHAT CAN A FRANCHISE OFFER YOU?

Let's assume you will select a solid, established franchise rather than a flim-flam operation (a distinction we will explore later in this chapter). Such a franchise might offer:

1. *Less Risk.* Since fewer than 10% of all franchises fail, you'll enjoy an appreciably better chance of succeeding. Nonfranchised businesses tend to fail at a 50% rate. McDonald's claims none of its franchises ever lost money, an impressive track record considering their 5000 outlets. Even if your franchise runs into trouble, there's a good chance the franchisor will buy your unit back to avoid a bankruptcy on its record.

2. *Management Support.* You'll need less prior experience. Nothing can replace experience, but most franchises include a training program and supply constant supervision and strict operational controls.

3. *Profits.* The typical franchise will earn more and reach the profit stage faster than will its nonfranchised counterpart. Even with higher franchise fees, the average franchise's return on investment will out perform the no-name business.

4. *Financing.* Few franchisors self-finance nowadays, but many will guarantee a bank loan, making it considerably easier for you to borrow money.

Why can a franchise provide these advantages? It offers:

1. *A Known and Accepted Trade Name.* Everyone's heard of Holiday Inn, Budget Rent-A-Car, Burger King, Dunkin' Donuts, and a healthy percentage of the other 1200 franchises. When you see a Holiday Inn sign you know what to expect, because the franchisor demands uniformity of product and service. Even if the name only has a regional or local reputation, the name creates sales and profits beyond what a no-name start-up might achieve.

2. *Location.* It's often difficult for independent businesspeople to land the better locations in shopping centers, malls, or other high-traffic spots. Competition for these locations grows so fierce that developers naturally select tenants they know can pay the highest rent, create the most traffic, and offer the strongest credit. Chains and franchises can offer those credentials.

3. *Economy and Efficiency of Operation.* This contributes to profits. Some franchisors include centralized buying and pass on the savings to their outlets. Efficient internal controls, budgeting, inventory control, merchandising, and layout and design all contribute to profit making. As one franchisor puts it, "We set up our Donut Shops so they're lean and mean, squeezing out 10–12% profits, while the independent mom-and-pop donut places are happy to produce 4–5%."

4. *Advertising and Promotion.* Operating many outlets under a common banner, the franchisor can actively promote the name and even conduct special promotional programs that nonfranchised owners cannot.

On the other hand, franchises present some disadvantages:

1. *Fees and Royalties.* It will cost you considerably more to buy a franchised business than a similar nonfranchised business. In many cases a good franchise, even in the fast-food field, may cost you over $100,000 in fees. You'll still have to pay for inventory, fixtures, and other start-up costs. And don't forget you'll usually pay royalties of 2–10% on sales.

2. *Down Payments.* While a franchisor may guarantee bank loans, they also require stiff down payments. For example, a typical fast-food franchise may cost you $150,000. The franchisor may support obtaining $90,000 in financing, provided you come up with the $60,000 balance from your own pocket. Many won't even consider creative financing, which is one of the most important ways to get people into businesses of their own. You may be able to find an independent business with comparable sales that is selling for the same $150,000, but you will be able to finance 80–90%. Steep down payments discourage many people from buying a franchise.

3. *Control.* The franchisor will dictate how you operate the business. While a franchisor's control may require you to operate more effectively and profitably than you would without its guidance and operating format, such rigidness can create a disadvantage. Through their own entrepreneurial knowhow or unique style, many entrepreneurs can perform considerably better than a franchise owner who is restricted

by a franchisor's rules. As you learned from the last chapter, some people aren't cut out to follow orders.

4. *Ownership.*   Another commonly overlooked disadvantage of a franchise is that you only own your business during the franchise period. That period may run 10 to 20 years, and may be renewed, but it's never 100% yours. Your contract may prohibit you from selling out or even leaving it to your family upon death.

5. *Flexibility.*   A franchise may not match your objectives for going into business. For example, if you only want an investment without putting long hours into the business, you probably won't qualify, because most strong franchises insist the franchisees work full time.

6. *Individuality.*   The selling point with a franchise is that their name and operating procedures produce more sales and profits than you could achieve on your own. This may be right, but it's not always the case. There are independent fast-food stands that outsell a McDonald's, or motels with a greater occupancy rate than can be boasted by Holiday Inn.

A TALE OF TWO FRANCHISES

A Loser   The word "franchise" turns Jack M.'s blood to ice water. He acquired one of 28 franchised superettes overseen by a local supermarket chain.

The franchisor leased the location in its own name, would pay the rent, and sublet to Jack. The franchisor provided use of the fixtures and allowed Jack to use the franchise name. The franchisor also provided all accounting services. In payment for the franchised name, rent, use of fixtures, and accounting services, Jack paid an initial franchise fee of $10,000 and continuing royalties of 15% of sales.

Jack, for his part, provided his own inventory, and had to operate the superette in accordance with a rigid set of operating restrictions. Even Jack's salary was limited to $12,000 annually, although Jack would be entitled to all profits from the franchise after payment of all operating expenses and franchise royalties.

Further, since Jack had to pay the franchisor a 15% royalty on sales, which turned out to be $50,000 on $350,000 the first year. Jack's year-end profits were a paltry $8,000.

Adding $8,000 to his $12,000 salary, Jack earned $20,000 from the franchise, while the franchisor earned $50,000 in royalties alone.

All the franchisor did was supply:

The lease (annual worth)	$12,000
Fixtures (annual worth)	5,000
(acquisition value: $20,000)	
Accounting services	1,000
Total value of services	
provided by franchisor	$18,000

Subtracting $18,000 from the $50,000 Jack paid the franchisor, you see that the franchisor basically charged $32,000 for annual use of its name, plus the initial fee of $10,000 besides. Is any franchised name for superette really worth $32,000 or 10% of sales?

Jack gave up the franchise, found another store of comparable size in the next town, signed his own lease for $10,000 a year, bought some used fixtures for $8,000 and moved over his old inventory. Freed from the franchisor's restrictions, Jack, a capable promoter, generated sales over $600,000 producing total earnings to himself of $72,000.

For another, less ambitious buyer, a $20,000 income might have been satisfactory, but it made little sense to entrepreneurial Jack.

And a Winner.   Tony S. ran his own independent small printing plant, but he achieved nothing but financial futility. Tony never earned over $25,000 a year with Empire Press, but today he earns over $50,000 with a Quick Copy franchise, in which he invested a mere $28,000. "Sure", says Tony, "I have to pay royalties to the franchisor, but it's worth it. After all, their name has created my profitable sales."

The moral of the story? Consider a franchise only if it can do more for you than you can do for yourself.

SELECTING YOUR FRANCHISE

Choosing a franchise differs only slightly from selecting a nonfranchised business. It takes three steps:

1. Select the type of business that most interests you and you'd most enjoy. It may be fast food, printing, a motel, or a pet shop. Virtually every industry has franchises. Ask yourself all the questions we discussed in Chapter 2.
2. Once you've pinpointed your target field, locate all the franchise opportunities in that field. If you select fast food, you'll find hundreds; if you pick printing, you'll see 12. Consult Chapter 3 for directories of franchise offerings.

3. Write to every franchise that appeals to you. Don't forget, as with any business acquisition, the more possibilities you uncover, the better. In a few weeks your mailbox will overflow with descriptive literature.

THE QUICK SCAN

You won't qualify for every franchise, and not every franchise will work for you, so use key variables to filter out some offerings.

1. *Required Investment:* $35,000? $50,000? They'll tell you. If you have only $25,000, weed out the franchise requiring $50,000. Unless you can come up with the investment or very close to it, you won't qualify. Many franchisors won't accept borrowed down payments, because they want you free of financial burdens, and consider a large cash commitment as a credit-worthy sign.

2. *Geographic Restrictions:*   Many regional franchises don't operate in your area. Cross them off your list. Even if they are willing to set up a franchise in your area, it might not work out, since you might not receive the close supervision and support you need and are paying for.

3. *History:*   Have they been franchising for less than five years? Newer companies are risky. But don't be fooled. Some will say they have been in business for 10–20 years. Close scrutiny reveals they ran one store for 7–15 of those years, or only recently started to franchise. As with any business, failure most often occurs in the beginning years. However, even the long-established franchise demands scrutiny. One long-standing Chicago based fast-food franchisor recently filed for bankruptcy, much to the surprise of its newer franchisees.

4. *Size:*   Do they operate a sufficient number of franchises to prove their approach works? Unfortunately no magic number exists. For example, I wouldn't express interest in a fast-food franchise with only 10 outlets after 8 years. It may be worthwhile, but a healthy operation in that industry should grow more rapidly.

Having checked these four variables, you'll have aimed your sights on franchises:

You can afford
Are in your area
With a track record

Those are the franchises you want to scrutinize more closely.

NARROWING THE RANGE

Among the companies that meet your criteria you'll discover a wide range of franchise prices. McDonald's, for example, sells its franchises for a minimum of $250,000, requires about $75,000 in cash, and projects 10% profits on sales of $800,000.

But XYZ Corporation sells its franchise for $100,000, requires $30,000 cash and projects 12% profits on sales of $500,000. Which franchise offers most?

You can examine that question from several viewpoints.

		McDonald's	XYZ
1.	Total profit: (sales × % profit)	$80,000	$60,000
2.	Return on initial investment: (profit ÷ down payment)	106%	200%
3.	Return on total price: (profit ÷ total price)	33%	60

Clearly, McDonald's wins in terms of actual dollar profits, but from a return-on-investment point of view, XYZ wins. If you invested $60,000 for two XYZ franchises you'd still be investing less money than for one McDonald's franchise and would earn considerably more. Would you throw away McDonald's brochure and dial for an appointment with XYZ? Not necessarily. You must take other factors into account:

How about risk? Can an investment in XYZ with its 18 locations be as safe as McDonald's with 5000?

What if you want to sell? Would you expect your investment in XYZ to grow as rapidly as an investment in McDonald's?

How about cash flow and financing terms? You owe a larger debt to McDonald's, but in light of higher dollar profits and more lenient terms you might end up with considerably more dollars in your pocket.

Contract terms? Maybe XYZ offers a limited 10-year contract, whereas McDonald's may offer 20 years with a renewal clause. What restrictions, controls, right to sell, or other costs do the two include? Who will train you better or work harder to help you create profits? There are hundreds of variables to consider.

Establish priorities. Which of the following interests you most?

Financial return
Safety/risk

Resale value and investment growth
Other contract terms
Personal factors

Since a preliminary review of the brochures won't provide sufficient information on which to base a decision, you'll need to play Sherlock Holmes again.

WHAT THE FRANCHISOR MUST TELL YOU

When you request information from each franchise, fortunately you'll get more than from any other business or investment you can acquire.

Federal law, through regulation of the Federal Trade Commission, requires that franchisors prepare and share with all prospective franchisees a *disclosure statement* containing essential information about the franchise. Undoubtedly the regulation came about due to widespread abuses in the franchising field. Several states require the same through state law, and in a few instances the state may demand an even more detailed *prospectus*.

The franchisor must provide you with the disclosure statement a few days before you sign the franchise agreement, and in some instances that's the earliest you'll see it. But you can still use the disclosure statement as an evaluation tool to guide an intelligent decision about pursuing any franchise. Ask for it as soon as you develop a serious interest in the franchise.

Here's what the disclosure statement *must* tell you.

1. Information identifying the franchisor and its business.
2. Identification and experience of each of the franchisor's officers, directors, and key management personnel.
3. A description of any lawsuits involving the franchisor.
4. Prior bankruptcies of the franchisor, its officers, or directors.
5. Information about the initial franchise fee and other required initial payments.
6. A description of any required continuing payments (royalties).
7. Information about the quality of goods or services used in the franchise, required suppliers, and goods the franchise must purchase from the franchisor or its affiliates.
8. A description of any available franchisor assistance in financing the purchase.
9. A description of restrictions on goods or services the franchisee is permitted to sell.

10. A description of any restrictions on the customers with whom the franchisee may deal.

11. The territorial protection the franchisor will grant.

12. A description of: the conditions under which the franchisor may repurchase the outlet or refuse renewal of its license; the restrictions on the franchisee concerning selling or transferring the outlet; how either party may terminate the agreement.

13. A description of the training program available to the franchisee.

14. A description of the involvement of any celebrities or public figures in the franchise.

15. Assistance in site selection to be provided by the franchisor.

16. Statistical information on the number of existing franchisees, projected franchisees, and terminated franchisees, including the number repurchased or not renewed.

17. A summary of the franchisor's financial condition.

18. A description of the extent to which franchisees must personally participate in the operation of the franchises.

19. A projection of franchisee profits and the number of franchisees achieving those profits.

20. A list of names and addresses of existing franchises.

As you can see, this information should form a sufficient basis for evaluation, but it's only useful if you thoroughly analyze it and make certain it's accurate. Since no governmental agency checks or reviews it, there's still opportunity for false statements.

Some of the disclosures deal with items contained in the franchise agreement, which we will discuss in a moment. However, you should concentrate on these aspects of any disclosure statement:

Items 1 and 2 deal with experience of the franchise management. How much experience do they have in the type of franchise you're buying? Do you consider that background sufficient to effectively manage the franchise system?

Item 3 tells you about pending lawsuits, which can divulge clues to operating problems. Almost every large franchise gets hit with lawsuits. Some are justified, some not. Have your attorney check the number of lawsuits against the size of the franchise system and obtain copies of suits to see if they share any common complaints.

Item 14 discloses public figures affiliated with the franchises. Don't assume public figures play an active role. They usually don't. If a franchise name is only as good as the public figure's name, a scandal could really hurt sales.

Item 16. History can tell you a lot. If they have terminated a lot of operations, why? Has the franchisor repurchased a lot of franchises to avoid bankruptcies? Why weren't some licenses renewed? Look closely. What happened to the others could happen to you.

Item 17. Have your accountant analyze the franchisor's financial statements. You want a well capitalized, profitable franchisor. Your franchise will never overcome a franchisor's weakness. Be certain that your franchisor's profit comes mostly from royalties rather than from franchise fees, because the former indicates strong ongoing health.

Item 19. Your accountant can help here too. It's easy for a franchisor to paint a picture of all the money you'll make, but have others consistently made that much? Remember, a new franchise usually doesn't reach projected profits for 2–3 years.

Item 20. Other franchisees can verify everything about the organization. That's why they're listed.

If the disclosure statement shows a reasonably clean and healthy history, and you don't foresee major problems in the terms of their franchise agreement contract, you're ready to ask the really tough questions.

WHO TO ASK FOR WHAT

Having negotiated several franchise acquisitions, and as an attorney for two national franchise companies, I've heard all the questions. It's the only way to find the facts.

Focus your interrogation on the following:

Existing franchisees
Failed franchisees
Suppliers
The franchisor

Interview them in that order, concluding with the franchisor. Grilling the first three will prepare you for the last one.

1. *What To Ask Existing Franchisees.*   Select at least five at random, because the franchisor will refer you to the ones most likely to give you favorable reports. Here's what to ask:

   a) When and why did you buy the franchise?

   b) Why did you select this franchise over others?

   c) How effective was the training program?

   d) Did the franchisor fulfill his obligations in setting up your franchise?

   e) What do you buy from the franchisor? Are his deliveries on time, his prices competitive?

   f) How effective is your area supervisor?

   g) How often does your supervisor visit you? What disagreements have you had?

   h) How effective is the advertising program?

   i) Who is the strongest competitor? What advantages or strengths does it have over you?

   j) Do the sales and profit figures compare favorably to what you expected?

   k) Are sales growing? Are profits growing?

   l) Has the franchisor honored the franchise agreement?

   m) What specific problems do you have with the franchisor? Are they being resolved?

   n) How many of the other franchisees do you know? What do they think of the franchise?

   o) Do you have any problems with the business itself?

   p) Are you satisfied with the franchise?

   q) Would you do it again today? Why? Why not?

You can ask many of these questions by phone, but it's best to visit the franchise to see it in operation. Some franchisees may refuse to talk to you or will provide guarded answers. Have the franchisor write a letter of introduction, confirming you as a prospective franchisee. Promise to keep results of all interviews strictly confidential.

Be realistic in assessing the answers. There's no such thing as a perfect franchise or one without run-of-the-mill business problems, including the intolerant franchisee who wouldn't be happy no matter what the franchisor did for him. I once interviewed a muffler shop franchisee who moaned and groaned, calling the franchisor a "dirty pirate." But he was sitting on a gold mine, so my client offered to buy him out at a bargain price. "No way!" shouted Mr. Miserable. "I'm making a fortune."

2. *What to Ask the Failed Franchisee.* Franchisees who have played the game and lost are usually unhappy and often place the blame on the franchisor. Try to dig out the true facts with these questions:

    a) Why did the franchise fail?

    b) What did the franchisor do to try to save it?

    c) Did the franchisor offer to repurchase the franchise? If so, on what terms?

    d) What were the positive points of the franchise?

    e) If location was the problem, would you consider the same franchise again in a different location?

3. *What to Ask Suppliers.* Since its suppliers do daily business with the franchise, they can provide a different and sometimes more objective perspective. Ask them:

    a) Are the franchisees required to buy from you?

    b) Have orders for goods increased per franchise?

    c) Do they pay their bills promptly?

    d) Do you know of any new product lines being considered?

    e) How do prices compare to prices for nonfranchised accounts?

4. *What to Ask the Franchisor.* When you meet with the franchisor make your appointment with someone at the management level. Many franchise companies delegate prospective franchise interviews to an in-house franchise salesperson or an outside marketing or franchise development firm. Though knowledgeable, these people want to sell you something and have not spent much time in the management of the franchise program.

Your questions should seek information not contained on the disclosure statement. For example:

    a) What locations are available?

    b) When will a franchise be available?

    c) Has a franchise ever been assigned to your area? What happened to it?

    d) What are the future plans for the franchise?

    e) May I see a sample franchise contract?

Of course you'll want to also ask the franchisor to clarify confusing points in the disclosure statement. For example:

    f) What are the details of the pending lawsuits?

    g) Why did prior franchisees fail? Why did some fail to renew?

    h) Does the franchisor own "company stores"?

i) What are its future plans for franchises versus expansion through company-owned outlets?

Before you start your interviews, you should isolate the principal terms of the franchise arrangement. These terms will form the basis of the franchise agreement.

FOUR MORE SOURCES TO CHECK

Most of your questions will be answered by the disclosure statement or by interviewing franchisees, suppliers, and the franchisor itself. But don't stop there. Check also with these four sources.

1. Most franchise corporations are traded publicly. This requires registration of annual and quarterly reports with the Securities and Exchange Commission. Request either from the SEC or the franchisor a copy of its most recent 10-K registration filing. It will provide more detailed financial and legal information on the condition of the franchisor than will a disclosure statement intended for franchisees. Have the 10-K report reviewed by your accountant and attorney.
2. Check with the Better Business Bureau in the state where the franchisor maintains its corporate offices to see if complaints have been filed.
3. The Attorney General in the franchisor's state, or the state agency that regulates franchises can tell you whether or not there are reported problems with the franchisor or if there are pending legal actions.
4. Call the International Franchise Association in Washington, D.C., to see if the franchisor is a member. It's a voluntary association so membership doesn't necessarily validate the franchise, but I have found most of the better franchisors belong.

NEGOTIATING THE CONTRACT

Before you try to translate the fine print in any contract, hire an attorney experienced in franchise law. If the franchise involves a major investment, you should retain a specialist. Surprisingly, despite the popularity of franchises (they account for 40% of all retail businesses), very few attorneys have much experience with them. Where can you find a specialist? Try the State Bar Association or the International Franchise Association in Washington, D.C., for a referral. Since an experienced franchise attorney not only knows how to protect you, but also knows what to negotiate and how to evaluate the franchise, you will be making a wise investment.

In the appendix of this book you'll find a franchise agreement we prepared for a health club franchise. It's comparable to what you'll find in most such agreements, although no two contracts are precisely the same.

If you're dealing with an established franchisor, particularly one in demand, you'll have little negotiating leverage. A take-it-or-leave-it attitude might frustrate you, but don't forget they built success on uniformity of operation. Can you argue with success?

Consider these aspects of franchise agreements:

1. *ice*
   a) What will the franchise cost?
   b) What are the initial franchise fees?
   c) What are the ongoing royalties?
   d) How often must you pay royalties?
   e) Are there any other hidden or start-up costs?
2. *The Physical Plant.*
   a) What are the specifications?
   b) What will you provide?
   c) What does the franchisor provide?
   d) Completion date?
3. *Location.*
   a) What is the proposed territory?
   b) Is the territory exclusive?
   c) What are your protections?
   d) Who can compete with you?
   e) Can the franchisor compete with you?
   f) Who finds the site?
   g) Who approves the site?
4. *Controls*
   a) Are you required to work the franchise?
   b) What are the salary limitations?
   c) Who controls hours?
   d) Who controls product selection?
   e) Are sources of supply limited or controlled?
   f) Are prices controlled?
   g) Is layout controlled?
   h) Are budgets or expenditures controlled?

    i)   What other policies or regulations govern you?

    j)   Is there an operations manual you must follow?

    k)   Can you advertise on your own?

5. *Support.*
   a) What training will you receive?
   b) What are the details of training? Location? Cost?
   c) Will you have start-up assistance?
   d) Who pays for a grand-opening launch?
   e) What continuing supervision will you have?
   f) Are legal or accounting services provided?
   g) Is inventory control provided?
   h) What other support can you expect?

6. *Advertising and Promotion.*
   a) What are the local or national advertising plans?
   b) Must you participate in all promotional programs?
   c) Is there a separate advertising charge?
   d) Will they assist in developing your own ads.

7. *Transfer and Death.*
   a) Can you sell, mortgage, or transfer your franchise?
   b) Can you transfer the franchise upon death?
   c) What are the restrictions on transfer?
   d) Does the franchisor have a repurchase option?

8. *Duration and Termination.*
   a) What is the franchise period?
   b) Is it renewable? On what terms?
   c) Do you pay a new franchise fee on renewal?
   d) Can you cancel the franchise?
   e) What constitutes a default or breach?
   f) Can you "cure" a default?
   g) Do you have an option on adjoining territories?

9. *Financing*
   a) What financing will the franchisor provide?
   b) What are the terms?
   c) What security must you pledge?
   d) Who is liable on the debt?
   e) What remedies does the franchisor have if you default?

Whether or not the contract terms are acceptable will primarily depend on whether or not they conform to general franchise standards and custom within the specific industry. Once you negotiate or review several contracts you'll be able to pinpoint questionable terms.

A franchise agreement can look like a one-way street, with the franchisor receiving all the benefits and rights while you shoulder all the burdens. Intimidating, preprinted forms certainly protect the franchisor. But you can negotiate some terms to better protect yourself.

CLAUSES YOU WANT IN THE CONTRACT

1.   Insist on a strict completion date for the franchise. Of all the potential pitfalls, none is more likely to occur than a franchisor promising a certain date, then allowing a 3- to 6-month delay due to zoning or construction problems. You, of course, have already quit your job. Your contract should provide that the franchisor pay you a weekly compensation if delays stall the project. Most franchisors will agree.

2.   Try to lower the initial franchise fee, which may be negotiable. The up-front fee to buy the franchise may mean less to the franchisor than the ongoing royalty percentage of sales, which is almost never negotiable. As the franchise becomes more popular, the franchise fee increases. A new franchisor may ask for a $10,000 fee. Five years later, after an established record, the same franchise may demand a $30,000 fee. If it recently increased the fee, the franchisor may agree to let you pay the earlier one, especially if you are a worthwhile buyer.

3.   Ask for the same interest rate the franchisor gets on its loans, which may be a point or two better than you can obtain on your own. For example, a franchisor may borrow the funds at 16% interest and plan to charge you 20–22%. If your franchise fails, the franchisor has risked little because it can step in and take over, retaining your sizable investment. Why should it also profit from your loan?

4.   Request a "right of first refusal" on adjoining or nearby available territories. Under such rights, before the franchisor can sell the territory to another franchisee, it must give you first opportunity to buy on the same terms. The franchisor loses nothing, but you have the right to expand.

5.   If you're considering the franchise merely for investment purposes, ask for an exception to the rule that the franchisee must actually operate and manage the franchise. Franchisors want a moti-

vated owner, not an employee operating the franchise, but I know several franchisees who convinced franchisors to accept them as absentee owners once the franchisees proved the quality of their appointed managers.

FRANCHISES TO AVOID

"Buying a franchise is like playing the horses," confesses Mike Yerardi, an attorney with extensive experience in franchising. "You never know who will come from behind and who will break a leg." But some never get out of the starting gate at all.

Avoid the following franchise set-ups:

Rack jobbing, vending machines, house-to-house sales, or deals requiring you to buy goods from the franchisor so you can "manufacture" the goods into a finished product for repurchase by the franchisor. Some may be worthwhile, but most are one step ahead of the Better Business Bureau or the bunko squad.

Companies that primarily make their money from the sale of equipment. These are not franchises in the true sense, so you should classify them as equipment suppliers. Manufacturers of coin-op laundries, dry cleaning, and car wash equipment often charge enormous fees over and above the value of the equipment, but provide little else.

A "franchisor" pushing a $2,000–3,000 "starter kit" that'll make you millions. Watch out! Something that easy usually isn't.

Pyramid schemes. With such a scheme you buy an area franchise and subfranchise to others, who in turn subdivide their territory to others in a never-ending cycle. There are legitimate area franchises, but law requires them to carefully define the number of subfranchisees they can establish.

With some common sense and careful investigation you can usually distinguish the flim-flams from the good franchises.

DIVORCE, FRANCHISE STYLE

A franchise relationship—as with any marriage—can end in divorce. Who ends up paying the alimony? Even though the fault may lie with either party, the franchisee usually pays through the nose.

Not long ago *The Wall Street Journal* reported that friction between franchisor and franchisee is quite common. Even at seminars conducted by the International Franchise Association, mending franchisee relations usually attracts a big crowd.

Franchisors often complain about franchisees not adhering to company policy. "The franchisee thinks he's running his own business," says one franchise director, "but he's only partially right. It still has our name on it." Unless you're prepared to run the business by the franchisor's rules, don't go into franchising.

Another franchise director cites another common cause for discontent: "The franchisee often resents paying the royalties, overlooking the fact that the franchise gave him a profitable business in the first place. It's the old 'what have you done for me lately?' complaint."

On the other hand, franchisees have a host of legitimate complaints against franchisors. Many revolve around minor operational problems such as lack of supervision or late deliveries. However, the most serious one involves attempted franchisor terminations, or arbitrary refusals to renew the franchise or allow resale or transfer. Some franchisors do try to terminate so they can reacquire the franchise either to hold as a company-owned outlet, or to resell for additional profit.

Perhaps it can be summed up best in the words of Don Jones, who has consulted to franchises for many years: "People think they're buying a business. But they're wrong. They're really buying a relationship."

YOUR TEN-POINT FRANCHISE CHECKLIST

1. Do you think you're the type for a franchise? Are you willing to adhere to company rules?
2. Have you selected the type of industry that would most interest you?
3. Have you established specific criteria for a franchise?
4. Have you reviewed all franchises that satisfy your criteria?
5. Have you selected an attorney experienced in financing?
6. Was the franchisor's disclosure statement carefully reviewed by you, your attorney, and your accountant?
7. Have you checked with existing and prior franchisees and suppliers?
8. Have you checked other valuable sources?
9. Do you understand the terms of the contract?
10. Has the franchisor thoroughly evaluated you to determine whether or not you are a suitable candidate for a franchise?

6

PINPOINTING THE RIGHT PRICE

Ask 100 experts to place a value on a business and you'll end up with 100 different answers, and the range will astound you. The reason is simple: Value is nothing more than perception, and we each bring to the valuation process our own ideas on what that "right" perception is.

The kid who sat beside me in the second grade taught me that lesson. I'll never forget the teacher shouting, "Marvin, how much is 2 + 2?" Marvin casually replied, "Depends." "What do you mean, depends?" screamed the teacher. Marvin the sage replied, "It *depends* on whether I'm buying or selling."

Years later Marvin wound up a millionaire, owning and operating a chain of motels and country clubs. It didn't surprise me. Good old Marvin knew "value" even in the second grade. He was smart enough to sell the right answers to the math homework for an exorbitant price—unless you decided to bargain and end up with the wrong answers. And if you didn't share Marvin's perception of value, that's exactly what you would get.

That's what makes the process of placing a value on a business so interesting. So few buyers and sellers share that same perspective.

Think of it. Every business is for sale at the right price. And any business can be bought at the right price.

Prospective buyers can pick from any of the 10 million small businesses, if they are willing to dip deep enough into their own pockets, and any of the estimated 20 million potential buyers might reach into their pockets, if they don't have to reach too far. True, realistic buyers and sellers inevitably find each other, but for every knowledgeable buyer or seller there are five others whose value system is on the blink. They invariably end up wondering about the deal that never was or worse—buying or selling at precisely the wrong price.

Admittedly, placing the right price on a small business is impossible. No formula is foolproof. No one equation can deal with all the factors that must be considered. At best, it's educated guesswork. Part of the process will depend on market conditions, other terms, and the self-satisfaction the business can provide you. However, these are purely subjective terms that must be coupled with objective analysis before you can arrive at your idea of value. Finding the value that will satisfy both buyer and seller is the most difficult part of the buy-sell process. The only "right" number is the one that convinces both parties that they are coming out ahead.

Marlene Rosen, vice-president of United Business Brokers sums it up this way:

> Sellers always ask what their business is worth. We have our own idea, but that doesn't matter. A business is worth whatever a seller can get for it. No more and no less. It's that simple.

That statement underscores the subjectivity of the valuation process. However, to zero in on the number that will make sense for you, an objective approach must be taken.

In this chapter you will find the "right" ways to look at any business, to gain a new perspective, and to determine just what that business is worth to you.

YOU DETERMINE VALUE, BUT NEGOTIATE PRICE

Don't confuse value with price. They are two different terms. And very seldom will value, using rational economic yardsticks, bear any relationship to what a business is sold for.

Value is what a business should be worth to you. *Price* is what you agree to sell or buy for.

How close the price comes to your value will depend on negotiation and "horse trading". Once you have ascertained the value of a business, it becomes your starting point for negotiating the price downward if you are the buyer, upward if you are the seller. More times than not, however, you'll find that the price you'll have to pay will be far below what you think it's worth. And there may be times where you'll have to reach beyond what you estimate the value to be to close a deal.

So your determination of value will only serve as a reference point. And it shouldn't surprise you if you end up with a business for a fraction of that value, or sell it for substantially more than you think it's worth. It only means that you're value system didn't coincide with your opponents. Perhaps you used different yardsticks.

Some recent cases from my files illustrate the point.

1.   A supermarket grossing $1,300,000 with a profitable history and tangible assets of $150,000 was quickly sold for $130,000 cash. that's $20,000 below the value of the "hard" assets alone, and about $120,000 less than the value I placed on the business. But if the business was worth $250,000 why did it go for $130,000? Answer: The seller recently lost his wife and wanted to relocate to California. He was willing to "cash out" for the first quick offer.

2.   A pharmacy with shrinking sales of $200,000 that could barely support its owner sold fast. The seller had planned to auction it when he found a buyer willing to pay $100,000. Answer: The buyer was blinded by the physical attractiveness of the shop. Emotion conquered logic.

3.   A client recently acquired a chain of hobby shops grossing $1,000,000, for a fraction of its inventory. And the buyer was able to do it with absolutely no cash of his own. How? Answer: The four partners who owned the chain were at each others' throats. They couldn't muster the cooperation to work together for a price that would benefit them all.

You've seen it for yourself. A business sells for a shockingly low price, or a lucky seller finally unloads his albatross for twice what he hoped to get for it. It happens all the time. Somebody's value system was satisfied by a ridiculous price. When you turn to chapter 9 you'll see the strategies to negotiate that best price. But for now, let's focus on your reference point— value.

FOUR COSTLY MYTHS

There are plenty of myths, misconceptions, and wrong approaches surrounding the business valuation process. Even experienced buyers have fallen victim to traditional or simplistic approaches that simply do not work.

Before we put you on the path to the proven ways to establish value, I will show you why you must avoid conventional yardstocks that don't measure up.

Here are four you must avoid.

1.   The Comparison Game.   Buyers and sellers alike look to the right and look to the left when they should be looking straight ahead. It's the comparison game. They simply glance around at what comparable businesses are selling for and assume it's the right value of their business.

That method doesn't work, because no two businesses are alike. When it comes to buying a house or a car one can comparison shop. However, the value of a business is tied to its own unique economic potential. Since earnings are dependent on the individual characteristics of the business— volume, expenses, loan terms, competition, and potential—even within a given industry few businesses have sufficient points of economic similarity to allow credible comparisons.

I recall a client who stumbled on the road to value by simply relying on the yardstick of some other deal. He was in the market for a hardware store and coincidentally found one grossing $500,000 annually, which coincided closely with another store that recently had sold for $135,000. He had an instantly established value for his business. But he was wrong. The other business had $90,000 in inventory, whereas his store only had $50,000. The other store paid $6,000 rent, but his landlord would require over $15,000. One by one the numbers differed—and so did the profit. Within two years my client lost his profitless business that cost him $130,000, while the store he measured it against continues to pump out healthy earnings. A business may have plenty of brothers but never a twin.

One exception to this rule is buying an existing franchised unit. Franchising is based on a high degree of uniformity. A McDonald's or a Kentucky Fried Chicken with equivalent sales should show near equivalent profits, as margins of profit, expenses, and other operating characteristics should follow chain standards.

The only reason for closely watching other business deals is to give you an idea of market conditions and demand for your type of business.

2.   The Magic Multiplier Fallacy.   There are a lot of magic formulas. A supermarket is supposed to be worth inventory plus one month's sales, a luncheonette should go for 3–4 months' gross, while a drug store should sell for about 100 days' sales. Some people call such a formula the "magic multiplier" method of valuation. I call it baloney!

No magic multiplier can establish the value, because the multiplier concept focuses only on sales volume. Sales may be one factor for establishing what a business is worth, but it's not necessarily the most important one. Profits are what count, but the multiplier method completely ignores profits by focusing on the top rather than on the bottom line.

The only time such a multiplier makes sense is if the profits of a business are always proportionate to its sales. But how often is that the case? If you examine 100 businesses in the same line, you will find little correlation between size and profit.

Some businesses enjoy phenomenal sales and phenomenal losses, while around the corner lies a little "sleeper" with small sales but consistently healthy profits. Which business would you rather have?

You may argue that you'd still put the higher value on the business with higher sales. Many buyers do, figuring they can whip costs and expenses into line, then enjoy enormous profits. Even in that case, value should be predicated not on sales but on predicted earnings.

Several years ago I was walking by Korvette's department store in Manhattan. Just that morning The Wall Street Journal reported that Korvette's had suffered their eighth consecutive quarter of staggering losses. In front of Korvette's entrance a pushcart vendor was wheeling and dealing his way to prosperity by hawking hot pretzels and popcorn from a cart with a striped umbrella. I struck up a conversation with the vendor who laughed about the Korvette monster that occupied a full city block but couldn't earn a dime. "You know," he said, "I paid $1200 for my pshcart. I take home $300 a week and at the end of the year this little pushcart shows a $12,000 profit. Perhaps the Korvette stockholders should liquidate and turn the money over to me for a fleet of pretzel pushcarts."

If one only considers profits, the vendor is right. Nevertheless with the facts before them, how many people would put a higher value on a fleet of pushcarts than on a department store? Bigger is not necessarily better. It's only bigger.

3.   The Asking Price Myth.   Another common misconception that plagues buyers is the belief that value relates to "asking price". It may, from the seller's perspective, but seldom from the buyer's.

Unwary buyers use the asking price as an arbitrary threshold from which to bargain. As James Rice, a New York acquisition consultant states:

> Whenever you find a seller quoting a price, you'll find some naïve buyer truly believing that if he can knock 10–15% off that asking price, he has suddenly found 'value.' "

Don't be a hypnotized cobra swaying to the snake charmers tune. A case in point: a wholesale novelty firm recently failed. It turned out that the owner couldn't keep up with the mortgage payments, so the bank foreclosed. The owner's story was an old one. He simply overpaid for a business that couldn't generate sufficient profits or cash flow to pay that inflated price. The owner confessed that the seller originally quoted $150,000 and, after months of haggling, reluctantly accepted $120,000. "I successfully lopped $30,000 from the original price, so I assumed that $120,000 was a good deal." Chances are this buyer would have agreed to a $200,000 price if the owner had started out at $250,000.

A seller is the least qualified person to determine value from a buyer's perspective. With years of emotional attachment to the business and the obvious self-serving a high price would bring, sellers rarely have any idea what their businesses are worth. Ask any business broker. He'll tell you that 90% of all sellers put their business on the market at a vastly over-rated price. After the business sits unsold for a year or more, the seller gradually drops the price until it finally enters the reality zone, unless, of course, a unwary buyer comes along first.

Disregard the asking price. Start the valuation process by assuming the business is worth absolutely nothing. Then work your way up, qualifying every dollar.

4.　The Tangible Assets Mistake.　Do you think the value of a business is always equal to at least the sum of its tangible assets? Many buyers believe that if they can pick up a business for its tangible assets alone, they have landed a bargain.

Let's take it from the beginning. Suppose you have the chance to pick up a business with $50,000 in inventory and fixtures worth $15,000, for a total price of $65,000. What makes that inventory worth $50,000 or the fixtures worth $15,000? Only the probability that those same assets can make money. Without profits all you get are assets that will eventually end up on the auction block for a fraction of what you paid. A business might be worth substantially less than the book or replacement value of its tangible assets. The business needs profit before assets represent any value.

I learned this lesson many years ago when I went into a partnership to buy out a launderette. The seller "justified" his price of $25,000 by pointing out that he paid $30,000 for the equipment just a year earlier and the depreciation on it was negligible. My partner and I never did think about profits— past, present, or future. Our eyes were glued to the assets. How could we go wrong, since we were only paying the "fair value" of the hard assets? Six months later we sorrowfully added up over $12,000 in operational losses and auctioned the equipment for $10,000.

I never made the same mistake again. Without potential profits a business is worthless. And so are its assets.

DEVELOP A NEW PERSPECTIVE

Enough negative talk. Now it's time to learn how to calculate the value which can influence the price of any business.

Consider this two-step process:

1. Understand the many factors that control value, and
2. Calculate what the business is worth to you, based on profit projections.

Let's take each step carefully.

FACTORS THAT CONTROL VALUE

A business' worth is a composite of hundreds of variables. Some are significant and can cause wide fluctuations in value; others are relatively minor, but can still influence a reasonable price. Some factors are external, whereas others relate directly to the business and to the proposed structure of the deal.

Because so many different factors exist, it's impossible to develop one right mathematical equation that uniformly applies to each business deal. Surprisingly, two businesses with exactly the same earnings will sell for two entirely different prices. Why? If profits are the goal of an investment, why should equal profits warrant different prices? The answer is that when one considers a sufficient number of factors, subtle differences will force value up or down.

From my experience, the most important value-controlling factors are:

1. *Supply and Demand.* This remains the first law of economics. The value of a business reflects the number of buyers available compared to businesses for sale. You must determine whether it's a buyer's or a seller's market. In periods of high unemployment, displaced workers seeking their own businesses can create a ground-swell that increases business values by 10–20%. Northland Management Corporation, a fast-growth holding company with retail stores throughout New England, reports that they have to out-bid an army of potential buyers to make acquisitions, even when they project earnings that don't quite justify the final price. Even local economic conditions can set the pace. When a Chevrolet plant in Framingham, Massachusetts, closed, laying off thousands of workers, hundreds of businesses that barely attracted a nibble were sold quickly, and in many cases for more than the original asking price. Remember this as you approach the market. Value is not created in a vacuum. Competition (or the lack of it), for the acquisition can be a roller-coaster ride.

2. *Nature of the Business.* Every business has its own peculiar characteristics. Years ago you couldn't give away small grocery stores. Today the small convenience store, such as 7-11, has become a money-maker. Brokers generally report that independent drug stores, hardware stores, liquor stores, and clothing stores that face stiff competition from big discounters move very slowly and at sluggish prices. On the other hand, fast-growth service firms, restaurants, and wholesale firms are in continuing demand. Businesses that are easy to operate and don't require specialized training can bring a higher price simply because they attract the broader market. If you know your line, you know its peculiarities. Take that into consideration when you estimate value.

3. *Risk.* Are you risk-oriented? To many buyers, the lack of risk is a key inducement to stick a higher price tag on a business. In such a case I might willingly agree to a premium price. If you have little to lose, you can afford to be generous. But when you are locked into a substantial loss should you fail, then you have to approach value with a cautious eye.

Only a few weeks ago our law firm was prepared to file bankruptcy for a large stationery supply firm. Along came a buyer who thought he could turn it around. We allowed him to purchase the seller's shares in the corporation for $5,000, and another $95,000 to be paid over five years contingent upon the company earnings. If the buyer succeeds, my client will end up with $100,000 more than he could get under any other alternative. Was it overpriced from the buyer's perspective? Of course not. If the business makes it he'll be happy to pay the $100,000. If not—well what did he have to lose besides time and effort?

4. *Down Payment.* Buyers are worried about how much cash they need to invest. Price resistance goes down as the down payment goes down. Our firm has been able to rapidly sell many businesses with such attractive terms that price becomes a secondary consideration. Of course, a reduced down payment adds risk in the form of other required financing. However, lowering the down payment demand makes the business accessible to more buyers, and many buyers with high aspirations but little cash will pay a premium for the opportunity to get into their own businesses.

Many sellers have reported that they had little trouble selling their businesses for the top price once creative financing and a low down payment requirement was available. I share that experience. Many buyers literally ignore price itself once they're satisfied that they can raise the few dollars to buy the business, and that the business can pay off the loans.

5. *Financing.* Certain financing arrangements can eclipse price in importance. Astute buyers always consider price in relation to financing, because the two together determine the total payout for the business. High interest rates since 1980 have depressed business values in the same way that they have softened the demand for real estate, automobiles, and other major consumer items. Consider the economic impact of 22% interest on a 10-year, $100,000 loan versus the same loan at 15% interest. The difference is about $35,000. In such a case, a buyer might insist that the seller absorb some of that cost by lowering the price. Kenneth Barron of Northland Management Corporation has adopted an increasingly common position on acquisition valuation: "If the financing requires interest in excess of 15%, we charge the excess against the value. If the seller, however, does the financing at less than 15%, we're willing to add the interest savings to the valuation." Interest is one financing criteria that can effect value but, in the minds of some buyers, cash flow can be even more important. Many buyers place a premium on a long-term payout (8 years or more) recognizing that this can insure a surplus cash flow they can use for expansion or modernization. The pay-back period can also put a lid on price. Buyers will limit a price to what the business can afford to pay back out of its own profits and cash. They want a loan that can be self-liquidating. By compressing the loan into a short term, this self-liquidation can evaporate. In Chapters 7 and 8, you'll find effective financial strategies that can dramatically change the value of a business.

6. *The Human Element.* Don't forget "chemistry." Chemistry between the buyer and the business of his dreams can cloud his objectivity, pump up his adrenalin, and create a weakness for an inflated value. The objective value of the business never alters, only the *perception* of that value.

Too many financial writers discussing business valuations never mention this phenomenon. However, having handled over 1500 transactions, I can assure you from first-hand experience that the rationality of the numbers seldom sells the buyer, but rather it's what the business does to the buyer's mind. For the small business buyer it's probably 80% psychological and 20% arithmetic. It may be an ego trip or a certain life-style. For the unemployed, the business may represent a tonic for anxiety and insecurity. A seller may simply be too tired or aggravated to continue, or perhaps his energies are directed to a new career. That's the human element to which both buyer and seller can respond. Buyers may talk numbers, but they're dreaming dreams. And it's dreams that bounce value around.

Are there other variables that influence value and price? Yes. The list is endless. Value is nothing more than putting 1000 ingredients through the Mixmaster minds of the parties and ending up with a concoction satisfying to each, and the end product is always different.

NAVIGATING BY THE NUMBERS

By now you know you can't determine value by mathematics alone. Nonquantifiable factors will always enter the picture and play havoc with your value system. However, the numbers are still important and must be the cornerstone of your value system. Bring objectivity to the valuation process. No matter what else you may think about the business, you must wrestle with the numbers until they become acceptable to you.

Here's how:

1. Calculate what the business will earn for you.
2. Determine how much you are willing to pay for those earnings.

Follow the step-by-step methods in the next few pages.

PROJECTING PROFITS

Human considerations aside, the purpose of business is to make money. There's no substitute for earnings. And if profits are your goal, then the size of those profits must dictate the value of the business. Therefore, you must accurately project just how much a business is likely to earn for you.

Looking at the seller's profit and loss statement won't give you all the answers, because profitability under his management will be somewhat different than under yours. I don't suggest you disregard the seller's performance; it can give you a foundation from which to build your own numbers. Historical analysis can help you anticipate certain ongoing costs and expenses. Although the seller's profitability (or lack of it) may influence price, a buyer must consider what the company can earn for him. In short, you are buying the future, not the past, and the past becomes relevant only to the extent it can forecast the future.

Statistics prove that past performance does not always hold up under new management. Buyers usually expect to equal past performance, but a study conducted by Northeastern University shows that 80% of the buyers surveyed responded that they thought they could *improve* profits by 50% or more.

How accurate were they? Of the 80% who believed they would greatly increase profits "under new management":

55% earned *less* money than their predecessors.

25% only nominally increased profits, or continued to operate at the same level of profitability.

15% increased profits by 49%.

Only 5% of the respondents fulfilled their prophecy by actually increasing profits by 50% or more.

I conclude that those interviewed didn't *project* profits, they only *predicted* them. There's a big difference. Most buyers look at the business through rose-colored glasses, assuming they can do better than the old management. As the survey showed, that's a dangerous assumption. Had new owners *projected* profits, they would have taken off the rose-colored glasses and realistically extrapolated the numbers.

When I counsel prospective buyers, I use a *proforma* profit and loss statement. Before I even allow a buyer to think price, I put him through the exercise of planning his profit profile. Not only does this quantify earnings expectation, it forces the buyer to think through virtually every phase of the business as he would operate it.

To get to that bottom line, the buyer starts at the top with sales and works his way down, through anticipated cost of goods and every last expense. Once he defines, justifies, and verifies each item on his projected P&L, he can measure forecasted earnings with some degree of confidence.

Let's journey through a typical income statement, asking how your numbers will differ from the seller's, using the Projected Income Statement as your step-by-step guide.

Sales. You know what the seller's sales are. Or do you? What if he skimmed 10–15% off the top to beat the IRS? Such a deflated figure may be to your advantage, but perhaps the seller padded his sales. Using the seller's sales as a basis, what volume can you generate? How will you achieve those sales? When? How certain are your forecasted increases? Play it cautious, because if you overestimate sales (which is a common error) you are creating a fallacy.

Cost of Goods. Your margin of profit, both as a percent of sales and in dollar terms, will differ from the seller's. You may add or delete new product lines, change the merchandise mix, alter pricing, or buy on better (or worse) terms. Any of these modifications can materially change the cost of goods and gross profits.

Projected Income Statement

Name of Business:_____

	Seller's	Year 1	Year 2	Year 3
Sales	$	$	$	$
Cost of goods				
Gross profit	$	$	$	$
Expenses:				
Owner's salary				
Payroll				
Rent				
Depreciation				
Utilities				
Advertising				
Insurance				
Other (list)				
Total expenses	$	$	$	$
Pretax profit	$	$	$	$

Buyer's Projected 3-YEAR Profit:

Year 1	$	
Year 2		
Year 3	_____	
Total for 3 years	$	
÷ 3 =	$	Average profit before debt payments

Owners Draw. Disregard what the seller declares as a salary. Plug in a personal salary that represents fair value for your time, effort, and talent. If you understate your salary, you are artificially subsidizing earnings. There are plenty of owners who draw anemic salaries and then proudly boast that they have a profitable business. Conversely, I can point out the owner of a health club that works 15 hours a week and draws a $75,000 salary and continuously wonders why the business loses money. Salary is what your management effort is worth. Profits are the return on your investment. Don't confuse them.

Payroll. As a major expense item this requires close evaluation. This is another area where you are wise to disregard the seller's numbers. He may pad the payroll with family or, conversely, have family working for a pittance. Base your payroll on one question:

What would it cost you to efficiently staff the organization if you had to start from scratch? Watch this one carefully.

Rent. Before you proceed too far in deciding the value of the business, examine the lease. In all probability, you will have to negotiate a new lease, and rent could increase dramatically. You may have to pay two to three times the seller's rent.

Utilities. An acquisition and subsequent renovations and modernization can expand this expense. New signs, refrigerated units, lighting, and air conditioning in an energy-intensive business justify calling in an electrician to estimate costs based on how you will set up your operation.

Depreciation. This "paper" expense serves as a tax shelter. The seller may have "fully depreciated" his assets so he has no depreciation to shelter profits. Conversely, your accountant may structure the deal to give capital assets a high value and then accelerate depreciation that can totally eliminate any projected profit. That's legitimate strategy from a tax angle, but it hides the earnings you're trying to measure. To avoid that distortion, use a figure that approximates the true decrease in value of the assets.

Advertising. As a new buyer, you will probably plan an advertising and promotional launch to reach your customers and projected sales. On the other hand, sellers usually are winding down their advertising.

Insurance. With additional inventory, new fixtures, and lender's demands, you may have to increase your insurance coverage. You may even be assessed at a new rate. Obtain a firm estimate in advance from your insurance broker.

Calculate any additional expenses. What about shipping or delivery costs? Will you sub contract some work? Regardless, walk through the business as you will operate it, considering every cost item. Only then can you project potential profit. Anything less is prediction, and you may as well glance into a crystal ball.

I saw a buyer purchase a tavern for $100,000 on the assumption that the seller was making a $10–15,000 annual profit. Unfortunately, it turned out that the seller's brother-in-law owned a wholesale liquor distributorship and sold to the seller at his cost. The buyer, of course, had to pay the "long price," so his cost of goods shot up by 15%. Next came a few payroll surprises. The seller had his entire family working for nothing. Replacement labor increased payroll by $12,000. And of course, along with the business came a new lease with a $5,000 increase. One by one new costs and expenses piled up. The seller's $10,000 profits quickly became the buyer's annual $20,000 loss. It could have been avoided with a few hours of careful investigation and projection.

The opposite is also true. Many potential buyers to rashly reject businesses they could easily convert into money-makers by relying on the seller's dismal performance. Most closely held businesses show little, if any, profit. Owners either hide sales or pad expenses to nullify taxable income. I don't endorse it, but it happens. Frankly, I have seen few small businesses with substantial profits, although many of these same businesses do, and can continue to, generate healthy earnings. I'm not concerned about your tax return. That's for your accountant and the IRS to worry about. My objective is to answer that one important question: What will that business *really* earn for you?

Don't confine your projections to the first year. Estimate profits for three years and average them. Oftentimes it will take two or three years to reach peak profits. Beyond three years, projection turns into mere speculation.

PUTTING A PRICE TAG ON PROFITS

Assuming you have painted an accurate picture of profits, what are you willing to pay for those profits? Your answer will become the numerical value you place on the business.

Financial writers refer to this approach as the capitalization method, or return on investment (ROI). It's a good approach, as far as it goes, and is the method recommended by most business analysts, and even by the Institute of Certified Business Brokers. It's not difficult, and you have probably used it to help decide on investing in stocks, money market funds, or savings accounts. You know what you're putting in and what you expect to take out. With a business you do the same thing, except you reverse the process. If you know what earnings will be, all you have to do is determine the investment that will make those earnings happen.

Let's assume you project a $20,000 profit. Assume further that you want a 20% return on investment (value of the business). The formula would be as follows:

1. $$\frac{\text{Projected Profits}}{\text{Required Return on Investment}} = \text{Value}$$

2. $$\frac{20,000}{.20} = \text{Value}$$

3. $$\$100,000 = \text{Value}$$

The calculation is simple enough. You may look at it as simply figuring out how many years it will take to recoup the price from profits. If you want a total payback in five years and the profit is $20,000 value to profits is a multiple of 5.

The big question is what multiple or return on investment is acceptable to you?

Some books suggest a return as low as 10%. Others insist on 30% or more. That dramatic swing indicates that the business with profits of $20,000 may be worth anywhere between $66,000 (33% ROI) to $200,000 (10% ROI).

Ask Harold Geneen of IT&T, and he'll have his own corporate criteria for assessing a possible acquisition. But you're not Harold Geneen. To you a business represents more than just another acquisition or pyramiding of numbers on a balance sheet.

As a small business owner, the business will represent more than a simple return on investment calculation. What you will demand on the financial end may be greatly influenced by what the business provides you in human terms.

Let me illustrate the point with a few quotations from buyers who gladly purchased businesses that will give them a smaller return than they could get in a bank.

1.   A buyer of an art gallery reports, "I've invested over $50,000 to buy the business and probably won't earn more than I could earn in my prior secretarial position, but I always wanted to own my own gallery."

2.   From an ex-schoolteacher: "I finally bought a small dress shop near my home. There were better opportunities around from a price/profitability standpoint, but this business is just the right size and type for me and I can be near by children."

3.   Dropping out of the corporate rat-race, a high-powered executive now owning a gift shop on Cape Cod says, "Before I'm through the business will cost me over $100,000 and I'll only be able to take home a salary of $20,000 and perhaps another $10,000 in profits. Sure my $100,000 would earn more in a money market account, but then what would I do—go back to my ulcer job?"

These are the human needs I mean. Buyers willing to sacrifice a better return that an alternate investment represents in exchange for a satisfying career, the security of his own paycheck, or as one buyer puts it, "the hell with somebody else's idea of the 'earning power of money.' As long as a business gives me a comfortable living and the enthusiasm to get up at 8:00 A.M. and open the store, what else really matters and how can you put a price tag on it?"

As I write this book, I reflect on my own investment criteria. If I were to invest in a business as a passive investor looking only to the return on investment element, I'd set my minimum goal at 25–30%—and this presumes a fair degree of safety. If liquid and safe money market accounts promise me 15–18%, it's difficult to rationalize any lesser return on a small business venture.

If anything, my views are conservative. Many other passive investors demand 100% or more. In many of these cases the return comes from growth or from selling out at a substantial profit in a short time.

You will have a different perspective. You are an owner-investor. Unlike the passive investor you will consider all the factors, including those bottom line profits.

TURNING THE NUMBERS INTO REALITY

Apply the capitalization method to practice. Suppose you *do* want a 20% return; if so, the business shouldn't cost you more than 5 × annual profits.

That's where all those variable factors come into play, and what you originally demand as a return changes as other aspects of the deal come into focus during the negotiation process.

Years ago a partner and I wanted to acquire a small supermarket. My partner would manage it and we would divide the profit.

The business had an inventory of $80,000 and fixtures with a replacement value of $30,000. As part of the deal we would assume $25,000 in accounts payable. We estimated that we would have to immediately invest about $30,000 to renovate the store with new lighting and other improvements.

Constructing our forecasted income statement, we believed we could generate annual profits of about $25,000. So, what was the business worth?

Here's how we stacked the numbers against the 20% return we wanted.

$$\frac{\text{Profits}}{\text{Value}} = \text{ROI}$$

$$\frac{\$25,000}{\text{Value}} = 20\%$$

$$\text{Value} = \$125,000$$

There it was. By our calculations the business shouldn't cost us more than $125,000 if we were to reach our 20% ROI goal. However, that value was based on buying the business free and clear of any liabilities. Oftentimes you will have to purchase a business subject to its debts, in which case you have to subtract the debt from the price to show the seller what's going into his pocket. So we would pay $100,000 to the seller and assume the $25,000 in debt. But what about the $30,000 in renovation costs needed to reach profitable sales? That too is part of the investment formula. If we paid $125,000 for the business and then spent another $30,000, our total investment would be $155,000—and our return would drop to 16%. To stay within the $125,000 expenditure we'd have to buy the business for $90,000, less the liabilities of $25,000.

That was our thought process as we entered negotiations. Did we end up with that price? No. First the seller reminded us that our proposed $90,000 price for the business itself was less than the replacement cost of the inventory and fixtures. This was certainly a logical point.

But the more we talked, the more our perception of value changed.

The seller agreed to finance $70,000 of the final price with a 7-year, 12% note. The favorable financing would justify adding $10,000 to value in our minds.

I realized the seller wouldn't require me to sign the note. All I could ever lose on the deal was my small investment, so the negligible risk factor warranted another $5,000.

The long-term potential was good. We could envision making even more money after three years. That was worth several thousand dollars more.

On the negative side, our accountant predicted some cyclical cash-flow problems with the business. The business could self-liquidate the note, but only if we retained the profits in the business. Down went value by $10,000.

Back and forth we went. Each positive feature weighed against the negative. As each factor of the deal came into clearer focus, our estimate of value changed.

We finally agreed to pay $115,000 for the business (less the liabilities). When we added the renovation costs, the package would cost us $145,000.

We didn't earn the projected $25,000 in profits. In fact, profits consistently hovered around a disappointing $15,000. That brought our return on investment down to almost 10%! Some you win, some you lose. But our experience typifies how it really works in practice:

1.   No matter how carefully you project profits you'll never end up on target. Your goal is to only obtain a rational expectation.

2.   No matter how you originally estimate value, don't expect to get the business at that price. Your values will constantly change as you consider additional factors.

COUNTING THOSE BIGGER DOLLARS

Remember my supermarket deal where I declared myself the loser because I only ended up with a 10% return? Well, three years later I rendered a new verdict. What I thought was a 10% return turned out to be more than a 100% return per year. In three short years we tripled our investment!

How did it happen? We sold the business for $240,000. After paying off the balance of the seller's loan (about $45,000 at the time of sale) and other business debts of about $35,000 my partner and I had $160,000 to split. That was $80,000 each. And we each invested only $22,500 of our own money to buy the business and pay for renovations. The $80,000 profit in three years equaled about $27,000 a year return on our one-time initial investment of $22,500.

That shows you another approach to business valuations. You must consider not only the operational profits but the growth, or appreciation, factor. How much more can you sell the business for as compared to the purchase price. Realistically, you can measure this return not against the price, but rather against what you personally invested to get that business.

Speculators and turnaround specialists use this approach and, considering their objectives, it makes sense. They'll take over a business with as small an investment as possible, build it up, and sell out for a handsome profit. The capitalization method means little or nothing to them. What is important is that they buy the business at a low enough price so there will be a sufficient profit spread between purchase and sales price to make it all worthwhile. How much of a profit spread will depend, in turn, on the required down payment and on the effort needed to build the business to the point where it can be sold for the healthy profit. Entrepreneurial types often look for distressed businesses with just that game plan in mind.

As one entrepreneur explained: "I shoot for a deal where I can sell the business for at least 50% more than I paid within two to three years. If I can keep the down payment and my own out-of-pocket costs down to 10–20% of the purchase price, I'll end up with more than a 100% annual return. That's how I look at value—is it low enough so I can cash out for that 50% more?"

Walk with him through a typical deal. He spots a business for sale and, after analyzing it, concludes he can make it profitable and sell it for $300,000 in perhaps two years. Therefore, his top offer can't exceed $200,000. Should he buy for $200,000 and sell for $300,000 and do it all for only a $30,000 down payment, then he will have achieved an annual return of $50,000 on his $30,000 investment—and that's tenfold what any bank will give him. That's how the speculator measures value.

WHAT IS GOOD REALLY WORTH?

WHAT IS GOOD WILL REALLY WORTH?

Typically, sellers will quote an asking price based on asset value. For example:

1.	Salable inventory at cost	$100,000
2.	Collectable accounts receivable	30,000
3.	Furniture, fixtures, and equipment (replacement cost)	30,000
4.	Good will	100,000
	Total asking price	$260,000

In Chapter 10, I show how to evaluate the tangible assets so you can make sure you get what you pay for. But take a hard look at good will. What does it really represent? Is it worth $100,000?

Pick up 10 different books and you'll find 10 different definitions. Sellers often use the wrong definition, equating it with a "going concern" and pointing out that the business has an established history. In many cases it's only a history of heartaches and losses. And many "going" concerns are going—into bankruptcy.

For you, good will means one thing: the business *will* make money. However, a business with potential profits is never worth the same as a business with profits in motion, because it will take your talent and effort to create those profits.

Use this rule of thumb. If an unprofitable business *can* make you money, don't pay more than one year's expected profits for good will. Anything beyond that is excessive.

Profitable businesses may deserve a value equal to 1–5 years' profits. One factor that can suggest a lower or higher range is the question of tangible assets.

A service business without tangible assets may earn $20,000. Conversely, a retail business with tangible assets worth $100,000 may also earn the same $20,000. From a capitalization viewpoint the businesses would have an equivalent value. But you do have the intrinsic value of the $100,000 in tangible assets with the retail store.

A business with substantial tangible assets will, of course, sell more than will a service business with equivalent earnings, as the inclusion of tangible assets may modify the capitalization rate; however, it will never replace it. If the seller demands a good will payment that puts the total price of the business beyond your acceptable rate of return, pass it up. Good will is only one component of value. Don't agree on a figure that makes the total price unworkable.

FIVE QUESTIONS YOU MUST ANSWER

Put your own perceptions of value to the test. Once you think you've found that "right" value for a business, ask yourself these questions.

1. Do you know what that business really means to you? What are your objectives? Are you buying it for a livelihood, for speculation, or for passive investment?
2. Do you know what that business will earn for you?
3. Do you know what return on investment you demand considering your investment objectives?
4. Will that business give you the return that's acceptable to you?
5. Are you satisfied with the other key points of the transaction—the down payment, financing, and risk?

If you find any "no" answers, go back to the drawing board—your idea of what that business is worth to you hasn't been sufficiently defined.

As one financial writer aptly states, "The most successful business people are those who know how to spot the right investment opportunities—and figure out what that business is worth to them."

7

FINDING THE MONEY

"Financing a small business isn't difficult," laughs one business professor. "All you need is a wealthy relative." If you don't have a rich aunt, you'll learn in this and the next chapter that plenty of money is available to business buyers who know where to look.

There's no mystery to it. Almost any business qualifies for financing, and almost any buyer can obtain that financing.

THE TWO LAYERS OF FINANCING

Suppose you found your perfect opportunity tomorrow, a profitable hardware store grossing $400,000, which you could buy for only $100,000. Where would you get $100,000? Would you dig into savings for a down payment, borrowing the balance from a bank? Of course, that's the conventional approach.

But let me ask a few questions.

1. If you had $100,000 in the bank, would you invest it all in a business?
2. If you only have $10,000 in the bank, should you borrow? How much? From whom? Under what terms?
3. What if you have no money in the bank? Should you forget about buying your own business?

I can't imagine a situation in which you should answer yes to the first question, but if you have money for a down payment, you should be able to obtain the balance through conventional financing discussed in this chapter. If you have little or no cash of your own to invest, you'll learn all about creative financing in Chapter 8.

Let's return to my questions. How would you finance the $100,000 for the hardware store?

THE ADVANTAGES OF BORROWING

When acquiring a business you should use as little of your own money as possible. If you borrow as much as the business can safely repay, you'll reap the benefits of leverage.

1.   You'll reduce your risk if the business fails. What would happen if you invested your own $100,000 and the business failed? Since you'd have to satisfy creditor claims before you would be entitled to proceeds, it's doubtful that you would recoup a dime. However, suppose you invested only $30,000, borrowing the $70,000 balance? You'd limit your risk to $30,000. If you personally guaranteed the $70,000 loan, the lender will have secured his loan with a mortgage on all the business assets, giving him first claim to their proceeds at auction. You'd only be liable for the difference between the proceeds and the loan balance. Perhaps the lender will recoup $40,000 from the auction. If your loan balance was $50,000 you'd still owe $10,000. So your total personal loss would be your $30,000 investment and the $10,000 deficiency owed on your guaranty, or $40,000. Had you invested the entire $100,000 you would have lost the $100,000.

2.   Borrowing lets you hold onto your available cash for other needs, such as improvements to the business, expansion, or unexpected contingencies. Many buyers use all their available cash for a down payment and start without adequate working capital. Once you commit your capital to buying the business, you'll have a hard time regaining that cash from the operation of the business.

3.   Interest payments on borrowed funds are tax deductible. If you invested your own $100,000 in the business, and tried to repay it to yourself over time, you'd pay taxes on the repayments, while it would be treated by the IRS as taxable dividend income. And the business would lose its interest deduction.

4.   Earnings from borrowed funds can surpass the cost of obtaining them. Assume you borrowed $70,000 at 18%, which would amount to about $12,500 a year in interest. You may pump your own $70,000 into another business or investment to produce $50,000 in profits. Leverage would have put you ahead by $37,500. So why not borrow instead of using your own money. But where should you look for money? Small businesses have three immediate choices:

a)   The seller
b)   Banks
c)   The Small Business Administration

WHY SELLER FINANCING IS YOUR BEST BET

Don't start your money search by rushing to the bank. You want the seller to finance the purchase by accepting your secured note for as much of the purchase price as possible. Let's carefully consider these advantages:

1.   Because people looking to sell a business are not interest-hungry, it should cost you far less to finance through them. If the seller agrees to finance a substantial part of the price at attractive interest rates, he's really helping himself by cementing a deal.

As I write this book, the prime lending rate that commercial banks charge their best customers hovers around 17%. As a small business person you won't qualify for the prime rate, but will have to pay somewhere between 3–5% above prime. Therefore, you can expect to face an interest rate from banks of about 20–22%. The SBA? They'll charge you even ½–2% more than the banks.

On the other hand, the typical seller may settle for 10–14%. Why would a seller accept 12%? He could get no more from such "safe" investments as a bank certificate of deposit or money market account. And wouldn't most sellers agree that their investment in a business they know intimately is "safe"?

A 24% bank loan for $100,000, payable within five years, would cost you over $60,000 in interest charges. The same loan from the seller at 12% will cost you about $30,000. The seller doesn't lose a dime, but you could come out $30,000 richer.

Though most sellers prefer to avoid financing your purchase, small business seller loans actually outnumber bank loans two to one, and most sellers lend at interest rates 5–7% below what a bank would charge.

2.   You can usually extend a seller's financing over a longer payback period. The length of the note can mean the difference between large monthly payments that could sink you, and easily handled payments that fit nicely into your cash flow and that may even provide some excess cash for business expansion, improvements, or a salary increase.

While most banks look for a three- to five-year payback period, sellers understand their business' cash flow limitations and may finance the purchase over a five to seven-year period. Larger trans-actions, where the purchase price exceeds $150,000–200,000 may win 10–12-year terms.

How about a 20-year pay-out? One buyer of a large lumber yard selling for $300,000 needed $180,000 to finance. A local bank was willing to lend it at 20% interest, payable in five years. Annual loan payments would be a staggering $55,000. The seller decided he'd finance the same $180,000 at 15%, payable over 20 years. Annual loan payments would shrink to about $15,000. Why was the seller willing to stretch the loan out for 20 years? He didn't need the money and looked at the loan payments as a 20-year annuity.

3.   Sellers may also finance a greater percentage of the purchase price. Banks usually won't go beyond 60% of the purchase price, and they'll only lend that much on strong collateral; even the SBA stops at 50%. However, sellers frequently accept financing for 70–80% of the price. Why? For several reasons. First, they already have their money tied up in the business. Selling to you on favorable terms may be the only way to eventually turn the business into cash. Second, consider collateral value. A bank knows that if you default they'll have to sell the assets at auction for 10–20 cents on the dollar. But not the seller. If he properly protects himself, he can step in, take the business back, and continue running it. Unlike banks and the SBA, bound by strict rules and regulations, a seller is limited only by his own negotiating posture and financial circumstances, both of which can work to your advantage.

4.   If you want effective recourse against the seller in the event that he breached a warranty or falsely represented his company, your note to the seller establishes that remedy. Problems may arise no matter how carefully you or your advisors check out the business. Recently a buyer acquired a fabric shop that had $60,000 in undis-closed liabilities. Fortunately our contract provided he'd have recourse against the seller for such a misrepresentation. Since the buyer owed the seller $80,000 on financing, we could simply set off, or deduct, $60,000 from the debt. If the seller received all cash, we'd still be chasing him to make good on the $60,000.

5.   Banks and the SBA are collateral-hungry lenders, who will try to gobble up all the personal assets you own to back up the loan: your home, car, stocks, and pet parakeet. Sellers want collateral too, but they'll usually settle for a mortgage on the business, rather than on personal assets. Why gamble everything you own?

6.   Best of all, sellers won't foreclose the first time you miss a payment.

To a bank you're just a statistic. Once your loan runs 60–90 days late, the president calls some junior loan officer on the carpet, and within hours they're on your back.

A seller only has to answer to himself, doesn't operate with a lot of red tape and regulations, and he understands your cash flow problems because he faced them himself. He can assess the true condition of the company without panicking. Besides, he probably enjoyed the business himself and would enjoy watching you suceed much more than taking the business back.

PUSHING THE RIGHT BUTTONS

How do you convince sellers to finance your purchase?

Few sellers will suggest that they finance the purchase, insisting instead on all cash. You know seller-financing benefits you, so all you have to do is persuade sellers that it will help them too.

1.   Call their bluff. The seller will keep saying "no" as long as he believes you'll give in and head for a bank. Convince him you'll only be heading for another business. It's all part of the negotiating game. Who will capitulate first? Don't let it be you. If he had a cash buyer in the wings, he wouldn't even be talking to you.

2.   Ask why he's reluctant to finance. Does he need the money? In most cases seller-financing can resolve both your needs. Perhaps he wants to buy another business or the funds to relocate. Once you know the reason, you can try to meet his immediate needs. In one recent example, a buyer convinced a seller to finance $40,000 towards the purchase of his $50,000 appliance store. Originally, the seller held out for the entire $50,000 claiming he needed it to buy a retirement home. The buyer made an interesting suggestion. "Finance the $40,000 and if it turns out you need the $40,000 you can use the note as collateral to borrow your $40,000 from a bank and I'll split the additional finance charges with you." The seller never did have to borrow against the note, as he fortunately found a home with a large assumable mortgage.

3.   As another selling point, why not concede a slightly higher price in return for advantageous seller financing. The seller of the $100,000 hardware store may go along with substantial self-financing if you gave him his very best price. Financing is only one negotiating point. Price is another. You'd probably do better buying the business for $110,000 with the seller financing $80,000 on a six year,

14% pay-out, than you would buying the business for $100,000 and looking to a bank for financing.

4.   Use your attorney to propose a loan arrangement with plenty of security. Sellers legitimately want to know their money will be as safe as possible. Of course, a promise is not necessarily a payment.

TURNING PROMISES INTO PAYMENTS

Put yourself in the seller's shoes. If a buyer can convince a seller that promises will turn into payments, a seller may agree to finance 60–70% or even 80% of the purchase price. But how can you do that? There's only one way: by the rule of calculated risk.

If a seller hasn't sold before, and even if he has, he may not know how to structure the loan to provide himself maximum protection.

You want to protect the lender's loan as much as he does, because you will undoubtedly have to guarantee it personally. Should the business fail and a liquidation result, you want the lender to recoup as much as possible from the business so he won't be chasing you for it. Suggest these guidelines:

1.   Collateralize the loan by a first mortgage (security interest) on all the corporation's assets. This provides the lender first claim on all proceeds upon liquidation which, of course, will eventually reduce your loan balance.

2.   Offer a personal guarantee. If the buyer is a corporation, its principal stockholders should also guarantee the note.

3.   Pledge the shares of stock of your corporation. Upon default, the seller can either foreclose on the mortgage, liquidating the assets, or he can assume the pledged shares and continue to operate the business. The stock pledge provides a valuable alternative if the corporation is reasonably solvent and worth taking over instead of liquidating.

These three essential ingredients are standard and offer minimum protection. However, several commonly overlooked methods can provide even further protection.

4.   Promise to maintain inventory levels. The primary risk the lender faces is that inventory will be gone by the time he forecloses. For example, the seller may sell a business with an $80,000 inven-

tory. If he is certain that upon foreclosure he'd end up with an $80,000 inventory, he really has little to lose but time, effort, and some legal fees. But what if the buyer depletes inventory to $30,000 before foreclosure? The lender faces a $50,000 loss and the only recourse he would have for any remaining balance would be your guarantee. The solution? The loan agreement should provide that you maintain an inventory at least equal to the inventory at the time of sale. If it drops below that level the seller can foreclose immediately, even if your payments are current.

5. Promise to maintain sales levels. Sellers argue, "What if the buyer ruins the good will of the business?" Good question. I have seen many businesses grossing $500,000 at the time of sale decline to $200,000 two years later. It's certainly not the same business the seller sold. Aside from convincing the seller that he can operate the business effectively, the buyer can commit himself to a performance standard, such as retaining sales at a minimally acceptable level. If sales drop below that level, the seller can declare a default and take back the business.

6. If the location is a valuable asset of the business, assign the lease to the seller. Ordinarily the buyer will obtain a new lease on the premises when buying the business. If the seller holds a mortgage only on the business assets, he can't reoccupy the premises and may have to auction the assets. With a lease, he can be back in business quickly.

Sellers may try to negotiate mortgages on the buyer's individual property, such as a house, to back up a loan. So will a bank and the SBA. But consider this: If the business you're buying for $100,000 isn't adequate collateral for an $80,000 loan, it's not worth the $100,000 you're paying for it. An effective compromise may be to grant the seller a personal collateral mortgage only for that portion of the loan that goes beyond what a bank would lend. For example, if a bank would loan only $60,000 on the hardware store, and demand a home mortgage as further collateral, why not ask the seller for $80,000 in financing, and a mortgage on your home to secure $20,000 of the debt. When the loan is reduced to $60,000 the seller would discharge the mortgage. Personal collateral to cover "excess financing" has cemented many a deal.

All the seller needs to ask is, "What will I recoup if the loan goes sour?" That's what he should agree to lend. But will he? Maybe. But what if the seller won't budge? You have no choice but to find another business with a more agreeable seller or try your next stop—your local banker.

BEFORE YOU MEET YOUR BANKER

Unlike a seller who is familiar with his business, its value, and its ability to repay the loan, a bank will require extensive documentation to justify a loan.

While large corporations understand the need for a well-documented loan proposal, buyers seeking capital for the acquisition of a smaller firm too often approach a bank much as they would if they were seeking a car loan or home mortgage.

However, to successfully land a business loan you must construct a businesslike loan proposal answering what I call the 5 Cs of loansmanship.

What are the 5 Cs?

1. *Character.* Do you have a history of good credit and personal stability?
2. *Cash Flow.* Does the business offer sufficient cash flow and profit after expenses to pay back the loan?
3. *Collateral.* If your loan defaults, will the bank have sufficient collateral to recover the balance owed?
4. *Capital.* What are you investing in the business? Banks are reluctant to lend to new owners who display neither investment capital of their own nor a track record.
5. *Coverage.* Are you insurable? The bank will want to liquidate the loan if you die or become disabled.

When preparing your loan application, follow this outline.

Loan Proposal

1. *Credit and Personal History* (Character)

    a) Name and address
    b) Marital status
    c) Employment history
    d) Education
    e) Personal assets
    g) Military status
    h) Bank references
    i) Credit references
    j) Outstanding lawsuits

2. *Financial Information on the Business* (Cash Flow)

a) Name and address of business
b) History and age of business
c) Tax returns for prior 3 years
d) Projected cash flow statement for loan period
e) Summary of proposed business changes
f) Lease or proposed lease terms

3. *Collateral for Loan*

a) Description of business assets
b) List of major equipment
c) Acquisition or replacement cost of assets
d) Liquidation value of assets

4. *Capital: Investment and Terms of Sale*

a) Sales price
b) Other financing available to buyer
c) Buyer's investment
d) Date of proposed purchase

5. *Insurance Coverage*

a) Insurability of assets
b) Insurability of buyer (or guarantor)
c) Existing insurance policies that may be assigned

6. *Proposed Loan*

a) Amount required
b) Loan period
c) Interest terms
d) Guarantors to loan
e) Collateral to be pledged

After carefully preparing your loan proposal in this format, test it the way a bank does:

1. Is your credit history sound? If you have a poor credit rating, try to erase or explain prior delinquencies or black marks.
2. Do tax returns show profitable history? If not, how do you propose to make the business profitable?
3. Does the cash flow statement prove you will have adequate cash availability to repay the loan? Can you justify the numbers?
4. Does the lease extend for as long as the loan?
5. Does the liquidation value of the collateral equal the loan requested?

Have your accountant prepare the financial information and take him to the bank with you. A banker will have more confidence if he knows an accountant stands at your financial helm.

A well-structured loan proposal will tell the banker more than what's in the proposal. It will tell him he's dealing with a pro.

KNOCK ON THE RIGHT DOORS

Since no two banks or bankers are identical, knowing which banks to approach can be half the battle. Approach commercial banks rather than savings banks, cooperatives, or credit unions, who specialize in personal, consumer, and real estate loans. If your business acquisition includes real estate, then you may want to consider these banks. However, I'd recommend splitting your loan, that is, using a savings bank for the real estate and a commercial bank for the business itself.

If you need a small loan (under $75,000–100,000), concentrate on smaller, local banks rather than on larger metropolitan ones. Match your loan to the bank. To the large bank you're a small fish. Even if a large bank approves the loan, your account may mean very little to them.

Since banks give preference to loans within their immediate geographic area, try banks near your business. They know the local market, and they want all your other business. Your best bet may be the bank presently servicing the business.

When seeking acquisition or start-up capital, check within the financial community to find out which banks are most aggressively making loans at this time. Successful borrowing will also depend on the cash availability of the bank. Money is a bank's inventory, and inventories can run low. A bank may be conservative one month, liberal the next.

After you find the right bank, you'll need to locate the right desk. Bankers are people, bringing to the evaluation process their unique personalities, prejudices, and style. Your ability to push a loan through will depend greatly on your ability to find a match to your personality, prejudices, and style. Some bankers will want a bushel basket full of information and never crack a smile. Others will prop their feet up on the desk and join in your entrepreneurial dreams. Don't expect a standard approach.

We routinely deal with nine banks in our area. One banker seems to judge a loan only by the collateral. Nothing else matters, so we refer our clients with extensive collateral to him. Another appears to place priority on management experience. The buyer with the track record is sent to knock on his door. Some prefer retailing, others manufacturing. Some prefer start ups, others won't touch them. In one case a buyer tried 12 banks to finance the purchase of a racquetball club. "Too speculative," they said. Finally the buyer met a banker who was a racquetball buff and had no trouble obtaining $200,000 in financing.

It helps to approach the top man in the main office, the president (if it's a small bank) or a vice-president in charge of commercial loans (if it's large). By-pass branch managers and all the bureaucrats. Years ago I represented a group looking for $25,000 to start a local business. First we stopped at the desk of a young man with a long title under his name: Assistant Vice-President—Commercial Loans. As it turned out, the "Vice-President" sat so low on the totem pole, he doubled as a teller during rush hours. After two frustrating months of delay he finally turned my client down even though we had a cosigner for the loan whose net worth was $3,000,000. When we objected to the president, he approved the loan after one hour of friendly conversation. We were lucky. When a junior loan officer or branch manager declines a loan, the bank will usually support the decision as a matter of policy. But even when a junior loan officer recommends a loan, a higher authority won't hesitate to override the decision. Don't hesitate to call for an appointment with the bank's top officer. His bank will earn plenty of profits from your loan.

NEGOTIATE THE BEST TERMS

There's a right way and a wrong way to structure a business acquisition loan. The following guidelines will help you do it right:

1. Request more money than you actually need. If you need

$60,000, ask for $70,000. This allows you to compromise during negotiations, but still obtain needed capital. If the business assets have a collateral value of $40,000–50,000, don't let that stop you from asking for more. In most transactions you should start by asking for 70% of the purchase price, knowing full well you'll probably end up with only 50–60%. Though policy will prevent some banks from going beyond 50–60%, others will, particularly if secured by sufficient personal collateral.

2.   Negotiate interest rates. Nowadays, banks hesitate to issue long-term loans at fixed interest rates because *interest rates may climb.* The bank will probably propose a rate tied to the floating prime rate. For example, the bank may offer a loan at "3 points above prime." An 18% prime rate results in a 21% rate for you. If prime increases to 20%, your rate correspondingly increases to 23%. For most small business acquisitions, interest at 2–5% above prime is reasonable, but if you have adequate collateral, you should negotiate for 2%. If the bank insists on 4% above prime, and that seems like the best deal after you've shopped around, ask for a decrease in interest as you pay down the loan. For example, at the point at which you reduce the loan balance by 40%, the interest on the balance falls to 3% above prime. A percentage point or two sounds small, but it can put thousands of dollars in your pocket. Doesn't one percentage point on a $100,000 loan put $1,000 in your pocket each year the loan is outstanding?

3.   Demand the longest loan period possible. Many buyers accept a three-year note, even though the business can't possibly repay it that fast. Your cash flow statements may predict you can, but don't forget those are only projections. You may have had your rosy eyeglasses on, and your banker may have borrowed them to review your situation. Shoot for a minimum five-year payback. If you can pay quicker, fine. However, you might have better use for that cash (salary, improvements, expansion) and would rather continue paying interest. In any case, make certain your contract contains the right to prepay without penalty.

4.   *Don't* pledge additional personal collateral, such as your home, without a fight. The bank will push for it, and even pretend it's standard procedure. Don't fall for it. It's negotiable.

5.   *Don't* falsify loan applications. A material misrepresentation can lead to criminal prosecution and even prevent you from discharging the debt through bankruptcy.

6.   *Don't* settle for the first loan offer. There are plenty of banks

to compete for your business. Having spent time putting together your loan proposal, shop it around to four to five banks for the best deal. You will see some surprising differences between the offers.

STRUCTURING YOUR BANK LOAN

How you structure your bank loan is very important. Don't borrow the money personally. The loan should be a direct obligation between the bank and your corporation. Your personal involvement should be limited to guaranteeing the loan.

With the loan directly between the lender and the corporation, the lender will have a mortgage on the corporate assets to shield you from unnecessary liability on your guaranty. Your corporation will also make payments directly to the bank with the interest qualifying as a tax-deductible expense.

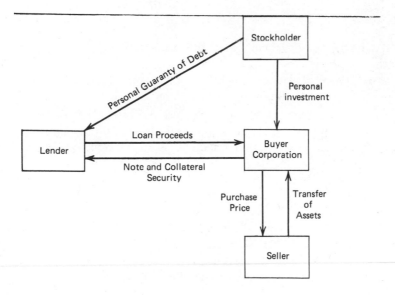

EXHIBIT 3. The Right Way

Many buyers erroneously borrow personally from a bank following this outline:

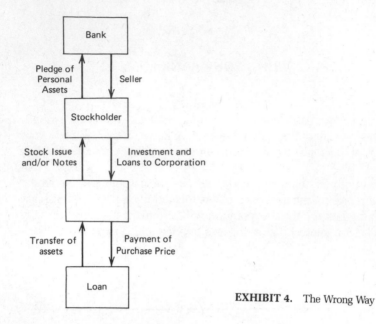

EXHIBIT 4.   The Wrong Way

The distinct disadvantages of this arrangement are:

1. Payments by the corporation on the bank note are taxable to you, since the corporation is not obligated on the bank note.
2. The bank has no claim against the assets of the corporation, and would not be entitled to proceeds upon a failure. Conversely, the bank would look to your pledged personal assets for payment.

Review your loan structure with your accountant and attorney to make certain you structure the loan to your benefit.

WHAT TO DO IF THE BANK SAYS "NO"

Don't be discouraged. Explore four alternatives

1. Find out why the bank declined the loan. You may not realize it at first, but the bank may have done you a favor. If they discovered a

weakness in your proposal, you may be able to strengthen it before approaching the next bank. You should consider the bank not as an adversary but as an ally in evaluating the soundness of your loan—and your acquisition.

2. Try several more banks. In many cases five banks will refuse before the sixth accepts. On the other hand, constant rejections may be a sign of a fatal problem in your loan proposal. Find that flaw and fix it.

3. If a bank declines your request for $70,000, ask if they will lend less. Try to trigger a counter-offer from the bank. Virtually any business can justify some loan.

4. After several banks turn you down, but you still think the loan is justifiable, approach the Small Business Administration. That's one advantage of being turned down by banks. To the Small Business Administration that qualifies you as an applicant.

THE REAL STORY ON SBA LOANS

Frankly, the SBA is the last resort for long-term acquisition loans. Many buyers knock on the SBA's door first, by-passing sellers (the best source) and banks (the second choice).

There are several reasons why I hesitate to send a buyer to the SBA:

1. The SBA will only consider you for a loan if you cannot obtain a loan from a bank. Think about that for a moment. If your proposal was sound, you wouldn't need the SBA. Through the process of elimination the SBA involves itself in weaker or even illogical deals. Though we all know business people who started with SBA financing and succeeded, I know many more who accepted SBA funds when they had no chance of succeeding in the first place and quickly ended in bankruptcy. When the SBA loses, they lose only a few dollars, but you lose everything. A sound acquisition plan should attract seller or bank financing. If it doesn't, you should probably redesign it.

2. The SBA has a fixed policy on collateral. If you own it, they want it. With a bank you have a strong chance of avoiding a mortgage on your home, but not with the SBA. Think carefully about what you're prepared to lose if the acquisition doesn't work out.

3. The SBA, as with most governmental agencies (except the collection division of the IRS), are slow movers. It can take two to three months to push an acquisition loan through. Admittedly, the SBA is working hard to speed up the process, but there can still be

a delay beyond what you can afford. If you plan to try the SBA, find out from the SBA how long it will realistically take to obtain an answer. Make certain the seller will wait that time period. Don't forget, many sellers want a quick sale.

4.   You may pay higher interest on an SBA loan, as much as 2–3% more than what a bank would charge. The reason for the higher interest is that you are actually borrowing from a bank and paying bank rates, however, the SBA guarantees the loan and adds up to 2.75% to the bank rate in return for the guarantee. Many banks will lower their interest rate to you considering the SBA guarantee, so the total interest won't always be higher.

5.   The SBA usually demands a higher down payment from the buyer, oftentimes limiting their involvement to 50% of the purchase price.

Does an SBA loan offer any benefits? A few:

1.   An SBA loan may allow 7–10 years for repayment. In this one respect an SBA loan may beat seller or bank financing.

2.   The SBA will accept businesses located in distressed areas,whereas most banks won't.

3.   Your credit rating doesn't have to be strong for an SBA loan. The SBA favors applicants whose credit cannot meet bank requirements.

4.   The SBA tries to favor minorities and women. If you qualify, the SBA may be a good bet.

The SBA offers two types of loan arrangements. A local bank participates in most of the loans. The bank lends the money, but the government guarantees 90% of the debt. If you borrow $50,000 from the bank under an SBA loan, the bank could never lose more than $5,000. Still, an SBA guarantee won't necessarily enable you to find a bank willing to participate. I have several buyers with a guaranty commitment from the SBA, but they're still finding it hard to line up a bank. Banks are reluctant to get involved in any "problem" loan, even at minimal risk.

It's unlikely, but possible, that you can obtain a direct SBA loan without bank involvement. Only if you can't secure a participating bank will the SBA consider a "direct" loan.

DO YOU QUALIFY FOR AN SBA LOAN?

Strict requirements govern SBA acquisition financing. As with all bureaucracy, the criteria fill several pages of regulatory fine print. However, if your business generates sales of less than $2,000,000 (it may be slightly higher with certain industries), you'll meet the sales or size requirements.

To quickly find out whether or not your loan will qualify, visit your nearest SBA office before you begin the laborious paper work.

In fact a visit to the SBA office may point you in the direction of other government loans programs better suited to your needs. Bear in mind that government loan programs constantly change. So do their criteria. Certain industries or special situations can receive specialized loans.

Scan this extensive list.

KEY FEATURES
OF SBA'S PRINCIPAL LENDING PROGRAMS

U.S. SMALL BUSINESS ADMINISTRATION • WASHINGTON, D.C. 20416

	BUSINESS LOANS *	ECONOMIC OPPORTUNITY LOANS *
	Direct, Immediate Participation and Guaranty Loans	Direct, Immediate Participation and Guaranty Loans
WHO IS ELIGIBLE?	Most businesses including farms that are: (1) independently owned and operated and not dominant in their fields; (2) unable to obtain private financing on reasonable terms; (3) qualified as "small" under SBA's size standards, based on dollar volume of business or number of employees.	Low income or disadvantaged persons who have lacked the opportunity to start or strengthen a small business and cannot obtain the necessary financing from other sources on reasonable terms.
LOAN PURPOSES	Business construction, conversion or expansion, purchase of equipment, facilities, machinery, supplies or materials and working capital.	Any use which will carry out the purposes shown above; generally, the same as other business loans.
MAXIMUM AMOUNT	$350,000** to any one borrower is the maximum SBA share of an immediate participation loan, where SBA and private lending institution each put up part of loan funds immediately; and the maximum SBA direct loan, one made by the Agency. For guaranteed loans, made by a bank and partially guaranteed by SBA, the maximum is also $350,000 normally but may be up to $500,000 for exceptional circumstances.	$100,000 to any one borrower, as SBA share of loan.
INTEREST RATE	6% per annum on direct loan and SBA share of an immediate participation loan. On the bank's share of an immediate participation loan, the lending institution may set reasonable and legal rate with a maximum ceiling set by SBA from time to time. On a guaranty loan, bank may set legal and reasonable rate, with a maximum ceiling set by SBA from time to time.	On direct loans and SBA share of immediate participation loans, the rate is set periodically, based on a statutory formula. Bank rate same as on other business loans.
MATURITY	Maximum of 10 years as a rule. However, working capital loans generally are limited to 6 years, while portions of loans for construction and acquisition of real estate may have maximum of 20 years.	Maximum of 15 years. Working capital loans generally limited to a 10-year maximum.
TYPE OF COLLATERAL	Real estate or chatel mortgage; assignment of warehouse receipts for marketable merchandise; assignment of certain types of contracts; guarantees or personal endorsements; in some instances assignment of current receivables.	Any worthwhile collateral which is available or will be acquired with the proceeds of the loan.

*Under the Handicapped Assistance Loan Program, financial aid is available to handicapped individuals to start or operate small firms, and to nonprofit organizations which employ the handicapped to make a product or provide a service. Further details at local SBA office.

**At times, SBA may have lower ceilings in order to conserve limited funds.

EXHIBIT 5. Key Features of SBA's Principal lending Programs

OTHER DEALS—OTHER SOURCES

Small business buyers can have delusions of grandeur. After pounding the pavement from bank to bank, and after a final "thumbs down" from the SBA, they begin to visualize venture capital.

Perhaps a Business Development Corporation (BDC) will finance them? No? How about a loan from a Small Business Investment Corporation (SBIC)? Are you in a minority group? Perhaps you can attract the Minority Enterprise Small Business Investment Corporation (MESBIC)?

The names change but they all share certain characteristics. They are each owned and operated by venture capitalists who capitalize their company through a combination of their own money and government loans. They then lend and/or take partnership positions in small business ventures.

Are you becoming excited? Don't. They won't lend you $70,000 to buy Harry's Hardware, $50,000 to acquire Sam's Deli, or $120,000 for Dwight's Dry Cleaners. They want fast-growth ventures in the more exotic fields of high technology, computers, or biological engineering.

However, if you believe your company can attract venture capital, consult A. David Silver's, *Upfront Financing* (Wiley). It's an excellent book and can tell you everything you need to know about this area of high finance.

Headed for a franchise? As you've seen in Chapter 5, most well-established franchise firms solve your financing problems by including financing as part of their program. Most franchisors provide 50–70% of the funds directly, or guaranty your loan to a bank. With a strong franchisor guaranty, financing is relatively certain. Interest rates under franchise financing tend to be slightly higher than bank rates, since franchisors (like the SBA), may add on another interest point or two in return for their guaranty. The advantage is that they oftentimes can provide a longer pay-out as loan payments are carefully structured to the anticipated cash flow of the franchised unit.

Similar to the franchise concept are dealerships. If your target business features or is limited to a particular product line, you may qualify for supplier financing. For example, you might finance a car dealership with the help of the auto manufacturer, who will accept the inventory and parts as collateral. A friend recently wanted to buy a shoe store featuring a certain shoe manufacturer's line. The manufacturer loaned $60,000 toward the purchase price of $90,000. When the business features a specific manufacturer's product, always consider supplier financing.

Are finance companies on your shopping list? Some books may disagree with what I have to say, but I don't consider finance companies a suitable financing source for small businesses. Their interest rates are prohibitively steep, loan terms are dangerously short, and collateral (business and personal) demands are excessively high. That's why these firms are so profitable. There are specialized finance firms geared to specific industries. The restaurant industry, for example, may have several finance companies routinely making loans to restaurant buyers or for start-ups. Typically, they rely on equipment for callateral. The only time I suggest finance companies is when the capital needs are relatively small or if the business has exceptional profit potential to overcome the adverse loan terms.

Finally, we come to the money brokers or "capital finders." You'll spot them advertising in newspapers and trade journals, but perhaps they'll spot you first. As in any industry, they have their good and bad players. The two items to watch in dealing with money brokers is their advance fee and the likelihood that they'll find you your money. Many finders take a $1,000–5,000 advance fee and never deliver. Others can tie you up for months, and even with their best efforts fail to find the financing. Money brokers of necessity work with lenders who accept risk that conventional lenders refuse. So you'll pay the price should they find the money. It may require 25–30% interest. Commonly you'll have to give up some ownership in the business. Be guided closely by your accountant and attorney before you call in the money brokers.

Will you find your financing? If you have your sound acquisition and a logical plan why others should end you the money, you'll succeed. Inability to find the money can also be success in disguise. Can all those lenders be wrong in evaluating your business?

KEY POINTS TO REMEMBER

1. Seller financing is your best bet.
2. Package your seller financing request to reduce the seller's concerns.
3. Banks are like snowflakes. No two are alike. Match your deal to the right bank.
4. Draft your loan proposal to answer the 5 Cs: credit, cash flow, collateral, capital, and coverage.
5. Banks will negotiate. Remember you want the *most money*, the *least interest*, and the *longest term*.
6. Structure the loan so the business, not you, is the direct borrower.
7. Don't try the SBA unless you're convinced you can't find a willing bank.
8. If you strike out with seller, bank, and SBA financing, ask yourself the important question—do you really have a solid plan?

8

COMING UP WITH YOUR DOWN PAYMENT

Walter T. only had $10,000 in the bank, so the $30,000 down payment he needed to buy Fairmount Bakery drove him back to his job as a milk truck driver.

The $40,000 needed to swing the purchase of Highland Pharmacy spelled doom to Nick G., who still fills prescriptions for a giant chain. Nick never could raise more than $15,000.

Could Jim and Harry B. come up with $60,000 to acquire the White Swan Dry Cleaners? Unfortunately, the brothers could only scrape together $24,000.

But Fairmount Bakery sold to a buyer with only $5,000 of his own money.

Two weeks after Nick walked away from Highland Pharmacy, a buyer purchased it using only $10,000 of his own cash.

And the shrewd buyer who picked up White Swan Dry Cleaners didn't spend a dime of his own money.

Unusual stories? Not at all. Small business buyers can purchase good, solid, profitable businesses with small down payments or without any cash at all.

Consider the facts:

Many buyers never buy because they can't raise the down payment they *think* they need to buy a business.

Other buyers usually buy too small a business to match their small pocketbooks, though they could buy a considerably better business with their limited cash.

Sellers who impose high cash-down demands have a hard time selling but could satisfy their objectives through creative financing.

It's too common a story. A seller will put his business on the market for

$60,000, and demand at least $30,000 in up front cash. They don't ask the important question: "Will buyers with $30,000 be interested in my business? Can the qualified buyer who only has a $5,000–10,000 down payment still satisfy my objectives and help me sell quicker?"

For their part, buyers who listen to such demands reason that they can't qualify for the business with only $5,000–10,000 and never ask: "Could I both satisfy the seller and buy the business with only $5,000–10,000? Do I *really* need $30,000?"

In most acquisitions you can answer those questions positively. The seller wants as much as possible, the buyer either has little to invest or refuses to invest that much.

How can the two come together? Let's examine some buyers and sellers who bridged the financing gap.

WHO NEEDS MONEY

John L. wanted to sell his hardware store for $100,000 cash, and Sid Craven had picked it out of half a dozen similar ones for sale.

Though Sid found the major financing building block for the deal at a bank that agreed to loan him $60,000 over five years, what about the remaining $40,000?

With $60,000 secured from the bank, Sid asked John to estimate the liabilities that John owed business creditors. John quoted $20,000, which he planned to pay at the time of closing, since he wanted to turn the store over to Sid free and clear of liabilities. Hearing that, Sid persuaded John to allow him to assume the liabilities and deduct an equal amount from the price. Now Sid only needed $20,000 to close the deal.

He approached the broker, who had introduced him to John and who was due a hefty $10,000 commission from the sale. "Lend me $5,000 from your commission to be repaid over two years," suggested Sid. The broker, not wanting to lose the sale and his commission agreed. Only $15,000 to go.

After some sleuthing, Sid learned that one major supplier provided the store over $100,000 a year in merchandise. Quickly tallying the supplier's profit from the account, Sid asked them for a $5,000 loan which would help him buy the business and insure that it remained a loyal, profitable account. They couldn't refuse.

With $90,000 in hand, Sid wasn't about to stop only $10,000 short. Since the terms of sale called for John to guaranty a $60,000 inventory at the time of closing, Sid suggested that John reduce the inventory to $50,000, putting the $10,000 cash in his own pocket while correspondingly reducing the price. Why not? John didn't care where it came from.

Sid swung the deal using everyone's money but his own:

$60,000	bank financing
20,000	assumed liabilities
5,000	broker loan
5,000	supplier loan
10,000	inventory cash conversion
$100,000	sales price

The net result?

The seller enjoyed the same net cash he would have gotten had Sid walked in with his own $100,000 check.

The broker salvaged his commission.

The creditors don't care who pays them.

The supplier's loan guaranteed the supplier strong profits for many years to come.

Numerous other tactics can bridge the gap between price and your meager bank account. Whenever I conduct a business buyer seminar most people ask, "Do these techniques really work?" They certainly do. In my book *Own Your Own/The No Cash Down Business Guide* (Prentice Hall), I show over 200 ways that buyers with limited or no capital can start or buy a business. Here's some highlights of the more common methods.

PYRAMIDING THE SELLER LOAN

Sellers may say, "I'll sell the business for $100,000 and finance 50–60% of the price." Before accepting, you would have to find $40,000 from other sources. Since sellers in such cases would hold *first* mortgages on the assets of the businesses, you can rule out bank or SBA financing because both demand a first mortgage as security.

Why not issue a counteroffer? "If I obtain a first mortgage from the bank (or SBA) for the $60,000, would you accept a second mortgage for $20,000?" Your advantages are obvious. With the bank's $60,000 and the seller's $20,000, you have $80,000 in place and have cut your cash requirements from $40,000 to $20,000.

The seller may see one advantage and one disadvantage. Though the seller would end up with more immediate cash (the bank proceeds of $60,000 plus a $20,000 down payment you'll get from other sources), he may feel that your $20,000 note isn't as safely collateralized as his original $60,000 note would have been. Now the bank's $60,000 mortgage takes precedence over his second mortgage. To solve the seller's security problem, you may, for example, propose a relatively rapid pay-down of his $20,000 note over a one- to three-year period. Few businesses fail within the first two years following takeover. By then the balance owed the seller would have shrunk substantially.

If you encounter the likely situation in which the seller agrees to finance part of the price, try to use his financing not in place of bank (or SBA) financing but in addition to it. Such bank/seller financing can in most cases create building blocks worth 70–90% of the purchase price. Now let's return to the $20,000 down payment I said you'd get from other sources.

TURNING LIABILITIES INTO AN ASSET

Assume the seller agreed to your counter-proposal. At the closing you would hand the seller your $20,000 down payment, the bank's $60,000 check, and your $20,000 note. The seller would have $80,000 in cash and would be obligated to pay his creditors before he could sell you the assets of the business free and clear of claims. But what if the liabilities totaled $20,000? After writing checks to his creditors the seller would leave the closing with only $60,000 cash. Propose that instead of giving him your $20,000 down payment, which will only go to creditors, you assume them yourself. He ends up with the same net cash, but you've used his creditors to finance your down payment.

The only objection a seller could pose to that proposal is that he (or his corporation) would still remain liable to the creditors if you failed to pay them. To solve that problem, indemnify (protect and reimburse) him from creditors' claims if you do not pay. If the seller still wonders whether your indemnity provides adequate protection, resolve his fear by granting him security (a further mortgage on the assets and/or a pledge of your shares of stock in the corporation) to back it up. In some cases, buyers have granted real estate mortgages on their homes to secure the obligation, however most buyers can avoid that through effective negotiation.

If that tactic doesn't work, ask the principal creditors to release the seller from his obligations in return for your assumption of the debt. Many creditors are willing to accept eventual payment from the buyer because they want to continue doing business with the buyer.

In this example, assuming $20,000 in trade debt wouldn't be unreasonable because it probably approximates the normal debt level for the business anyway. Upon takeover, the buyer would be "turning over" the debt by paying the seller's balance first, then building up a corresponding debt of his own through new purchases. A buyer can usually pay off the seller's debts within 30–90 days from date of takeover.

What if the seller had only $10,000 in debt? If you assume the $10,000 in liabilities, you only need $10,000 more. Fine. Always close the gap by cutting your cash needs by any amount possible.

If the seller had $40,000 or more in liabilities, you could structure the financing with the same $60,000 bank mortgage, but instead of a $20,000 second mortgage to the seller, you'd ask to assume the $40,000 in debt for the full balance of the purchase price.

Some finance experts may argue that $40,000 in immediately due liabilities would place too great a financial strain on the business. That's a possibility, and your demand that the seller partially reduce the trade debt from the $60,000 he'd receive at the closing would probably meet strong resistance. Why should the seller use his cash proceeds from the sale to allow you to buy without cash?

Don't allow excess debt to unduly concern you. It represents a powerful financing tool, not an insoluble operation problem. As a practical matter, you can ordinarily restructure currently due accounts payable to suit what the business can pay within a reasonable time.

Assumption of liabilities often works because the sale of small businesses ($50,000–200,000) involves transfer of assets from the seller to the buyer, rather than acquisition by the buyer of the stockholders' corporate shares. Review Chapter 10 for details. When a seller assigns assets to the buyer, the customary terms dictate that the seller will pay existing debts at closing so the buyer can acquire the assets free of creditor claims.

On the other hand, if you were to buy the shares of stock in this same $100,000 business, the price you'd pay for them would reflect the corporation's existing liabilities. Assuming $40,000 in liabilities and $100,000 in assets, the seller could expect $60,000 cash for his stock. Obviously, you couldn't use the liabilities as a financing mechanism, so if you need creative financing with existing liabilities you should avoid buying shares.

However, if the seller's liabilities are excessive, you may find it advantageous to buy shares of stock because the shares have little or no residual value.

Such a strategy helps take over insolvent or debt-ridden companies. One recent buyer parted with only $10,000 to acquire the shares of an intriguing but floundering hobby store chain. For eight months the business sat on the market with a $280,000 asking price. Several buyers nibbled and a few even shopped for bank financing, but no bank would lend more than $140,000. The seller was candid, insisting he needed $280,000 cash to cancel $240,000 in debts and net $40,000 for himself. Perfect! Financing fell into place with creditors' money. In return for his shares in the company, the buyer agreed to a $10,000 down payment and $30,000 in notes with payment conditional upon the buyer's ability to compromise creditor claims below $160,000. Rather than face a bankruptcy dividend, the creditors agreed to a 50% settlement payable over three years. The buyer is still paying the seller on his note, but she enjoys writing her checks.

SELL YOUR SUPPLIERS

You won't be the only one to profit from you business. Your business may put even more profits into your suppliers' pockets.

Ask yourself a simple question. If your suppliers stand to make money from doing business with you, why not call upon them to help with the down payment that will help put you into business?

Remember how Sid approached the hardware supplier for $5,000 towards the down payment? The $5,000 represented only 5% of the $100,000 in business, or $20,000 in profit, the supplier would earn over the next year from Sid's hardware store, and the supplier would even make money off the interest on the loan. As Sid would say, "Suppliers are willing to extend credit to a new buyer *after* a take-over, why not *before*, especially if doing so will make the take-over possible?"

Supplier loans would happen quite often if more buyers simply asked. Suppliers seldom turn down a reasonable request. Don't call it charity. An advance loan is only another form of credit.

As one leading wholesale drug firm president states, "Twice prospective buyers asked us to advance a loan to purchase a business. One account was good for $200,000 in annual sales, so we could justify a $20,000 loan toward his $60,000 down payment. We'd be foolish not to. We earn over $24,000 in annual profit from that account, plus the 18% interest we charge for the loan."

The supplier loan also worked for Bill F. Bill, one of my more entrepreneurial clients, already owned one heavily mortgaged liquor store when he located a second profitable one for sale. With $120,000 in bank and seller financing lined up, Bill only needed $40,000 to reach the $160,000 sales price.

Bill confidently marched in to see the president of his wholesale liquor supplier. Hitting the supplier with a look of despair, he confided, "I've got a problem. As you know, my present store buys about $600,000 in liquor from you per year. I have a chance to buy a second store, but its present wholesaler wants me to do business with him so badly he offered me a $50,000 loan toward my down payment, and an extra 2% discount above what you give me, provided I buy through him for both stores. I guess they really want the combined $1,200,000 volume. I want to do it, but I had to give you a chance to match their deal, we're such old friends." Do you think Bill received the $50,000 loan? He had his check the following week, spending $40,000 to buy the business and $10,000 for working capital. Why? Because he employed logic, psychology, and plain business sense.

If you are a cash-shy buyer who would otherwise qualify for a business, make a list of existing and competitive suppliers. Concentrating on the primary suppliers, try to structure a loan proportionate to the value of the account. If the supplier stands to earn an annual gross profit of $20,000, ask for a $10,000 loan. Within six months the supplier would have recouped the loan from profits and could still look forward to a loan pay-back with interest. The pay-back period for the loan may be anywhere from one to four years, depending on the size of the loan and the cash flow of the business, but that usually concerns the supplier less than his ongoing profits. Suppliers, like any lender, want security, so grant them a mortgage on the business and a personal guaranty.

Prove your buying commitment which, in turn, proves the suppliers will win future business, thus motivating them to make the loan. Be prepared to offer the supplier an agreement that if your purchases fall below certain levels, the loan will fall due immediately. That affords the supplier some protection against you taking his money and switching to a competitive supplier.

Don't let the supplier lock you in with unfavorable terms as penalty for the loan. You want the same prices, discounts, and other benefits that comparable accounts receive.

Your success will depend on competition among suppliers, the present value of your account, and your expansion potential or future good will. Perhaps the most important is the supplier's confidence that you can effectively manage the business into a profitable account.

Taverns, restaurants, and other businesses with concessioned juke boxes, cigarettes, pinball or other vending machines always represent an opportunity for advance loans. Typically, the vending company and the business owner split the profits 50/50. Two or three high-volume machines can generate $15,000–20,000 annually for the owner. Many vending machine firms willingly advance up to the first year's owner's commission to obtain a concession lease. But every industry has its opportunity. As long as suppliers are making money off you, you'll have a willing audience.

THE HELPING HAND FROM BROKERS

In Chapter 3 I mentioned the possibility of a loan from the broker, and you've seen how Sid convinced the broker to lend half his commission to help with the down payment. Let's expand.

Never overlook the importance of the broker as a source of cash. When you consider that the average conventionally financed small business acquisition requires only a 20% down payment from the buyer, and the seller must pay a 10% commission to the broker, the seller uses 50% of your cash investment on broker's fees. In many cases the seller demands the cash needed to pay the broker.

Brokers earn their livings from commissions. They will always resist your idea that they kick in part of their commission to close the deal, but faced with losing a deal, they seldom refuse. If you convince brokers you can raise the capital from other sources, they'll bluff you right down to the wire. As usual, success depends on effective negotiation.

Except for some very large firms who won't loan on commissions as a matter of policy and to avoid precedent, about the only brokers who will refuse are those who have a long-term exclusive on the business and other active prospects in the wings.

If you ask the broker for a loan, don't borrow more than 50% of his commission. The broker also has expenses to meet. The loan should be secured by the business assets, carry reasonable interest, and be payable within 12 months.

TAPPING INVENTORY FOR CASH

A seller based the price for a business on certain asset values at the time of sale. For example, the price may be $100,000 based on an actual $60,000 inventory at the time of sale. If the inventory at the time of take-over has fallen to $50,000, the price would drop to $90,000. Sid asked the seller to reduce inventory levels by $10,000 and take the proceeds from the business without replacing the inventory. The seller obtained $10,000 that would otherwise come from the down payment. If your seller complains that the cash removed from the business may be taxed as ordinary income rather than as capital gains (a lower rate), make an adjustment to compensate for the additional tax. But keep in mind the seller will pay a smaller broker's commission on the lower sales price, a fact that may offset increased taxes.

For example, $10,000 received by the seller from inventory conversion would incur a $4,000 income tax liability, if the seller is in the 40% tax bracket. If the same $10,000 came from the sale of the business it would be taxed at the 20% capital tax rate creating a $2,000 liability. So the net tax difference is $2,000. However, if a broker is involved, the seller would save $1,000 on brokers fees, as the selling price is reduced by $10,000. Therefore, the net loss to the seller is only $1,000. Why not simply add the $1,000 to the seller's note if the seller has this increased tax liability and questions the point.

Excess inventory can work wonders even on a larger scale. In one case a cosmetic shop selling for $140,000 was sold by using excess inventory in place of a down payment. The cosmetic shop had $90,000 in merchandise, but only needed $50,000 to operate profitably. The astute buyer proposed that the seller reduce the inventory by $40,000 over the following two or three months and turn it into cash. With $40,000 in the business bank account, the seller redeemed (sold back to her own corporation) some of her outstanding shares, with the corporation paying her $40,000 for the shares. Next, the seller reduced the price of the business to $100,000 allowing the buyer to acquire it with a $50,000 bank loan, seller financing for $30,000 and the assumption of $20,000 in still-outstanding liabilities. The buyer had his profitable business with no cash down and the seller was able to walk away with $40,000 cash (taxed at the favorable capital gains rate), and her $30,000 note besides. Excess inventory can close the gap.

TAKING THE CASH OUT OF CASH FLOW

Intentionally increasing liabilities can improve cash flow and can generate enough money to replace a down payment. Suppose you came across a business selling for $100,000 and you have assembled $90,000 in financing. The seller tells you he has no liabilities and therefore none you can assume. Suggest that the seller operate the business for a month and incur $10,000 in debts but, instead of paying the bills at the end of the month, simply take the cash as income and have you assume the $10,000 in liabilities. Other than adverse tax consequences, the seller would only be taking the $10,000 down payment out of cash flow rather than your pocket. He would end up with the same amount of cash.

In many cases, assets include accounts receivable. If your $100,000 business includes $10,000 in accounts receivable, ask the seller to retain the receivables and reduce the price—and the down payment—accordingly.

One of my clients creatively tapped cash flow when she acquired a supermarket for $300,000 but was short $20,000 at the time of closing. Passing papers on a Friday afternoon, she handed the seller $280,000 in bank and certified checks and her personal check for $20,000. The seller never questioned the noncertified check and cashed it the following Monday morning. My client used the whole weekend's sales receipts to cover the check. You may not have to play such a questionable game. However, many sellers will accept a series of post-dated checks to be cashed on a periodic basis after you take over. In a recent transfer of a small wholesale carton factory, the buyer candidly told the seller he could come up with $70,000 towards the $78,000 price, but would need the cash flow of the business to cover the final $8,000. The seller agreed to accept four checks for $2,000, each dated one month apart. When a seller trusts and has confidence in a buyer, it's not hard to close the financing gap. Between them they can tap cash flow for a down payment.

THE SIMULTANEOUS SPIN-OFF

Your target business may have certain assets you can convert to cash and apply to the down payment at the time of sale.

When the Johnsons spotted a restaurant for sale on Long Island, they scraped together $180,000 of the $200,000 sales price. Finding the last $20,000 presented an obstacle. Shrewd old Mr. Johnson eyed the parking lot bordering on a busy beach, then negotiated to lease the parking lot to someone else during the day, reserving its use for the restaurant at night. He demanded $20,000 in advance rent. The lease and the purchase of the restaurant occurred simultaneously. The Johnsons only had to turn their rent check over to the seller to reach the magical $200,000.

Biscayne Wholesale Plumbing Supply used a similar strategy to acquire another plumbing firm. To raise $80,000 toward the down payment, Biscayne simultaneously sold and leased back from another firm the fleet of trucks included as part of the assets.

Every business has hidden assets you can turn into cash. Consult this checklist:

Disposable fixtures or equipment.

It may be a computer, cash registers, excess office furniture, or any other tangible item not needed in your operation of the business.

Customer lists.

The business' customer lists can have a value to related but noncompetitive businesses, and they will buy or rent your list with payment in advance. A buyer for an artificial brick manufacturer prearranged the rental of customer lists with the names of 10,000 homeowners who recently acquired brick. A tile manufacturer paid $5,000 for the use of the list, adding to the cash available for a down payment.

Trademark and patent rights.

Why not prenegotiate valuable territory or licensing rights and use the advance fee toward a down payment. It worked for a buyer of a well-known burglar alarm company who arranged to license the name to seven burglar alarm companies in other states, and collected $10,000 from each, conditional upon his acquiring the business. The $70,000 was all that was needed to close.

Sublet or concessional space.

Here you can line up a tenant to occupy excess space, collect rent in advance, and apply it to the down payment. It was a solution for the Johnsons and for others. One supermarket buyer found a print shop to occupy its 8000 sq ft basement, with the entire $24,000 first-year rental payable in advance. In another case, a buyer for a car dealership arranged for renting billboard space with a $9,000 advance rental.

Excess motor vehicles.

Biscayne Wholesale Plumbing Supply showed you one way to do it. Frequently a business includes personal or delivery vehicles that are either not required or can be rented. Why not prearrange their sale for the down payment.

To make these, or perhaps other, hidden assets work for you, follow this step-by-step approach:

1. Locate an asset you can sell, without hurting your business.
2. Arrange the sale, lease, or money-raising transaction in advance, but make it conditional upon your closing the transaction.
3. Make certain the asset isn't mortgaged under your financing plan so you have the authority to sell. Your attorney should review this.
4. Coordinate the sale of the asset with closing the deal so you can use the money to fund your acquisition.

Study your target business before you buy. What assets can you turn into cash to make that sale happen?

DO YOU REALLY NEED A PARTNER?

Do you need a partner to clear the confidence hurdle or to provide management skills? In either case a partnership may be wise. They can also supply money, but watch your step.

If your partner only has money to invest in the business, you may be paying an exorbitant price for a few dollars. For a capital-intensive business, or one that is unable to attract alternate sources of long-term debt financing, a partnership may be not only the logical but the only solution. However, any buyer who can put together a financing package for 70–80% of the price should avoid partners for the remaining funds. If you borrow money, once you're through paying it off you're through with the lender, but once a partner gives you his cash he's with you forever.

If you are tempted to look for an investing partner for those few final dollars, try to structure the arrangement so you can buy your partner out in the future. For example, you may need a partner to invest $20,000 to match your own $20,000 to buy a $140,000 business. Perhaps your partner would sign an option for you to acquire his interest for $30,000 within two years. Your partner may consider the return worthwhile. He'll analyze the risk, and what this $20,000 could earn in other investments over two years. He may decide his $20,000 would yield $6,000 interest in a far safer or more liquid investment and decide a $4,000 premium is not sufficient to justify the investment. Perhaps he'll counter-propose with a buy-out option at $35,000.

Don't let your investing partner forget that any profit on the buy-out will be taxed at a low capital gains rate, whereas interest from other investments will be taxed at the higher ordinary income rates. Maybe that will convince him to drop the option price to $32,000. Negotiate!

A buy-out option will:

1. Provide time to work down existing loans, and/or build the business so you can re-borrow to buy out your partner.

2. Allow you to dissolve the partnership should disagreement arise. Having a fixed, predetermined buy-out figure puts a ceiling on what it will take to dissolve the partnership, while retaining complete ownership of the business.

3. Insure that you will not have to share long-term profits or gains with a partner.

Essentially, a partnership structured along these lines displays the characteristics of both equity and debt financing. Your partner has an ownership interest in the business, but you have the right to pay his investment back (with a profit) to regain sole ownership. It may be at a steep price, but it's seldom as steep as what this same partner would walk away with many years later. Still, consider partnerships a last resort.

THE PAPER CLIP NET WORTH THEORY

So-called finance exports are probably screaming, "How can Goldstein tell his readers to mortgage themselves to the hilt and go into business owing a fortune? Doesn't he know a business should have a certain debt/equity ratio? Doesn't he know the dangers of undercapitalization? Doesn't he know he's breaking every rule in the book?"

Yes, I know I'm breaking every rule in the book, but those rules control other people's books, not mine. I prefer the "paper clip net worth" rule: a business can afford as much debt as its cash flow can reasonably pay. I picked up this term years ago, when I represented an astute buyer, Tom P., who only knew one word: leverage (using other people's money). He would only buy with 100% financing. On one particular deal Tom acquired a motel-restaurant with a potpourri of creative financing techniques. He has SBA loans, bank debt, and seller loans, layered by takeover of liabilities, and some supplier loans. OPM (other people's money) perfectly coincided with the purchase price of $380,000. Tom didn't put a nickel of his own in the deal. His accountant, the finance genius, ranted and raved how the business would collapse under the weight of the debt and finally shouted, "Tom! You don't even have a paper clip invested in this deal."

Tom looked up, reached into his desk drawer and threw a paper clip onto the desk saying, "Sure I do. Here it is." Tom was able to hold his creditors at bay until he could finally pay them down and build the motel-restaurant into a healthy business grossing over $2,800,000 and a net worth of close to $2,000,000.

Leverage frightens many buyers, whose accountants, playing by the book, scare them to death with debt. But many people know what Tom knew. Businesses seldom fail due to poor capitalization; they fail because they're unprofitable. Creditors will wait or will stretch out payments to match cash flow, if they can see the business heading in the right direction. Creditors, particularly those in a junior position, display tremendous resiliency. They usually have little choice but to wait.

On any highly leveraged acquisition, ask two questions:

1. Do the cash flow projections show that you can pay down a debt within some reasonable time?
2. What do you risk by gambling?

If I believed the company only had a 20–30% change of making it, I might make the acquisition if I had no significant investment or personal liability.

Conversely, if I believed the company could make the grade, I would be willing to contribute a heavier investment and personal exposure.

I have seen many buyers invest $50,000–60,000 of their own funds to buy a $100,000–120,000 business and fail. Others, like Tom, invest a paper clip and succeed. That's why I advise clients to invest as little of their own funds as possible, knowing it means little to future success.

Leverage, as Tom would define it, requires a carefully brewed mixture of adventure, management skill, luck, creditor patience, and common sense. As Tom is quick to point out, "It sure beats staying out of business because you don't have the money."

IT MAKES SENSE TO SELL FOR "LOW CASH DOWN"

Whenever a seller retains us, we expect to hear a line like this: "I want $100,000 cash for the business, but for the right buyer, I might be willing to 'hold $40,000–50,000 in paper.' "

What happens to these sellers?

1. They never find buyers with $50,000–60,000 in cash, because such buyers are looking for $400,000–500,000 businesses they can buy with leverage; or
2. They find a cash buyer but bargain the business away for $70,000 because no competing buyers exist; or
3. They bend their terms, sell the business for $80,000 with $25,000 down, finance $55,000 and then watch the business go down the drain ending up with only $20,000 of a $55,000 note.

Examine the objectives in selling a business. The typical seller wants:

1. the fastest sale possible
2. the best price
3. the greatest certainty of getting his money

Do you know how you'll best satisfy those objectives? Offer the business for sale to buyers with very small down payments. Here's why.

The number of available buyers rapidly decreases as cash requirements increase. A seller who insists on $100,000 cash is really talking·about finding a buyer with $40,000–50,000 to spend, assuming the balance can be handled through bank or SBA financing. But in the small business market a buyer with $50,000 is rare. If the same business were put on the market demanding only $10,000–15,000 down, the number of potential buyers doubles or triples. Reduce it further to $5,000–7,000 and the buyers flock to it. To select the best candidate to fulfill your objectives, you want a pool of qualified buyers.

Price? Don't offer the $100,000 business at the $100,000 price, but at $125,000. Can you get away with it? Absolutely. And for three good reasons. First, you have attracted large numbers of buyers to the business. You are bound to find many who would accept $125,000 as a fair price. Second, increased competition for the business inflates a business' sales price. Last, and most importantly, buyers consider price less crucial than overall terms and their ability to buy the business with limited cash. The limited-capital buyer won't haggle as much over price. He's happy with the idea that he can buy it at all.

Assuming the seller has agreed to a low down payment and creative financing, will he get paid on the note? Of course one worries about that with a smaller note, so the problem becomes acute when it involves $85,000 rather than $55,000.

Too many sellers are so busy looking for the front money they become sloppy when considering the safety of the balance. Reverse your priorities. Take a small down payment, get your best price, and concentrate on finding and negotiating adequate security for the balance.

How can you obtain more security from the buyer with a small down payment? Wouldn't such a person own fewer assets and be able to offer less collateral? Possibly. Then again, many buyers don't enjoy cash liquidity but do have sizable equities in their home or other assets. Adequate collateral, whether it be business, personal, or a combination of assets should be the essential ingredient in seller financing. Collateral—not cash—becomes the criterion for accepting the buyer.

Ray S. owned a $100,000 superette, which he advertised and listed with several brokers. His requirements were always the same: $50,000–100,000 cash up front. The nibbles were few and far between.

We sat down with Ray and agreed on a new strategy. The following week this ad appeared in the *Boston Globe*.

Superette For Sale
$450,000 sales. Good lease.
Profitable. $7500 down payment for
qualified buyer. South of Boston.
Phone: _____

In three days 86 buyers stood in line for the superette. The screening process began. We wanted the buyer with $7500 who could match it with a willingness to pay the $125,000 price and collateral to back up a hefty note.

We whittled the 86 buyers down to 20 who would buy at $125,000. Now we began to focus on collateral. Some buyers were so poor they quickly dropped out, and we soon narrowed the field to our one best prospect.

The sale finally came together on these terms:

Sales price:	$125,000
Financing:	
Cash down	7,500
Assumed liabilities	5,000
Principal on note to seller, with interest at 17% payable over six years	112,500
	_____
	$125,000

How safe was the financing? Ray held a mortgage on a business with a liquidation value of $35,000 even under the worst of circumstances. But Ray also had a second mortgage on the buyer's home ($60,000 equity) and a first mortgage on some farm land owned by the buyer ($30,000 equity). Ray couldn't lose.

Though Ray didn't walk out of the closing with any cash in his pocket (the down payment became our commission), he didn't need immediate cash. He was willing to give up small dollars today for larger dollars tomorrow. Perhaps a seller needs cash for another business, to buy a condo in Florida, or to take a long-overdue trip around the world. If Ray needed some cash he could either sell his note or borrow against it, because it's fully collateralized and yields high interest. Ray could probably sell the note for $100,000 and still come out ahead.

BUILDING THE FINANCIAL PYRAMID

Whether you're the buyer with little or no cash down, or the seller wanting the benefits of the leveraged sale, scan this financial pyramid to show you how you can find your own financing building blocks.

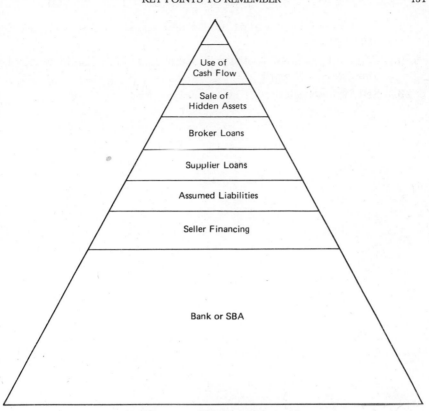

EXHIBIT 6. The Financial Pyramid

KEY POINTS TO REMEMBER

1. Don't fall victim to a seller's "cash down" demands. You can probably buy with considerably less.
2. Always build your financial pyramid starting with bank financing and letting the seller provide secondary financing.
3. Why not assume the seller's liabilities, to be deducted from your down payment?
4. Your suppliers offer an excellent source of down payment money.
5. Can you tap cash flow to get the seller his money without digging into your pocket?
6. Brokers can lend.
7. Look for hidden assets you can pre-sell to supply your down payment.

8. Don't accept expensive partners unless you *know* you can't raise the funds elsewhere.

9. Don't be afraid of leverage. Remember, today's liabilities can be tomorrow's net worth.

10. Sell for low cash down to get your best price.

9

NEGOTIATING YOUR BEST BUY

I'm going to make you an offer you can't refuse," said the Godfather in Mario Puzo's famous novel. Who wouldn't be confident with two "assistants" preparing cement overshoes in the background?

But you're not the Godfather. You need your own brand of bargaining power to land your best deal. This chapter will guide you through the negotiating process from beginning to end, sifting out the tactics, strategies, and gambits to put you ahead.

You can only achieve what you can negotiate, and the outcome of your negotiations is an agreement. How good will it be?

Will you buy at the rock-bottom price or overpay? How about financing? You know the best ways to finance. Can you get the seller to see it your way?

Will you find the seller's signature on your agreement or will it end up on another buyer's contract?

Successful negotiations don't require the persuasive powers of a Dale Carnegie, the sophistication of a Henry Kissinger, wit of a Will Rogers, or business genius of a J. Paul Getty. Be yourself. You only have one overall objective: cutting the best deal with your own style and approach. And there's never one best way to negotiate. Every situation demands its own tailor-made approach. You may close your best deal over a friendly cup of coffee. Perhaps it will be months of dickering before you tally the scorecard. But follow one motto: *work* for the best, but *prepare* for the worse.

Where do you start?

PUT ON YOUR POKER FACE

Did you spot a business that interests you? If so, you have already started the negotiation process. It began the minute you walked through the seller's door. While one eye scans the business, the other probes the seller for signals: "Does this seller really want to sell? How badly? Why? What will he settle for?" As the seller begins to tell you about the business and answers important questions, your ears pick up the hesitations, the pauses, the uncertainties.

The seller's radar is also spinning. "Does this buyer have money? How much? Is he serious? Is he anxious to buy? Does he like the business?" Negotiations begin.

The negotiation process continues as you pour over financial records, investigate and evaluate the business. You and the seller meet frequently, sizing each other up. The seller tries to detect anxiety. You look for signs of desperation. During this important prebargaining stage, most negotiations are won or lost.

Arthur lost. He left his poker face home as he scouted a motorcycle dealership in upstate New York with an inflated $180,000 price tag. Smiling like a kid in a candy factory, Arthur shouted, "Hey, this is just what I've been looking for!" Twenty minutes later he was haranguing his accountant to drop everything to check out the books. Bright and early the next morning, Arthur showed up with a beautiful set of plans for promoting the business. The seller looked forward to spending his $180,000.

Anxious Arthur started with a $160,000 offer. "Can't do it" insisted the seller. Two hours later Arthur's bid was up to $170,000. "No way." Next day Arthur dashed back. "Okay, okay, I'll pay $180,000." "Hate to disappoint you but I decided not to sell" replied the seller. "What do you mean?" screamed Arthur. "Just yesterday the business was for sale for $180,000." "That was yesterday. Today it's $225,000," shrugged the shrewd seller. "But I'll tell you what," he deftly added, "I'll let you have it for $215,000." Did Arthur pay it? You bet. The seller later confessed he was prepared to sell for a quick $140,000. Arthur would call it negotiation. He should call it capitulation.

Many buyers fall victim to their own enthusiasm, tipping their hands early in the game by showing too strong an interest in the business.

Remember these points:

1. The negotiations start the minute you come face to face with the seller.
2. Listen! Don't talk. You're there to pick up the seller's signals, not throw out your own.
3. Be patient. Don't rush the deal. You want the seller to think you have other deals pending and have neither the time nor the interest to strain yourself cementing a deal with him.

4. Successful negotiating depends on consistency. Everything you say and do should carry one message: the business interests you, you can handle it, but you can take it or leave it. The attitude you display before you sit down at the bargaining table inevitably determines what you'll win or lose at the table.

What's the seller up to while you're hiding behind your poker face? Let's see.

SMOKESCREENS: EVERY SELLER'S PLOY

Sellers come in all shapes and sizes, and they all play predictable games. Camouflaged by their own smokescreen you're bound to meet:

1. Mr. Just Testing.   Some sellers are the counterparts of the buyers who spend their lives looking but never buy. They advertise, and even negotiate, but they never close a deal.

Why do such sellers persist in wasting your time and money? For several reasons. Some only want to reassure themselves that their businesses are valuable. Others enjoy dickering with buyers. Finally, comes the seller who figures he'll put his business on the market at a ridiculously high price to see if one poor sucker might take the bait.

The only seller in this category worth dealing with is the one who sincerely wants to sell but can't quite tear himself away from his lifetime investment. Why not offer a job? This works especially well with the seller facing retirement.

How can you smoke out the testers? They never call in their accountants or lawyers because accountants and lawyers cost money and make his hobby very expensive. Whenever you suspect you're up against a tester, ask him to have his accountant work with your accountant to go over the books. That's when the tester usually backs out.

2. Mr. I Don't Really Want to Sell.   This character sits behind his big desk with his hands behind his head, saying, "My business isn't really for sale, *but* I'll entertain an interesting offer." This master intimidator wants you on the defensive, while he maintains the upper hand. But this same seller has beaten the bushes for the past three years looking for a buyer. He has run so many ads he's on a first-name basis with the local newspaper editor. Every night he kneels down beside his bed and adds to his prayers, "Please find me a buyer." If you don't realize that, you may begin your own begging and whimpering for a chance to shovel his goldmine.

There's only one way to pierce the smokescreen of Mr. I Don't Really Want to Sell: let him know early in the game that you don't really want to buy. The phone call will come.

3.   Mr. In Demand.   His strategy is to get you bidding against yourself by believing every buyer is banging down his doors. Last week he had three offers that he's still considering and tomorrow he expects two more. Mr. In Demand, is a very busy man sifting through all his wonderful offers. But since he's the benevolent type he'll add yours to the growing pile.

How should you react? First, tell him you don't care about other buyers or what they offer. Your only concern is what the business is worth to you. Next, let him know you can't be rushed because you have too many other businesses to consider. Don't worry about competition. Mr. In Demand has been running his ads longer that Mr. I Don't Really Want to Sell.

4.   Mr. Desperate.   This cunning creature peeks out from behind his smokescreen to entice you to take advantage of his desperation. "I've got to sell—and fast," he tells you, recounting his problems with his lower back. Maybe it's the broker handing you this yarn, but you see the message. Snap it up before it gets away. Today's your lucky day.

Mr. Desperate is seldom desperate. He just wants a fast offer to get the ball rolling so he can spend the next four months negotiating you up to his price when he's not busy playing golf with his bad back.

How can you be sure Mr. Desperate's not in trouble? It's easy. If he was he wouldn't be playing Mr. Desperate. He'd be called:

5.   Mr. Who's in Trouble?   Now here's where you'll find the *real* Mr. Desperate. Bill collectors are closing in, the landlord's about to throw him out, and the sheriff's hanging auction signs outside his door, but there he sits pretending he's on top of the world.

Faced with the seller who has to sell, but isn't likely to admit it, you can only use one strategy. In fact, this strategy can work wonders in bringing any of these game players out from behind their smokescreen.

THE BOGEY OFFER

It's strong medicine. As Paul V., a successful entrepreneur with a string of acquisitions would say, "When you meet up with a game-playing seller, you need a few of your own games to neutralize him." Paul's a master at the Bogey offer.

Paul recently pulled it on Ken T., who was trying to peddle his magazine distributorship. Ken was a combination type, not sure if he really wanted to sell the business, and with a line of buyers stretching around the corner if he did.

"How much do you want for the business?" asked Paul. "At least $250,000 *if* I sell," countered Mr. In Demand. Paul sized up the situation. "Well, it seems steep, but if I had some time to hustle together the money, would you give me a chance to buy?" Paul queried with tongue in cheek.

It was music to Mr. In Demand's ears. With a barrel full of wasted ads, he only pulled one paltry $140,000 offer months earlier.

Within a week Paul had his ecstatic seller's signature on the $250,000 contract, loaded with escape clauses. Now Paul went to work.

Three weeks later Ken received the anxious phone call from Paul. "I'm having trouble with financing. I'll have to drop the price to $220,000 to put the deal together." Ken reluctantly agreed.

The following week Paul pulled the "bad lease" ploy. "Sorry Ken, but with the lease your landlord's holding me up for, I can't see my way clear to pay more than $180,000." Ken's bubble began to leak more air.

The big day arrived. Ken showed up at the closing expecting $180,000. Paul only showed up with another story. "I just took in a partner," announced Paul. "He thinks it's a bad deal. My partner doesn't want to go ahead for more than $150,000. And he won't let me pay cash. He wants us to buy with $20,000 down and you, Ken, will have to finance $130,000." Ken's balloon burst. "I'll sue!" he screamed. Cleaning his eyeglasses, Paul quietly replied, "Go ahead, but on page 8 of the contract it says 'we must be satisfied with the financial records'; on page 7 it says something about our 'ability to find financing,' and besides," Paul added with his constant smile, "you only have a $2,000 deposit and a corporate signature on the contract. Our corporation only owns a corporate seal." Where's Paul today? Running his magazine distributorship, of course.

Paul rationalizes the bogey offer this way:

> Start with a low offer like other unimaginative buyers, and sellers will lose interest. After all, you're only one of the crowd.
>
> Start high, and the seller begins to dream his wonderful dreams and becomes psychologically committed. The trick is to slowly work their dreams down until you reach the price and terms *you* want.

Paul concludes: Do game-playing sellers deserve better?

SETTING YOUR LIMITS

Before you negotiate seriously, you must determine two numbers:

1. *The Buy Price.* What you'll first offer the seller. Of course, if you're a believer in the bogey offer, you'll start with the seller's asking price and work down. However, if you're the typical buyer dealing with the typical nongamesmanship seller, you'll start low. But how low?

2. *The Bye-Bye Price.*   The price (and terms) beyond which you'll refuse to go.

These two numbers establish your range. For example, you may discover a business for sale at $100,000. Will you initially offer $60,000? $80,000? Should you propose $10,000 down with the seller financing the balance? If the seller insists on unfavorable financing such as all cash, should you drop your Bye-Bye price to $75,000? Conversely, if the seller allows you to buy with only $5,000 down, should you increase your ceiling to $95,000 or even the $100,000 asking price if you peg the value at $80,000?

To decide, you must consider three inter-relating factors:

Price

Down payment

Financing terms

Be flexible. Evaluate the trade-offs. A high down payment demands a lower price, while attractive financing justifies a higher one. Get your Bye-Bye price in focus.

YOUR FIRST OFFER

Let's assume you locate a $100,000 shoe store that you value at $80,000. Here's a good rule of thumb to follow in framing your first offer.

25% below your estimate of value, if there is strong buyer competition or if the seller has a strong bargaining position.

40–50% below value if you have the decided upper hand.

Offer the most outrageous terms imaginable, because sellers display considerable flexibility on terms. If you're prepared to put a $20,000 down payment on the business start with $5,000. Don't be too timid to propose anything but conventional terms. Sellers can concede financing most easily without losing face. In many instances a seller hasn't thoroughly thought about financing. Most take the easy way out and simply say "cash." In any case, you can always give up a few concession points on financing to get your better price.

Don't ignore these rules. You may be tempted to come in with a more generous offer because:

1.   Your offer is well below the seller's asking price. For example,
one successful buyer spotted a kitchen cabinet business on the market
for $300,000. The buyer wisely valued it at $120,000. Even with the
best financing, he set his Bye-Bye price at $140,000. So he offered
$90,000 with $30,000 cash down and the balance through seller
financing. Think about it. Here was an offer, 70% below what the
seller was looking for. After some negotiation the parties agreed on
$117,000 with the same financing. More than 20 other buyers
considered this same business, but they were all too intimidated by
the seller's outrageous asking price to submit an offer. Don't forget—
sellers over-price; they may have no idea of what their business is
worth.

2.   Brokers may discourage low offers. Don't blame them. They're
only doing their job. A broker may tell you the seller is firm on his
$100,000 price, or that the seller already refused a $90,000 offer.
Ignore it. He works for the seller.

THE RIGHT WAY TO PROPOSE YOUR OFFER

Once you formulated an offer, you'll be tempted to meet with the seller.
Avoid the temptation if you're hitting the seller with unexpected terms. A
face-to-face confrontation demands an immediate reaction, and the reaction
will probably be negative. Put it in writing so he can mull it over.
You must:

Prove your offer is serious, even if unacceptable to the seller.
Allow the seller a chance to properly evaluate your offer and to
prepare a counter-offer.
Set a deadline for seller action.

Is there a broker involved? He's probably been pushing a pen in your hand
for weeks to sign an offer—any offer—to get the ball rolling. But now you're
ready. Put away the broker's standard offer form. It spells trouble. Brokers'
offer forms won't protect you. An offer in writing can be binding even if the
broker assures you it's harmless. Besides, you want your offer to be tailor-
made to serve your purposes.
That brings us to your attorney and the right way to make an offer. Your
attorney will prepare a letter offer that:

Sets forth your terms in detail.

Requires a timely decision.

Binds the seller, if accepted.

Provides you with your escape clauses.

Turn to the appendix and you'll see an offer letter used for a recent transaction. The terms are set forth in adequate detail, so the seller knows precisely what you're offering. Give the seller a specific date to accept by. Ten days is usually long enough. Have the letter state the offer is withdrawn if not accepted by then. This strategy forces a decision and prevents the seller from holding your offer while shopping for a better deal. Don't overlook the conditions or escape clauses. Your offer is conditional upon outside financing, a favorable lease, verification of the books by your accountant, zoning, or any other terms to be satisfied before you're bound. Money doesn't talk, it shouts. Enclose a binder check for $1,000 with a further deposit upon signing the formal contract. If a broker is in the picture, the offer and check should go to the broker. Have the broker hold the deposit in escrow, pending the closing or rejection of the offer. Never let the seller hold your deposit. Sometimes they forget to return it. If there's no broker, the offer *should* go directly to the seller, but your attorney should represent he's holding the deposit and will turn it over to the seller's attorney to be held in escrow pending a closing.

Most importantly the letter requires the seller's immediate decision to:

Accept the offer

Decline the offer

Make a counter-offer

Will he accept? It's not likely. If he does you made a mistake. A seller that anxious to unload the business would have settled for an even lower offer. Should it happen, why not use your offer as a bogey offer and negotiate downward? Don't forget—you're not bound, because you have your escape clause.

Will he decline or ignore the offer? He may, if he's already sold or doesn't intend to sell (remember Mr. Just Testing). But it may mean you have a very shrewd seller on your hands playing the waiting game for you to keep bidding against yourself. Follow up with an invite to counter-offer, but don't budge until he goes.

Chances are you'll receive a counter-offer. That's what you're waiting for.

HOW TO INTERPRET THE COUNTER-OFFER

There are two important messages in every counter-offer:

1.   Who's making the counter-offer? If the seller thinks your offer is high

enough to seriously interest him, he'll call in his own lawyer. That's why your offer went out on your attorney's letterhead. Test the seller. Is he now beginning to spend some money on his own legal fees?

2. What does the counter-offer say? You don't want stories, you want a specific counter-proposal. You offered $80,000. That's specific. If it's not acceptable, what is? "Something higher" isn't an answer. You're still bidding against yourself. How about what you proposed for financing? Make the seller give you details of the financing he's willing to go with. Let him put it in writing. Why not? You gave him your offer in a written, detailed proposal.

How low did the seller drop his price? Does he seem more interested in price or in financing? What terms does he appear flexible on and what seems non-negotiable? Measure, weigh, and read between the lines for the telltale messages.
    What's your next move?

APPLYING THE THREE-FOR-ONE RULE

With the seller's new terms in hand, your best move is to do absolutely nothing. Draw the seller out. Let him do the chasing. Test his interest. Once he finally reaches you, see if he'll bid against himself. If his counter-offer brought him down to $90,000 from $100,000, tell him it's not enough. Perhaps he'll drop another $5,000. In the meantime you're still at your original offer.
    The strategy is to make the seller concede points at a faster rate than you. Use the three-for-one rule. For every $3.00 the seller comes down you increase your offer by $1.00. Perhaps financing is the more important issue. If so, concede some on price but make him concede even more in financing.
    Either you'll find the seller foolish enough to throw away his concession points and let you win the game by default, or he'll stop the game for the favorite trick in every seller's arsenal.

THE PHANTOM OFFER

The phone rings. On the line is the broker saying, "Hurry, hurry, another buyer's about to beat your last offer." Stretching the seller's fantasy into an outright lie, he may even tell you he has the better offer in hand, waving the signed offer and a fat deposit check before your eyes. He wants you to pull out your checkbook and beat the offer.
    Lock up your checkbook. Look closely at the other buyer's offer. Who made it, the seller's mother-in-law? Even if it is a legitimate buyer, why hasn't

the seller accepted it? Dissect the offer carefully. It probably contains nine pages of conditions and clauses no intelligent seller would accept.

Interestingly, you can help your own cause by creating a few phantom buyers of your own.

Here's how a shrewd buyer, Joan S., handled it. For three weeks she negotiated the purchase of a printing plant with a $180,000 price tag. Joan calculated the business to be worth about $120,000, so she offered $95,000. Within a week the seller backed down to $150,000, while Joan rose to $105,000. Fearing an impasse, the broker called Joan. "If you want to save the deal, you better work fast. A buyer just offered $140,000 and the seller's about to grab it." However, Joan played the waiting game for a few more weeks and the business remained unsold. The "buyer" turned out to be the seller's bowling team captain.

Now it was Joan's turn. First she sent in an old college friend who offered the seller $60,000, "and not a dime more for this run-down business." The following week Joan's second phantom, a neighborhood friend tossed in a quick verbal offer of $40,000 to "cart out whatever's salvageable." The seller, battered by two low-ball offers, began to reconsider. Two weeks later Joan's third phantom popped into the seller's plant. "How about $50,000 for a quick sale?" The seller's thoughts turned into nightmares as he began to wonder what the business was really worth. Joan's $105,000 began to look good. Soon he called Joan. "My 'buyer' couldn't raise the financing, maybe we can talk about it some more . . .?" Three days later Joan bought the business for $112,000.

COMBATING THE "I CHANGED MY MIND" SELLER

Sellers play all sorts of tricks. How about the seller who suddenly plays hard to get? Usually the seller will simply say he changed his mind, hoping you'll plead and beg to renew interest.

To counter this play, consider a "phantom" offer on another business. Let word trickle back to the seller.

In the seller's bag of tricks sits "the business is suddenly too good" routine. A competitor just filed bankruptcy. The seller just landed a major new account, or for some reason orders started flooding the company. That may be true. Check it out. Perhaps you should revalue the business.

Barry L. found a bluffing seller. Negotiating for a real estate firm, Barry was up to $90,000 and the seller was down to $125,000. No progress was in sight. The seller decided to reverse direction and increase his price to $160,000. "The listings and house sales are piling up too fast to sell the business for less," said the bluffing seller.

Barry decided to make things interesting. He had a friend locate an empty store located across the street from the seller's real estate firm. Renting it for $125 a month, two days later a big bright sign announced:

> **Opening Soon—Acme Reality**
> Nine Full-Time Brokers
> and Lowest Commissions in Town

The perplexed seller hurriedly turned the business over to Barry for $110,000. Barry's friend removed the sign and the store still stands empty. Dirty pool? Not to Barry.

HANDLING THE HOLD-OUT SELLER

Your seller may not be playing tricks, but may still refuse to lower his price to what you're willing to pay. He may have over-valued his business, but may also believe that you under-valued it. This particularly affects new business offerings when the seller hasn't had sufficient opportunity to test the market and become realistic. Until such a seller has watched a dozen prospects shake their heads and walk away, further negotiations are probably a waste of time.

Maintain close contact with this type of seller. You don't know when he'll realize your offer wasn't so ridiculous after all, so periodically remind him you're still interested.

Sometimes financing, rather than price, creates the stumbling block, particularly if the buyer proposes substantial seller financing. Delve deeply into the seller's thoughts and you'll usually discover he's more worried about your ability to pay than he is about the terms themselves. Slap your credentials on the table. Build seller confidence. Reveal your plans for the business. The seller may not want to offend you by bringing up the subject or creditworthiness, so don't wait to be asked. Sell yourself.

BRING IN YOUR TEAM

Your accountant and/or attorney play a role in the negotiating process. Don't have your attorney negotiate directly with the seller (beyond sending the original offer letter), but he can be brought in to:

1.   Simultaneously negotiate with the seller's attorney. This is

the "platoon system." While you're working on the seller, he keeps a constant dialogue going with the seller's counsel. The advantage is that if negotiations break down on one level, they may be maintained at the other.

2. Probe the seller's real concerns. Lawyers have their own language. No one else seems to understand them, but they talk very straight to each other. For example, a client may report that, try as he might, the seller can't be persuaded to finance $80,000. All the buyer can learn from the seller is that the seller needs the cash. The buyer's attorney hears a different reason from the seller's attorney: "My client (the seller) won't finance because your client went bankrupt three years ago." Now the cards are on the table. You can deal with it.

3. Take over negotiations once you've gone as far as you can go. It's a common strategy. The buyer spends two months negotiating a deal, finally working the seller down to $90,000 and a certain financing plan. Close but not quite good enough, reasons the buyer. But he shakes hands anyway and agrees to turn it over to his attorney to draft the papers. His attorney, in true deal-killing fashion, finds flaws. Back to the drawing board, as the buyer's attorney tries to wrangle the final few points to improve the deal and improve his fee.

Sellers, of course use all these same strategies. That's why you want to flush the seller's attorney out of hiding right from the start. Let him do his hard bargaining while you're negotiating rather than come in later and try to change the hard-fought terms. If you think you can match him without help from your own attorney during the initial stages, then hold your attorney in reserve so he can come in later to put in his final shot.

SALVAGING THE COLLAPSED NEGOTIATIONS

Most negotiations suffer a communication problem. There may be an initial meeting or two, but beyond that it's usually telephone calls and letter writing. You talk to the seller, your attorney periodically touches base with the seller's attorney, and eventually a deadlock sets in.

There's only one possible cure. I call it the do-or-die session. Give it one final try. Call the seller and ask him for a meeting with the accountants and attorneys for both sides. A conference among all the players can produce results. Define the unresolved issues. Your advisors may spot solutions you overlooked or may be able to drive certain points home. Six heads are better than two.

From my own experiences, it salvages at least 50% of the deals that otherwise would go by the board. A certain chemistry can come about once the participants are all brought together.

In one recent case, we had a buyer deadlocked with a seller over several substantial issues. The seller still demanded $150,000 with $60,000 down, but the buyer was holding firm at $120,000 with $25,000 down. Lesser points of disagreement involved interest, length of note, and whether or not the buyer should grant a mortgage on his home to secure the note. The bargaining was going on for two months, but all headway stopped. The broker did his best to keep negotiations going but was unsuccessful.

A do-or-die session was called and the points of contention were defined. We asked the seller what was negotiable and what was non-negotiable. He admitted the issue of the house mortgage may be reconsidered. It was starting point. We matched it by upping the interest 2%. One by one the issues narrowed. We'd throw out a proposal and the seller's team would huddle in another office and come back with their counter-proposal. Back and forth like ping pong balls went the negotiating points. After a seven-hour marathon the deal was closed with both parties reaching an approximate middle ground.

That's how it happens in the real world. Sometimes buyers and sellers are so busy posturing and positioning and playing games that they overlook the one essential element of every negotiation—sincere communication and the willingness to really listen to the other side and help satisfy his needs.

BE PREPARED TO TAKE A WALK

Remember your Bye-Bye price and terms? That's the point at which you leave the bargaining table, never to return.

Buyers frequently become emotionally married to a business. They start the negotiation process with a firm fix on how high they're willing to go, but during the process they become increasingly committed to buying. Sure, they'll negotiate as hard as they can, but even when the negotiations bring them well beyond their original "Bye-Bye" price or terms they capitulate.

Ronald S. comes to mind as a classic example. He found a country inn for sale in northern Maine. The seller was asking $260,000, but Ron had it appraised at $170,000 which confirmed his own estimate. Ron started out the right way by setting his limit at $185,000 with perhaps another $5,000–10,000 with liberal financing. It was a well-conceived Bye-Bye ceiling. Starting with an equally sound $150,000 offer, the seller quickly showed he wasn't about to come down as rapidly as Ron was going up. "$250,000," said the seller. "$180,000," said Ron.

Logic was leaving, emotion was setting in. During the negotiation period Ron was proudly announcing his soon-to-be acquired business. He was psychologically committed. Giving the final bye-bye to his Bye-Bye figure, he bought at $240,000 cash.

Don't let it happen to you. You have defined your ceiling when you start. That's when you're objective. Until you are handed the keys, the business isn't yours and may never become yours. There are other businesses available. So don't lose the objectivity to walk away when the right deal can't be hammered out.

BEWARE THE STRANGER FROM AFAR

Strange people appear between the day you shake hands with the seller over a hard-fought agreement and the day you both sign contracts.

The "advisor from afar" may suddenly appear on the horizon. Who's the advisor from afar? It may be the seller's uncle from Scarsdale, who thinks his nephew is crazy to sell the business so cheap—or to sell at all. Perhaps it's his grandson who just completed High Finance 202 during his sophomore year at Podunk University, with his own wrinkle on how the deal should come together.

Of course, if the seller's late-arriving attorney and accountant haven't been party to the negotiations and haven't blessed the agreement, you can be certain it won't fly. But you have already learned to pull them into the act early.

These strangers can quickly undo what has taken weeks or months to put together. Unless they plant a thought that has been overlooked in the original negotiations, you should stand firm.

You may have your own strangers. Opinions come cheap. Beware of your own strangers as well as the seller's.

What about the last-minute *genuine* competing buyer? Should you walk away or boost your offer? There's only one answer. If a matching offer puts you well above your ceiling, just forgo the deal. You know what the business is worth to you. On the other hand, if you reached verbal agreement, for a price below your ceiling, don't stand on principle and walk away. It's only business.

There's only one way to avoid meeting that stranger from afar. Once the seller gives verbal agreement, demand a written agreement as soon as possible. About 40–50% of all handshake agreements fall apart during this critical period. The longer you wait, the better the chance that you won't obtain the seller's signature. Don't allow your attorney to delay. Have agreements signed quickly, even if it's only a binding letter agreement. A carefully prepared letter or formal agreement with appropriate escape clauses will let you wriggle out if you discover problems later.

HOW THE WALK-AWAY ARTIST WORKS

Some buyers, armed with a signed agreement and an awareness that the seller can't wait to pick up his check and deliver the bill of sale, play a final trick of their own.

Clara T. was a master walk-away artist. For three months she bargained the seller of a drapery shop down to $40,000, with $10,000 down and a note for $30,000. The big day arrived. The seller had his bill of sale in his vest pocket and said his final good-byes to his employees. His bags were already on their way to his condo in West Palm Beach.

Clara showed up at the passing with a dismayed look. "The damned landlord," she muttered. "He won't give me a lease for $500 a month. He wants $550." "So?" countered the seller. "My agreement with you makes the closing conditional upon my obtaining a lease on terms acceptable to me. $550 a month is not acceptable." The cornered seller could see it coming. Clara the walk-away artist walked away with the business for the hurriedly changes terms of $38,000 with $6,000 down.

It may not be an intentional maneuver. Oftentimes a buyer has a good reason to back out, leaving the seller the option of either conceding more points at the last moment or losing the sale. With less frequency it's the seller dodging a sale through a hidden escape clause. Protect yourself!

1. Make certain all conditions and escape clauses are satisfied well in advance of the closing. Don't leave any last-minute loopholes.

2. If you're a seller, make certain the buyer has his financing lined up and a lease ready.

3. What about the buyer's deposit. It is large enough so he won't take a walk or, if he does, will it at least make it worthwhile?

4. Never put yourself in the position where you have to go through with the sale if the other side threatens to back out in return for some concessions. Don't leave your job (take a sick leave). Don't sign a long-term lease in that new town or buy a house near the business. Remember, the business is not yours until you own it. Even with the signed agreement you may face some last-minute bargaining. You know when negotiations begin, but when do they finally end?

SOME FINAL POINTERS

1. *Learn all you can about the seller.*   Learn about his problems, motives, inclinations, and pressure points. Buying a business requires more than investigating the business. You also have to investigate the seller.

Put yourself in his shoes and bargain from his perspective, and from not yours alone.

2. *Don't let emotion distort logic.* Feeling elated by something unrelated to the transaction can make you unnecessarily generous. Any good negotiator will tell you that most people do there best negotiating when they're not in a good mood. Take this into consideration when negotiating with the seller. He's human too. If you detect a seller's bad mood, postpone the meeting. Emotion destroys more deals than money ever will.

3. *Don't fall for "higher authority."* If the seller can't, won't, or doesn't take the authority to finalize terms, make certain you're dealing with a person who can make decisions. The field is full of shrewd negotiators who'll listen to your concession points and then tell you they have to check with someone else before they can make their own concessions. ,

4. *Dont knock the seller's management ability.* It has destroyed many negotiations. Buyers frequently believe they can hammer a lower price by pointing out how poorly the seller has operated the business. Sellers take such criticism personally. Rather than scoring negotiating points, the buyer only antagonizes the seller and sets up a negotiating barrier.

5. *Be patient.* A business represents a considerable investment, and it's a complex transaction. Negotiations can't be rushed without paying a steep price. As one buyer sums it up, "It took me four months to bring the seller down from $160,000 to $120,000. The way I look at it, I was paid $10,000 a month for negotiating."

Successful negotiation always pays big dividends.

=10=

CLOSING THE SALE

Every acquisition has a long ancestry. Negotiations give birth to the terms that form the basis of the final agreements between the parties.

It's at this stage that the attorneys and accountants attempt to hone the final terms to provide their clients with maximum legal protection and tax benefits, consistent with the generally agreed upon terms.

As stated in the prior chapter, one major advantage of early advisor involvement is to resolve legal and tax matters during the negotiation process, rather than to attempt to rearrange the agreed-upon terms later. It's not unusual for buyer and seller to reach tentative agreement only to find their advisors rejecting the agreement for legal or tax reasons.

The buyer's counsel is interested in:

Obtaining good title to the business assets.

A favorable tax basis for resale and depreciation purposes.

Protection against false statements of the seller and undisclosed or potential liabilities.

Adequate indemnification and security from the seller.

In contrast the seller is interested in:

Protecting his loan on any seller financing.

Favorable tax treatment of gains from the sale.

Severing liability ties, present or future.

These issues are resolved not only through the contract, but in the design of the take-over itself. This chapter will show you how those objectives typically are resolved.

ANATOMY OF AN ACQUISITION

If the seller is incorporated, the sale of the business can be accomplished by either of two methods:

Transfer of assets

Sale of shares in the seller corporation

1. Transfer of Assets.   When the seller operates as a sole proprietorship or as a partnership, the sale must be conducted by a transfer of assets, as there is no corporation in existence to acquire. Over 60% of all small businesses, however, operate under a corporate form of organization creating the dual alternative.

Under a transfer of assets, the seller conveys to the buyer title to the defined assets. The buyer typically sets up his own corporation to accept title, and simultaneously enters into a new lease on the business premises.

2. Sale of Shares of Stock.   With a sale of shares, the buyer acquires the shares of stock from the stockholders in the corporation. Upon take-over of the seller's corporation, the selling stockholders resign their officerships and directorships. The buyer, as the new stockholder, then elects his own.

There can be a modified approach, where the selling stockholders sell (or redeem) their shares back to the corporation that acquires it, and the corporation then sells new shares to the buyer. The selling stockholders divest themselves of ownership in the corporation, and the buyer, through simultaneous acquisitions of the new stock issue, takes over as the sole stockholder of the corporation.

The purpose of having existing stockholders redeem (sell back to the corporation) their stock is to obtain a mortgage on corporate assets to secure any payments due from the sale of their shares. If the stock was transferred

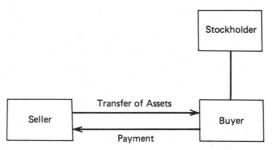

EXHIBIT 7.   Transfer of Assets Method

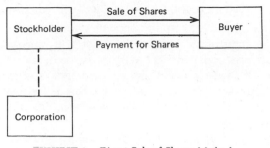

EXHIBIT 8.   Direct Sale of Shares Method

directly between existing and new stockholders, the sellers couldn't look to the corporation for a mortgage to collateralize any payments due under the sale, since the corporation wasn't a party to the transaction. Therefore, the redemption method, rather than the direct sale of stock method, is useful only to assist in securing seller financing. Since there is no other distinction between the two methods, the redemption and direct sale of stock method will be discussed as one.

How the Decision is Made

When the buyer has the alternative of acquiring either assets or shares of stock, the decision will be based on the importance of each of these five points:

Liability Considerations.   A transfer of assets reasonably assures the buyer that he is acquiring the assets free of any liabilities of the seller. The buyer's counsel can protect against creditor claims through compliance with the Bulk Sales Act (to be discussed later) and by a check of existing liens or encumbrances of record. Once these steps are taken, the buyer has no further concern over the seller's liabilities.

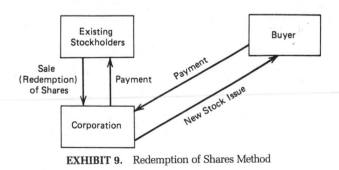

EXHIBIT 9.   Redemption of Shares Method

On the other hand, a stock transfer only gives the buyer ownership of the seller's corporation, together with any known or unknown liabilities that may exist against the corporation. Usually the seller will represent the extent of the known liabilities, and this debt will be factored into the price for the shares of stock. Of greater concern are the unknown or contingent liabilities. It may be a subsequent tax audit for prior years, a lawsuit by a customer injured on the premises, or a product liability claim. The possibility of subsequent claims are endless.

The concern over unknown or unlisted liability prompts most buyers to decide in favor of acquiring assets instead of stock. The risk may be reduced, however, by a thorough evaluation of the corporation's books and records to determine the likelihood of future claims. Additionally, most buyers insist that the seller indemnify the buyer for any unlisted liabilities that may arise, and secure the indemnity with either personal assets of the seller, or a right to deduct such claims from any payments due the seller under the sale.

Existing Contracts and Leases.   A corporation holds certain contracts and leases. It's not always possible or advantageous to transfer these contracts to the buyer as part of a transfer of assets. This is usually a strong argument in favor of acquiring the shares.

For example, the corporation may hold a favorable 10-year lease for its premises at $1,000 a month. Upon a sale of shares the same lease would remain in effect, since it's the same corporate tenant. With a transfer of assets, the buyer would be obligated to negotiate a new lease for its own tenancy. If the landlord demanded $2,000 a month, the transfer of assets would have a decided $120,000 disadvantage, based on the increased rent.

The same problem may exist with franchise or licensing agreements, distributorship contracts, or other contracts that can't be assigned to a buyer.

Certainly, a buyer can check to see if existing contracts can be assigned to him on the same terms and conditions to determine whether or not contracts are a problem.

From the seller's perspective the issue is of equal importance. Consider the problem of a corporation with a nonassignable, 10-year distributorship agreement. If the corporation sells the other assets of the business, it's essentially terminating operations and couldn't perform under its agreement. The resultant breach could create extensive liability for the seller. In this case, the seller would logically demand a sale of shares to keep the corporation intact and avoid the breach.

Financing.   The financing structure will, in large measure, determine whether it will be a sale of assets or shares.

If the corporation has a high debt level, the buyer can effectively utilize the debt to be credited to the purchase price. Take the case of a corporation with assets valued at $100,000 but with debts of $80,000. The buyer could acquire the seller's shares for only $20,000.

Although the debt can be assumed by the buyer even under a transfer of assets, creating the same financing package, it would be considerably easier to accomplish it through a stock sale.

When the assets of the corporation are secured by a mortgage or other lien, the transfer of assets can't be undertaken without approval of the mortgage holder. In our prior example, if the $80,000 in debt was secured, the creditor may require full payment to allow the transfer, or would allow the transfer only with new and less favorable financing terms.

Credit Rating. The corporation's credit rating can be either an advantage or a disadvantage in acquiring assets.

A good credit rating favors the purchase of shares to obtain the continued benefit of the rating, as a buyer's newly created corporation will start with very little credit availability.

Conversely, a buyer may do better to rely on a new corporation with no credit rating than to take over a corporation with an adverse rating.

This can be an important issue, particularly when the buyer is relying on credit to compensate for the lack of initial working capital or to build depleted inventories.

Tax Considerations. The tax aspects of an assets versus stock transfer are twofold.

A tax-loss carry-forward, of course, favors the acquisition of shares to maintain the benefit of the prior losses to shield future profits from taxes. The IRS Code provides many ways to benefit from tax-loss carry-forwards as well as many conditions to qualify. Therefore, the actual advantage would be nalyzed by the accountants.

The second tax consideration tends to favor transfer of assets. The corporation may have fully depreciated its capital assets, providing the buyer of shares no further depreciation expense. If assets are acquired, the buyer may allocate a high percentage of the acquisition price to capital assets and use that price as a basis for depreciation.

For example, if a corporation has fully depreciated the assets, but sells all the assets for $100,000, allocating $50,000 for the depreciable assets, the buyer would have the benefit of the $50,000 future write-off. Even for the small business in the 18% tax bracket, this benefit is worth $9,000 in future tax savings.

The seller corporation would have to pay a capital gains tax on the $50,000 sale, however, this may be of no practical importance if the corporation is to be liquidated within a short time after the sale. The tax consequences to the seller can only be decided by a review of the seller's liquidation plans.

The decision to acquire assets or stock seldom rests entirely on any one of these issues, but rather on a balancing test of all of them, and must be decided by the accountant and the attorney as well as by the client.

CONTRACT TERMS THAT PROTECT YOU

After the structure of the transaction is decided, a contract can be prepared that contains all the agreed-upon points. In the appendix of this book you'll find model agreements for both an asset and a stock transfer, although the content and protections are much the same.

Every contract should cover these questions:

1. What assets are to be sold? The asset description should be detailed so no confusion or misunderstanding exists as to what is being acquired. For example, an itemization may include:

a) All merchandise inventory existing at the time of sale.
b) All furniture, fixtures, equipment, tools of the trade, and signs. (The description may be broadened to include all tangible personal property, and the major items should be described on an appended list.)
c) All existing supplies at date of transfer.
d) All good will of the business, including all customer lists, rights to the name, and transfer of existing telephone number. (If the name is trademarked, it would include an assignment of trademark. If the seller intends to utilize the name in other locations, the respective rights to the name should be delineated.)

2. What assets are to be retained by seller? Although a description of assets to be transferred should imply the assets not intended for sale, it is best to expressly state the assets the seller will retain. Frequently these include:

a) All cash on hand and on deposit at time of transfer
b) Motor vehicles (particularly personal-use vehicles)
c) Tax rebates, insurance proceeds, prepaid deposits
d) Claims against third parties
e) Credits due from suppliers
f) Real estate
g) Securities or equities in any corporation or entity

h) Accounts receivable
i) Notes receivable

Of course the list of assets to be sold and retained will be decided on an individual case basis.

3. How Will Accounts Receivable be Handled? If the buyer is to acquire accounts receivable, their valuation must be decided. Rather than arbitrarily discount older receivables, it's best to acquire them at face value. Receivables uncollected after a specific time period should be transferred back to the seller for full payment.

Frequently the seller will retain receivables, which creates an operational problem. The seller will be inclined to notify the accounts to mail payment directly to him. This puts the customers on notice that the business has been sold and may impair good will. Aggressive collection tactics by the seller can also destroy the acquired good will.

A better method may be to allow the buyer to bill and collect the seller's receivables and turn the payment checks over to the seller once a week. Payments should first be credited to the seller's receivables and next to any new charges generated by the buyer. Any bills outstanding beyond 90–120 days can be turned over to the seller for collection.

4. What is the Purchase Price? The total purchase price should be allocated among the assets being sold in order to establish the acquisition price of depreciable assets. For example, the contract may read:

$30,000	for inventory
50,000	for fixtures & equipment
3,000	for supplies
7,000	for good will

As a buyer you will want to allocate as much of the price as possible to fixtures, equipment, and other depreciable capital assets so you will have as high a depreciation deduction as possible. Conversely, as little as possible should be allocated to the good will.

7. How Will the Purchase Price be Paid? The purchase price ordinarily will be divided between:

a) The down payment
b) Assumed liabilities (if any)
c) Amount financed by seller

The down payment should be for a fixed amount and should not increase based on an adjusted price, as the adjustments may exhaust the buyer's cash availability. If the liabilities to be assumed are ascertainable, the list should be annexed.

The seller's financing should adequately define the terms, collateral, and guarantees. It's suggested that counsel prepare all the loan documents in advance and make them exhibits to the agreement, so no disagreement develops at the time of closing on the language within these important documents.

6. How Will Inventory Adjustments be Made?   When a business that contains inventory is sold, the purchase price should be based on an agreed-upon inventory level. For example, the total agreed-upon price may be $100,000, conditional on inventory valued at $50,000 at the time of closing. However, the inventory at closing may turn out to be $45,000 or $55,000, thereby decreasing or increasing the purchase price. In turn, that creates two other questions: a) How will inventory be tabulated? and b) How will the adjusted price be handled?

The valuation of inventory should be conducted by physical tabulation immediately prior to the sale. The parties should agree on a professional inventory tabulation firm to impartially tabulate and value the inventory. Inventory tabulators can be located through wholesale firms within the industry or in the yellow pages.

The agreement should state that the valuation shall be binding upon both parties, and that the fees be divided between buyer and seller.

Many buyers and sellers decide they'll conduct the inventory valuation between them. This very seldom works out, as disagreement inevitably appears. Always use an outside firm.

The valuation formula should also be defined in the agreement. Use acquisition or invoice cost rather than a discount from retail, as the buyer may mark up goods to inflate value. Don't overlook cash and customary trade discounts. The objective should be to buy at the seller's net acquisition price. Certainly shopworn, unsalable, or defective merchandise should be rejected from tabulation; however, items of questionable value should be left to the tabulators to set a partial value.

Any adjustment to price should be applied to the financed portion of the price, not to the down payment. Where the seller isn't financing any part of the price, the buyer should have the seller agree to finance any excess price based on a higher inventory, as the buyer's cash and financing may equal only the unadjusted price.

Another worthwhile clause is to control the permitted inventory adjustment.

As an example, if the inventory value is to be $50,000, set a ceiling of perhaps $55,000–60,000 and a floor of $40,000–45,000. Many sellers drain

inventory to increase their immediate cash, which leaves t
Of course, this creates the problem of replacing the inven
payable basis instead of the longer payout of seller finar
to discourage a seller from "loading" the inventory with
or other low-priced liquidation inventory.

7.   What About Other Adjustments?   Buyers and s̲_
and prorate these items at the time of closing:

a)   Insurance premiums (if buyer takes over the seller's policy)
b)   Rent and other occupancy costs
c)   Deposits with utility companies
d)   Payroll and payroll taxes
e)   Vacation and sick leave time
f)   Fuel oil
g)   Inventory sold after tabulation
h)   Prepaid licenses and fees

Advertising in the yellow pages is not customarily apportioned, although it
can be a matter of negotiation.

Adjustments due the seller from the buyer can be considerable. The cash-
tight buyer should request that adjustments due be added to the seller financing.

8.   What About the Seller's Liabilities?   If the buyer is to acquire the
assets without assuming seller debt, the agreement will expressly state the
"assets are being sold free and clear of all liens, encumbrances, and liabilities
or adverse claims." That simple clause in itself doesn't provide all the needed
protection. The buyer will have to take these additional steps to fully protect
himself:

a)   Comply with Bulk Sales Act: Every state has a Bulk Sales Act that
     requires the buyer to notify the seller's creditors of the intended
     sale not less than 10 days prior to the sale. The buyer provides the
     seller with a list of creditors stated accurate under oath. If there's
     strict compliance, the buyer will take the assets free of creditor
     claims, assuming no prior objection to the sale. The agreement
     should provide that the seller will comply with the Bulk Sales Act.
b)   Check of liens and encumbrances: Mortgages (security interests),
     goods sold on conditional sale, tax liens, and creditor attachments
     must be a matter of public record to be valid against a buyer. Your
     attorney will check the public records for their existence and make
     certain they are paid and discharged by the seller at the time of
     closing.
c)   State taxes: In many states a buyer must obtain a tax waiver from
     the state to acquire assets free of unpaid state taxes owed by the

seller, even though there's no tax lien of record. Your attorney will know whether or not this is a requirement in your state.

d) Seller indemnification: A buyer should insist on an indemnity agreement whereby the seller will pay or protect the buyer from any claims made by the seller's creditors. If the seller is a corporation, the principal stockholders should personally execute the indemnity. Any notes owed the seller should contain the right to offset creditor claims, and if that doesn't provide adequate protection the indemnity should be secured by personal assets.

e) Escrow: Many buyers additionally require the seller to place a sufficient portion of the purchase price in escrow as security to protect against unsettled creditor claims. In some cases this may be adequate protection without need for other safeguards.

Where liabilities are assumed, either the specific creditor list or the aggregate amount should be defined. There is no need to comply with the Bulk Sales Act where the buyer assumes liabilities as the buyer expressly agrees to pay the debts.

9. What Protection Does the Seller Have if the Buyer Doesn't Pay Assumed Liabilities?   The agreement should reciprocally provide that the buyer agrees to pay, indemnify, and save the seller harmless from any claims arising from assumed debt. This may be secured by a mortgage on the business assets, a pledge of shares by the buyer, personal guarantees, or personal collateral pledged by the buyer.

10. What Other Warranties Should the Seller Make to the Buyer?   A buyer should insist on each of these additional warranties:

a) The seller owns and has good and marketable title to all the assets to be sold. (If any items are not owned but leased, held on consignment, on loan, or on conditional sale, they should be set forth on a disclaimer list attached to the contract.)

b) The seller has full authority to sell and transfer the assets and to undertake the transaction.

c) The financial statements (or tax returns) shown to the buyer are accurate in all material respects. The tax returns or statements should be attached to the agreement.

d) No litigation, governmental proceedings, or investigation against the business is known to be pending.

e) The seller has no knowledge of any developments that would materially affect the business.

These warranties are usually sufficient under a transfer of assets, but would require considerable expansion under a sale of shares. Turn to the redemption agreement in the appendix to see the warranties made in a stock sale.

11.   What Are the Rights of the Seller to Compete?   The seller (and its principals, if the seller is a corporation) should execute a covenant not to compete with the acquired business, as competition detracts from the value of the good will.

The covenant not to compete should define a specific geographic radius and duration. It's enforceable to the extent reasonable to protect the good will. For businesses where the specific customers can be defined, the covenant should prohibit solicitation of these customers by the seller.

There can be important tax consequences under a covenant not to compete. If the covenant doesn't contain specific payment, the Internal Revenue Service may apportion a part of the purchase price to the covenant and then tax the sellers at the ordinary income rather than at the capital gain rate. Therefore, sellers should insist that the covenant recite the only compensation for the covenant is the sum of $1.00 (and not any part of the purchase price).

The buyer may ask for a part of the price to be payment for the covenant, since the buyer can then deduct the payments as a business expense over the duration of the covenant. Although a negotiable point, most small business acquisitions favor the seller's position.

12.   What if There's Casualty to the Business Prior to the Closing?   The contract should provide that upon any casualty (fire, water or sprinkler damage, etc.) to the premises or to any material part of the assets, the buyer should have the right to rescind the agreement.

The casualty clause should extend to the shopping center, or other major adjoining tenants relied upon to draw customers.

13.   What Restrictions Should be Imposed on the Seller in Operating the Business Prior to Closing?   This is a particularly important provision to insure that the seller maintains the good will and efficiency of operation for the buyer. The minimum conditions should be that the seller will:

a)   Maintain customary business hours.
b)   Not change prices beyond the ordinary course of business
c)   Not terminate employees, without good cause.
d)   Not conduct a going out of business or liquidation sale.
e)   Not discontinue charge accounts, deliveries, or other existing service policy.
f)   Not terminate relations with suppliers.

g) Preserve the good will of the customers, suppliers, and others having business relations with it.

14. What Conditions Should Attach to the Agreement? The buyer should make the agreement conditional upon any external factor on which full performance is dependent. The most common examples are:

a) Lease: The buyer would make the obligation to close conditional upon his obtaining an acceptable lease for the premises. The terms of the proposed lease should be negotiated with the landlord in advance of the closing and even in advance of the negotiations. Therefore, a copy of the intended or required lease should be appended. The seller would agree to terminate his present lease upon sale, with acceptance of termination by the landlord. If the seller's lease is to be assigned, the contract would be conditional upon the landlord's assent to the assignment and acknowledgment that the lease is in good standing.

b) Financing: If the buyer is relying on outside financing to fund the acquisition, the terms of the proposed financing should be spelled out. The seller should insist that the condition be satisfied by a certain time prior to the sale, or the contract may be voided. This protects a seller from waiting until the date of closing to find out the financing condition hasn't been satisfied.

c) License transfers: If the buyer is obligated to obtain new licenses to operate the business, the contract should be conditional upon the buyer obtaining the licenses. As with all conditions, the buyer should agree to use best efforts.

d) Transfer of contract rights: If the buyer is relying on a transfer of contract rights (franchises, distributorships, or other third-party contracts), the agreement should be conditional upon acceptance of the transfer.

The conditions for performance are extremely important to a buyer and should be foreseen and communicated to counsel for inclusion within the agreement.

15. What Happens to the Books and Records of the Business Upon Closing? Under a transfer of assets the financial and tax records would remain the property of the seller.

Records relating to the good will of the business should be transferred to the buyer. These would include customer lists, trade secrets, pricing infor-mation, catalogues, and invoices relating to assumed liabilities.

The seller should also deliver any warranties on any equipment being transferred.

Where a seller may have need to refer to transferred records, the contract should provide that the buyer will maintain the records and make them reasonably available to the seller.

16. How Should Disputes Under the Agreement be Resolved?   Most contracts are silent on this point, which of course means protracted litigation in the courts if disputes cannot be resolved. This can be expensive and time consuming, and can create years of delay.

I believe a far better approach is to provide for binding arbitration to settle controversies. The *American Arbitration Association*, with offices in every major city, will hear and resolve disputes within a matter of months, and their findings have the same authority as a court judgment, if the parties agree to it in the contract.

17.   When Should the Closing Be?   Buyers should favor the earliest possible closing date to prevent any work-down of inventory or impairment of good will. The only time delay should be the interval necessary to obtain financing and to satisfy the other conditions of closing.

Many sellers also prefer an early closing for personal reasons, but others want the time to convert inventory or receivables to cash, or to otherwise manipulate the finances to their advantage.

For most transactions, a 10–45-day interval is an acceptable range. If the business is approaching the busy season, timing is obviously more critical. That's when most disputes arise. When negotiating, the parties should consider the approaching selling season as a bargaining point to influence price or other terms.

Buyers should be aware that even when a contract specifies a closing date, the parties have a reasonable period of time thereafter to perform. The buyer should insert a provision stating "time for performance is of the essence," if he intends to hold the seller to the exact closing date.

A contract to buy or sell a business, like any other legal document, must be designed to match the transaction. No two are or should be identical. Therefore, your agreement may contain most but not necessarily all these points. Conversely, you may need added provisions to protect yourself. This, of course, leads to two additional and perhaps most important points:

> *Don't play lawyer:* Unless you happen to be an attorney, you can't
> handle the transaction yourself, any more than you can play doctor

and remove your own tonsils. Buying or selling a business is serious business involving serious money. Don't try to save on legal fees; it will cost you far more in the end. You may be convinced, but every attorney can tell you stories of the do-it-myself crowd who signed (or prepared their own) contracts without legal representation, only to end up in a barrel of trouble. Never sign any offer, binder, or agreement before obtaining your attorney's approval.

Talk to your attorney: A well-prepared agreement is a collaborative effort between attorney and client. Your attorney knows the law but doesn't necessarily know the peculiarities of your business, the conditions you need, or other operational safeguards needed in the contract. In almost every instance where I have seen a problem contract, the problem was not in the legal draftsmanship but in the absence of practical considerations that should have been furnished by the client.

Prepare your contract well. Your acquisition is never stronger than the printed word.

THE FOUR BEST WAYS TO AVOID LIABILITY

You never know what will go wrong after you sign the contract. Many buyers discover problems with the business not covered in the contract, others find better opportunities at the last moment, and still others want to abandon the deal for personal reasons. It may even be a matter of last-minute fright.

All these possibilities raise the inevitable question asked by all buyers, "How can I get out of the contract?" You may not be able to walk away unscathed, but there are steps you can take to reduce your losses.

1. *Keep your deposit to a minimum.* Don't put down a larger deposit than you can afford to lose. If you're buying a $100,000 business you may be able to get away with a $1,000–5,000 deposit. Brokers and sellers will push for more, but most sellers will agree to a small deposit. Buyer impulse and anxiety for the business induce them to act in haste and repent in leisure. When you write your down payment check, ask yourself whether you'd mind losing it.

2. *Try a liquidated damage clause.* Buyers mistakenly believe that all they can lose on default is their deposit. This is not so. If your contract calls for a $100,000 selling price and you breach with the seller forced to sell to someone else for $80,000, you can be held liable for the

$20,000 actual loss. If your contract provides that the seller shall retain your deposit as liquidated damages upon default, then the deposit is all you can lose.

3. *Buy through your corporation.* You should be incorporated to operate the business, so you'll need to set up a corporation to take title to the assets. Your strategy should be to incorporate prior to signing the contract so the contract is between the seller and your corporation. This may shield you from personal liability in the event of default.

4. *Use your escape clause.* You've seen conditions to compel performance that should be in the agreement. There can be many more. Verification of books by your accountant, or other unilateral conditions can be your escape route, and most sellers (and their attorneys) seem to go along with it. Why lock yourself in?

5. *Avoid personal guaranty.* Since you're signing through a corporation, don't defeat your purpose by needlessly guaranteeing the contract or other buyer obligations. Always ask, "What do I stand to lose if the business doesn't work out?" Put the business to the risk: benefit ratio test.

BETWEEN SIGNING AND CLOSING

The days between signing and closing can be critical for the buyer. During this period his objectives are to:

1. Identify any major hidden problems with the business that may dissuade him from closing.

2. Acquaint himself with the business for an orderly and efficient management transition.

3. Maintain control over operations to preserve the good will of the business.

4. Help coordinate the fiscal affairs, buying, inventory levels, merchandising, and payables to put the business on the correct footing for subsequent take-over.

These objectives can only be achieved if the seller agrees to give the buyer full access to the business premises. Many sellers resist. Most refusals are based on a fear of warning employees, customers, or suppliers of a pending sale they are afraid may not materialize. Sellers may be justified in taking this position until the conditions are fully satisfied and the buyer is committed to the acquisition.

Aside from these considerations, the relationship between seller and buyer during the transition period is more a matter of a cooperative attitude, which is not always possible after hard-fought negotiations.

Buyers and sellers should consider these guidelines:

1. New or replacement staffing during this period should be approved by the buyer. It's unfair to newly hired employees to discover that they'll shortly have a new employer who may not need their services.
2. Special orders, merchandising "deals," or other purchases out of the ordinary course of business should be cleared by the buyer.
3. Credit retention with suppliers is important. Payments during this period should be made to suppliers whose credit line is critical to the buyer.
4. Major contracts and orders accepted by the firm should be approved by the buyer if the contract is to be performed in part by the buyer.
5. Collection procedures on overdue accounts should be coordinated and approved by the buyer. Changes in prices, terms, credit, or service to key accounts also require close monitoring by the buyer.
6. The buyer should identify suppliers with whom he doesn't intend to do business and allow the seller to return excess or unsalable stock or to bargain for other concessions to settle accounts while the seller still has leverage with the supplier.
7. Inventories should be adjusted during this period to approximate the represented inventory at the time of closing. If the business has excess inventory, a coordinated sell-down should be undertaken with the buyer. One frequent problem is the seller who depletes fast-moving inventory. The buyer's goal is to assure replacement so he takes over with a healthy inventory mix.

COPING WITH LAST-MINUTE PROBLEMS

It's not often a closing occurs without a few last-minute stumbling blocks. What can you expect?

1. Disputes over broker's commissions: The broker sits there with his hand out while the seller tries to figure out how he can avoid the commission (cut it), or make you, the buyer, pick up part

of it. Resolution of commissions should occur before the sale, and should even be spelled out in the agreement.

2. Lease problems: Landlords have a way of making last-minute changes in the lease terms. The only way to avoid this deal-killing catastrophe is to obtain the landlord's signed lease well in advance of the closing and hold it in escrow pending the closing.

3. The missing link: What's the missing link? It's the wife, husband, partner, investor, or guarantor who was supposed to be a party to the transaction but suddenly backs out.

A buyer, for example, may represent a wife who will go along with granting a mortgage on the home to secure the note, but nobody ever hears it from the wife. The sale drifts along only to have the seller find out at the closing that the wife has no intentions of signing. The cure is apparent. Everyone required to execute any document at the closing should sign the agreement acknowledging their willing participation. Avoid last-minute surprises.

4. The equipment break-down gambit: It's frequently a last-minute point of contention. The parties show up quarreling over who's responsible for repairing a recently collapsed air conditioner, heating system, compressor, or delivery truck. As with most problems, it can be foreseen and handled in the contract.

5. The key man factor: Buyers planning on absentee ownership may be relying on a manager. You know what happens at the last minute. The buyer calls two hours before the closing to announce that his key man is no longer available and needs more time to find a replacement. The buyer should pay for the extension through an additional down payment to make certain that further delays in closing won't occur.

6. The attorney's final word: No matter how involved the lawyers are in negotiating or legal draftsmanship, they always enjoy changing or fighting for the last few points. If the deal was well thought out they can't be meaningful points, so it may be nothing more than grandstanding. It can be traumatic for a buyer and seller to listen to two attorneys with their last-minute posturing. The one best solution is for the attorneys to prepare and approve *every* document needed for the closing well in advance. They can then sit there and tell you how hard they fought over the papers two weeks earlier before they finally "agreed." At least you're spared the last-minute showmanship.

As one broker accurately states, "A closing shouldn't be the final round of a battle. It should be a happy ceremony. After all, isn't the seller getting his money and the buyer the business he wants?"

UNDER NEW MANAGEMENT

"Under New Management," in the words of Glenn Downing, the proud buyer of a local nightclub, "is more than a paper sign in the window. It's an emotion. When you turn the key for the first time you're a mixture of enthusiasm, bewilderment, pride, and hope."

Some day soon you'll be hanging your own "Under New Management" sign in the window. That's an important message to your customers. But what are you planning to do with the business to prove that you're not only "new" management, but even "better" management? The first 30 days may provide the answer.

MOVE SLOWLY—VERY SLOWLY

Henry Davidson, a successful owner of several discount stores recalls his first acquisition, a small soft- and hardgoods discount store successfully operating for years in the foothills of Vermont's Green Mountains.

"Grass didn't grow under my feet. Within the first week after buying the business I:

changed the name from 'Milton Hill Discount' to 'Davidson Discount';

cut back on the greeting cards, children's wear, and hardware sections;

added camera, toy, and hobby departments;

dropped prices across the board by discounting an extra 5%;

stopped all charge accounts;

fired three employees.

"Do you know what I discovered within the next several months?" added Henry.

"My customers resented the name 'Davidson Discount.' Losing the familiar 'Milton Hill Discount' sign was to the townsfolk like losing an old family friend.

"Sales dropped 40% because greeting cards, children's wear, and hardware were the best movers in the business.

"Cameras, toys, and hobby items bombed. Evidently nobody in town took pictures or was under the age of 18. If they were, they must be shopping for these items elsewhere.

"I found out the extra 5% discount didn't help in increasing sales. My customers didn't even notice.

"The store's charge customers refused to switch to cash or credit cards. You'll find them today buying, and charging, at my competitors down the street.

"I somehow managed to fire the three most valuable employees."

Henry concluded with this parting advice: "When you buy a business, move slowly. Move very slowly."

Don't be tempted to tear your business apart too quickly. It will take time to know the business, its customers, its employees, and its competition. It may take even longer to test its strengths and weaknesses. Make your decisions on what you *know* will work rather than on what you *think* will work. Move slowly. Very slowly.

WHAT'S IN A NAME? PLENTY!

A call to the sign painter may be one of your first inclinations. Deciding upon a business name can be a tricky affair. Put down the phone and think it through.

At the closing you paid the seller a sizable amount of money for good will. Part of that good will is the name you acquired. Just how valuable is that name?

It's common for buyers to underestimate the value of an existing name and overestimate the benefits of a new name. The decision may even be based on the blind pride in seeing the buyer's name on the sign while sacrificing the reputation, recognition, and good will represented by the existing name.

A name change should only be considered when:

1. The business has a poor reputation and a change is required to announce new ownership and improved operations.

2. The new name has a proven recognition factor with greater drawing power than the existing name. Certainly, chains and franchises are in this category.

3. When the business will undergo significant alterations in product lines, pricing, or other operational characteristics.

Even when a name change is useful, its timing is important. A new name will signal new ownership, and many customers who never shopped at the business before or who stopped patronizing the business will return to see what the new ownership is offering. For the first several months you may have made few changes so you're putting your worst, not best, foot forward. Why not wait until you have the business the way you want it before attracting your new flock of prospective customers? A name change doesn't have to be a sudden affair. It may be done in phases, gradually switching from the old to new name.

For example, when Bryan Donovan acquired Regal Motorcycle, he decided to switch the name to Bryan's Motorcycle. However, Bryan acknowledged the "Regal" name had a long-standing reputation, so rather than suddenly drop the name, his new banner read Bryan's–Regal Motorcycle. Two years later he dropped the "Regal" from the name, confident that it was no longer needed.

How will a name change affect your credit rating? An existing name with a strong credit rating is an important plus, just as a poor credit reputation can be a serious drawback. Make your name work for you with both customers and creditors.

EXPERIMENT WITH YOUR EMPLOYEES

From the first moment you take over, your employees will be eyeing your every move, just as you should be hard at work sizing them up.

What are your employees thinking? Will he fire me? Will I have to work harder? less? Should I hit him up for a raise? You'll have a few questions of your own.

Here are a few opening rules:

1.   Forget the seller's evaluation of his employees. When you buy the business the seller will give you his honest assessment of each employee and you should ask for it. But his assessment may not work for you. An employee may have had a personality conflict with the seller, or perhaps didn't provide the particular skills the seller needed. A new boss starts a new working relationship. That same employee may work twice as hard for you as he did for the seller and be three times as valuable as another employee who received top marks.

2.   If you plan to cut the staff, don't terminate employees until you've had a chance to evaluate them.

3.   Rumors can start an avalanche of resignations. Many new owners have needlessly lost valuable employees who grabbed new jobs on a rumor or suspicion of future terminations. Let your employees know their jobs are secure if they perform.

4.   For every employee in fear of a termination there's another who decides he's indispensable to a new owner and asks for a raise. Raises should be out of the question for at least six months. Make them show they deserve it.

5.   You'll bring to employee relationships your own personality and management style. Most personnel managers agree, however, that it's best to start with a detached attitude and gradually develop a less formal relationship until your relationship reaches the right tone.

6.   Don't overlook your employee's experience with the business; they know the problems and improvements that can work. The seller may have had closed ears to their suggestions, but you should listen carefully. A colleague of mine acquired a large wholesale firm, and at his first meeting with the employees told them he invited their written comments of how the business could be improved. Within five days he had a desk loaded with valuable suggestions. He also knew which employees had their thinking caps on.

7.   Establish the ground rules. Each employee knew what the seller expected of him, but they don't necessarily know what you expect. For the first few weeks you should probably not make any changes, except the most obviously needed changes in policy or duty. But even continuity of duties and policy should be communicated.

Your employees can be either assets or liabilities. How you handle them in the first few weeks can be the deciding factor.

CULTIVATE YOUR SUPPLIERS EARLY

No sooner will you open your doors when suppliers will start knocking it down to do business with you. As with employees, the early innings may determine the outcome of the game.

Start by taking a hard look at the present suppliers. They may have been doing business with the seller for years, so competitive suppliers recognizing the long relationship may have stopped bidding for the business. But you represent a new opportunity to sell. To keep your account, your existing suppliers must match the best prices and terms available elsewhere.

What's the best way to cultivate your suppliers?

1.   Scout out every logical source of supply. You never know who the most competitive supplier will be.

2.   Ask each supplier for a proposal. Don't focus on price alone, but on credit, promotional assistance, and service as well. For the poorly capitalized buyer, priority should be on credit since it's usually more important then a few pennies on price.

3.   If you're in a merchandising business and returns through suppliers are possible, it should be high on your negotiating list. Why? When you acquire a business you'll inherit a substantial amount of "dead" stock, or merchandise that may not fit into your merchandising plans. As one concession for obtaining your account, the supplier should be willing to accept your return goods even if the goods originally were purchased through another supplier.

Don't ignore this point. If you buy an inventory-intensive business you may be spending more time in the first few weeks returning merchandise than buying it. It's as good as money in the bank. I know one buyer who purchased a health and beauty aid store and convinced a new wholesaler to accept over $20,000 in merchandise for return credit.

4.   In certain retail fields, wholesalers and other suppliers will provide a merchandising team to come in and set up the store. It's quite common in the food, drug, liquor, greeting card, and hardware lines. Usually they don't charge for the service, but you may have to ask for it; they can supply expertise as well as workers.

5.   If you're not totally familiar with the concessions available from suppliers in your industry, ask someone who is. Suppliers can be a generous lot when they want your business, but are seldom as lenient thereafter. It's remarkable what suppliers will furnish. Some provide signs, others will supply display racks and fixtures. I have seen greeting card firms carpet an entire store in return for the account. You have to ask, but equally important you have to know what to ask for.

6.   All other terms being equal, it's probably best to stay with existing suppliers. The longevity of the account has a certain value. They may be more understanding about delayed payments than will a new supplier. Further, the existing supplier knows your business and its buying patterns. They can guide you better during the initial months.

7.   The one major benefit a present supplier may be able to provide a merchandising business is a computer printout, or sales velocity study, of individual product lines purchased in the past. Chances are the seller can't provide you with this information for planning your merchandising. It's an extremely useful and easy-to-use tool in the remerchandising of the business.

George Maloof, president of New England Wholesale Drug Company, offers this advice for new owners: "Never blindly accept the seller's suppliers as your own; the seller may be buying on noncompetitive terms without even realizing it. Pretend you started a brand new business and invite all competing suppliers to work for your account." It's good advice.

CREDIT: DO'S AND DON'TS

One of the first items on your take-over agenda should be to improve your credit rating through three objectives: a) to cure any existing credit problems, b) to line up additional credit, and c) to prevent future credit problems by working out payment plans in advance.

Take these steps:

1.   Cure Existing Credit Problems.   If you are acquiring an existing corporation, request a copy of its credit rating from any of the major credit reporting services. You may have already taken this step as part of the investigation of the business. Call *Dun and Bradstreet, TRW Credit Service,* and any local or regional bureaus monitoring credit within your industry. If you are unable to obtain the credit report directly, a subscriber or supplier can get it for you.

Adverse credit information may be deleted in several ways. First, if you believe you have a legitimate dispute with a creditor who filed an adverse report, you can submit to the credit agency your reasons for nonpayment. This will help clarify the record to future creditors. If the creditor's bill has been paid, you should ask him to withdraw the adverse report. He's not obligated to, but he may, particularly if you intend to have future business with him.

2. Line Up Additional Credit. If you started with a new corporation, you'll have to establish a credit rating. *Dun and Bradstreet,* for example, will solicit information from recently organized companies. You aren't required to submit information, but from my experiences you should cooperate. It usually creates a more favorable report than one listing inadequate information.

The second step you should take is to find three or four present or past suppliers who will give the company a favorable credit report. These suppliers may have done business with the seller's corporation rather than yours, nevertheless the distinction may not be important. Once you have your own current suppliers, always maintain a list of several who will issue favorable credit reports.

3. Prevent Future Credit Problems. Protecting your future credit rating is equally important. If you anticipate delays in payment because of start-up cash flow problems, let the creditor know about it in advance and work out a long-term payment arrangement.

Many buyers over-buy merchandise following an acquisition and can't pay from current cash flow. Within several months the credit rating is destroyed. This usually can be avoided.

The best policy is to forecast your ability to pay and negotiate extended payments before you buy. It's not surprising that many suppliers will go along with an extended payment plan for an initial stocking order, because they want your account and understand the cash flow problems and frequent need to build inventories following an acquisition.

Don't take your credit rating for granted. Periodically check out your report so you can correct or cure it. Remember, most businesses fail due to lack of cash flow. Credit is always an important component of cash flow. Make it work for you immediately.

LEAN AND MEAN

For a merchandising business this is the only philosophy to follow until you can measure product demand, competition, and proper pricing levels.

Don't be anxious to load the shelves with new product lines or to build inventory quickly until you know your merchandising strategy.

Once you take over, salespeople will try to load you up with every conceivable deal. Inexperienced managers fall victim to the deals hoping to increase gross profit. They overlook the importance of turnover, ability to pay, and whether or not the product line or quantity is even right for the business. It's an easy way to strangle. Refuse any deal until you know it fits into your final merchandising plan.

Pricing should be changed only when the final merchandising plan is implemented. As with over-buying, a second common buyer error is the belief that sales can be quickly built through lowered prices. Although it's beyond the scope of this book to discuss merchandising or pricing strategy other than in context to the acquisition transition, it's during this preliminary stage when pricing errors are likely to occur.

Whether it will make sense to reduce or raise prices in the future will require a careful sales/gross profit analysis. However, few customers can appreciate reduced prices unless it's coordinated with a new merchandising and promotional effort.

Liquidation of excess or undesirable inventory through "below-cost" sales promotions should also be avoided immediately after the take-over period. Just as a new buyer can't reasonably evaluate the inventory to be added, the same is true for inventory to be deleted or reduced.

One buyer of an auto supply store anxious to unload a basement full of a generic brand of antifreeze, ran a promotional sale at 30% below cost. After replacing the generic antifreeze with a national brand, the new buyer soon discovered the generic brand was the one in demand. It cost him over $5000 to learn the lesson—you never know what does or doesn't sell until you test your demand.

Any change in service policy should also be avoided in the first few weeks. Delivery, charge accounts, and other customer services may be quite important to the sales and profitability of the business, and they require careful consideration.

New buyers face a particular problem with existing, but slow-paying charge customers whose credit may have been stopped by the seller. These same customers have a tendency to ask the buyer to open their charge policies, hoping he either doesn't know their credit history or will be so anxious for sales, he'll overlook it. It can be a costly trap.

It always makes sense to review all credit histories with the seller, even when the seller retains the receivables. You should take over with complete familiarity of who's entitled to credit.

CUSTOMERS: WHO'S MORE IMPORTANT?

The transition from seller to buyer should include a closely coordinated effort to transfer seller good will to the buyer. Customer retention will depend on how successfully it's carried out.

The precise method to follow will, of course, depend on the nature of the business and the relationship between the seller and his customers.

Where personal relationships are close between seller and customer, as in a retail store or a small town, the seller should agree to remain for several weeks to personally introduce the buyer to the customer.

We recently sold an electrical supply wholesale firm with 200 accounts. The seller and buyer agreed that a proper farewell for the seller and introduction for the buyer could best be handled through a free dinner party for the 200 accounts. It gave the seller who did business with these accounts for many years a proper send-off. Of equal importance, the accounts met the buyer and heard some of his plans for the business.

Considering the importance of these accounts, the seller and buyer visited each account to resolve any outstanding problems and to define how the buyer could best serve the future needs of the customer. It was the right way to solidify customer relations for the buyer. With a small investment in time and money he didn't lose a single account.

Coincidentally, another similar-sized wholesale firm was sold that same week. The seller telephoned a few of his major accounts to say goodbye, saying very little about the buyer. The buyer, for his part, did nothing to extend his own hand and cement relationships. Competitors, realizing that accounts are most likely to switch when a business is sold, aggressively pursued them, and before the buyer realized it he had lost almost half his accounts.

Where personal customer contact isn't practical, the seller should at the very least undertake a letter to the customers thanking them for past patronage, telling them something about the buyer and his plans, and encouraging their future patronage. It may appear to be both common courtesy and good business, but too many sellers and buyers ignore its importance.

One reason for a seller refusing to participate in this easily accomplished effort is because the relationship with the buyer may have deteriorated during the negotiating or closing stages.

The sales contract may provide for the seller to issue a letter to customers simultaneously with the sale. If there's even a remote likelihood of no seller cooperation, it's even a good idea to have the letter drafted and signed in advance, with authorization for the buyer to mail the letters after the closing.

I recall one particular problem between a seller and a buyer originating at the closing over a bitter dispute over several closing adjustments. The seller begrudgingly went through with the sale, and several days later sent a letter to all the customers discouraging them from patronizing the business. It was a breach of contract since the seller sold the good will of the business, but it gave the buyer little practical recourse, as the seller already had his money and was moving to Florida.

Since that transaction I considered it worthwhile to escrow part of the purchase price for several months to discourage tactics of a disgruntled seller.

As a follow up to a seller's letter, a buyer should send his own letter or announcement, telling the customers about his future plans for the business. Many buyers prefer to take a low profile and defer announcement of the sale until they have the business changed to their satisfaction.

Customers understand that it takes time to bring about operational changes, so it's preferable to announce the sale and make introduction as early as possible.

Imaginative sellers and buyers can not only retain customers but can even build business for the buyer.

The best example was a well-conceived plan put into play by a seller and buyer of an Italian restaurant in a small town. Agreement on the sale was reached, but the closing was scheduled three months ahead. The clever buyer proposed that the seller conduct a free raffle for all customers within the three-month period. It provided the buyer with a customer list. Upon take-over, the seller and buyer offered a free buffet for the customers, with the raffle drawing to be held that same evening. The buyer footed the bill for the entire affair and the $500 grand prize color TV, but as he says, "It was a terrific investment."

What imaginative strategies can you design with the seller to retain—and build—customers during the take-over period?

LOOKING AHEAD

Your first few months in your own business will be a challenge. But look ahead and you'll see what so many other small business owners who have traveled the road before you have discovered.

Business ownership can be one of life's most satisfying and rewarding experiences. Why else would so many people hope and dream of their own business? But, as with most worthwhile things in life, it doesn't just happen. You have to make it happen. Others have and so can you.

12

PROBLEM SOLVING

The following questions have been selected as representative of those asked most frequently by business buyers and sellers. Names in all cases are fictitious.

1.Q: I have an opportunity to buy a general store together with the real estate containing the store, two upstairs apartments, and an adjoining gas station. The seller wants $220,000 for the business and the real estate. How can I determine the value of each?

A: When real estate is included with a business, the two must be valued independently. Start by setting a value on the business. If you believe the business is worth $100,000, then you're actually paying $120,000 for the real estate. To determine whether or not the real estate is worth $120,000, ask what a fair rental value is for the space the store occupies. Add it to the other rental incomes. That provides the gross rental income for the real estate. With a gross rental income defined, you should call in a certified real estate appraiser to place the value on the real estate. The key item to remember is that the business and the real estate must each stand on their own as fairly priced investments, and each has its own criteria for determining value.

Another reason for segregating the value is for tax purposes. If you don't allocate price between the business and the real estate, you can't establish your cost "basis" for each, creating problems with both depreciation write-offs and taxable gains when you sell.

2.Q: Should real estate be owned by the same corporation that owns a retail business? Our restaurant is incorporated and owns the building it occupies.

A. I almost always recommend that real estate *not* be owned by the

197

operating corporation. The reason is that any business can become insolvent, so why risk losing the real estate to business creditors? Many buyers take title to the real estate under their business corporation and build up a substantial net worth in the building, only to lose it when the business fails.

Depending on many factors, there may be some slight tax advantages in having the business own the property, but even more frequently the tax benefits argue in favor of independent ownership.

Whether you should take title to the property in your personal name, real estate trust, or separate corporation should be decided by your accountant and attorney.

Once real estate is owned by a separate entity, keep it arms-length from the operating business. Create a lease on fair rental terms, pay monthly rent to the real estate entity, and maintain separate accounts and books. If you mingle the cash of both entities you may lose the property to the creditors of your operating company.

3.Q: I am interested in buying an awning sales and installation business, but am at an impasse with the seller. I want him to agree that he won't compete with me by owning or working in a comparable business within 50 miles for a 10-year period. The seller wants the noncompete agreement to extend only for 10 miles, and be in force only for 3 years. What's reasonable?

A: A reasonable covenant not to compete is one that restricts the seller only to the extent actually necessary to protect the good will of the business you're buying. Beyond that you're not protecting the acquired good will but only preventing the seller from earning a living. The courts will not enforce an unreasonable noncompete agreement, and will cut it back to the area and time period it considers necessary to protect you.

Is 50 miles reasonable? It may be if you're in a rural area and encompass customers within a 50-mile trading area. It wouldn't be if you're located in the Bronx and can't claim customers beyond a 5-mile radius. That's the test. The time period is more questionable. I usually use a 10-year period in my noncompete agreements, and it has never been challenged. However, I can't say a court may decide that anything beyond 5–7 years is unreasonable. Certainly a court would consider the nature of the business and what you paid for the good will as factors.

You should negotiate for the most restrictive noncompete agreement that can possibly meet the test of "reasonableness."

4.Q: Two young buyers offered me an interesting proposition to buy my book bindery business. I calculate my net worth in the business to be about $50,000. The proposition is that they would take over my stock ownership without initial payment, but pay me 50% of the pretax net profits for the next three years. They tell me they can build the business to $60,000–75,000 profits within one year, so I'll come out ahead rather than sell my interest for $50,000 cash today. The business under my ownership shows a $15,000–20,000 annual profit, but perhaps with young blood it can grow. Should I accept?

A: Forget it. What you are offered is called the earn-out, or a sales price contingent on future profitability which you can't control or even measure.

A shrewd accountant can make paper profits disappear like cigar smoke in a drafty room. Even if you try to define the accounting procedures by which profits will be determined, the loopholes and the need to play detective speak against the deal.

If you are willing to sell for $50,000, why not propose a deal based on the "greater of 50% of profits or $50,000"? If you don't receive at least $50,000 as your share of profits over the next three years, the difference would then be payable. The buyers have the benefit of a "no cash" take-over, but you have put them to the test. If they're so confident they'll make money, why should they refuse? If they agree, make certain your attorney tightly secures the obligation.

While you're at it, you should look carefully at the appraisal that your net worth is only $50,000. With existing profits in the $15,000–20,000 range it may be appreciably higher.

A sale predicated on an earn-out only makes sense when the seller is about to throw the business into bankruptcy and walk away with nothing. He may never see more under his earn-out, but at least he gave nothing of value away.

5.Q: I am negotiating to buy a small lumber yard, but the one remaining point of contention is the valuation of accounts receivable. They have a face value of $120,000, however, many are 60–120 days old. How should they be valued?

A: Many books suggest a discount from face value be used. For example, receivables over 30 days are discounted by 20%; over 60 days 40%; and so on. There are several common formulas available.

I suggest you ignore them all. The far safer approach is to value them at their $120,000 face, but provide that any receivables uncollected after 90 (or 120) days be assigned back to the seller on a non-recourse basis, and that the seller repay you their face value. Of course, you want to make certain he honors his obligation to repurchase. This can be accomplished either by setting aside a reasonable sum in an escrow account or by providing in any note you owe the seller your right to "deduct said amount from next-due installments."

With this technique you pay only for what is actually collected. The seller, on the other hand, can try to collect any receivables he reacquired under the agreement.

6.Q: My concern is $12,000 owed the IRS for withholding taxes due from the bakery I am about to buy. Can my corporation be liable for the seller's tax liability?

A: I assume your corporation is acquiring the seller's assets rather than taking over his corporation through a stock purchase.

On a sale of assets the IRS can only go against the buyer if the buyer expressly agreed to assume the IRS liability. The IRS can only proceed against the assets sold to the buyer if there was a tax lien on file prior to the sale. The only other exception is where the buyer is not really a bona-fide purchaser for value but a "straw transferee" under a fraudulent conveyance.

Your attorney should check for existing tax liens, and if they don't exist, no claim can be levied against you or the acquired assets.

State taxing authorities may work under different rules. Some states have a "continuing tax claim" against assets even if no tax lien is on record. In these states the burden is on the buyer to obtain a tax waiver from the state to insure title free of state tax claims.

7.Q: The seller of the supermarket I'm interested in buying insists on a five-year employment contract as assistant manager as a condition of sale. His salary would be about $30,000 which is consistent with what we pay assistant managers in our other stores. Should we agree?

A: It depends whether he'll give you the performance consistent with your other assistant managers. But how do you know?

You may consider him qualified based on how he operated the store, but don't forget he was working for himself. Will he work as hard once he sells? From my experiences, many sellers who are protected by an airtight employment agreement don't put in the effort. Of course, that must be assessed on an individual basis.

An effective compromise may be a termination clause with a substantial severance pay provision; $5,000–10,000 may be in line. However, any termination based on good cause (theft, gross neglect, etc.) should be without compensation. Make certain you are protected upon termination by a noncompete agreement.

8.Q: A broker introduced us to a prospective buyer for our landscape business over a year ago. We hadn't seen either the broker or the buyer since then. Two weeks ago this same buyer approached us to sell. If we do sell to this buyer would we be liable for a commission?

A. Probably not. Most cases hold that where a broker abandons all efforts in creating a sale he abandons all claims to a commission. The tricky question is what time must elapse before the abandonment arises. In Massachusetts, for example, the time period is six months, according to a Supreme Court case. Other states may define it by statute or court decisions. Still others have yet to resolve the issue.

Only local counsel can provide the answer for your state, but in any event you should obtain an affidavit from the buyer that he has not been in contact with the broker since the particular date. You should also negotiate for the buyer to share in payment of the commission should the broker sue and prevail. Don't forget, he may also be benefiting from the lower price since you don't plan to pay the broker.

9.Q: I have an opportunity to sell my fast-food franchise for an excellent profit. The problem is that the franchisor is refusing me permission to transfer to the buyer. Can he prevent it?

A: The place to start is by reading your franchise agreement. It should state the conditions of transfer.

The contract probably says that franchisor approval is necessary. It may even grant the franchisor absolute discretion in approving any transferee. But don't let that stop you from purusing it. Several court decisions have held that a franchisor must have a bona-fide reason for refusing the transfer. The test is whether your buyer has the character, credit, capital, and capabilities consistent with successful franchise applicants.

If you're convinced your buyer meets the test, you may be able to force the sale through court action and may even obtain the support of the Federal Trade Commission.

The one problem is that victory may still give your buyer that uneasy feeling. As the "unwanted child," he certainly will have questions about future problems.

10.Q: What length lease should we require in purchasing a convenience store for $70,000? The landlord wants to give us a three-year lease and the seller tells us that's standard with the landlord (the seller has only received three-year-leases in the past). The seller assures me the landlord will renew the lease after three years.

A: You want to remember that the seller is already in business at that location. You're the one buying and paying $70,000 for the privilege.

A buyer should expect, as a minimum requirement, a lease of sufficient length to recoupe his investment from profits. If you project a $10,000 annual profit, look for a seven-year lease as your least-acceptable term. For an investment of this size I would want a 10-year lease, with an option to extend for one or two additional five-year periods.

If the landlord refuses to give you more than three years, define what the business would be worth if you had to vacate after the three-year period. Let's say it's $40,000. Now turn to the seller and explain that you want $30,000 of the price held in escrow and returned to you if the landlord doesn't renew the lease, or refuses to renew it without specified terms. Will the seller go along with it? Probably not. But you should go along with nothing else.

11.Q: The seller of a drugstore I'm interested in also owns the store block housing the pharmacy. Although he's willing to give me a long-term lease I also want an option to buy the real estate, which he refuses to grant. How can I make certain I have first opportunity to buy the building if he sells.

A: What you're looking for is a right of first refusal. Your lease should provide that if the seller decides to sell, and receives an offer acceptable to him, he will provide you first opportunity to match the offer and buy the property. If you refuse, he is then free to sell to the original offeror.

It provides you with the protection you want and should be acceptable to the seller as he still decides if and when he will sell and the acceptable price.

Your attorney will record the lease with this clause to put prospective buyers on notice of your prior rights to buy.

12.Q: Am I required to notify the seller's creditors when I buy his business?

A: Yes. has a Bulk Sales or Bulk Transfers Act requiring notice of intended sale to creditors. The laws on this are relatively uniform and summarily provide that:

1.   The seller will provide the buyer with a complete list of all creditors, in affidavit form and under oath.
2.   It is then the buyer's responsibility to notify the creditors of the intended sale at least 10 days prior to the sale. Notice must be by personal delivery or registered/certified mail.

If the buyer fails to comply, creditors have six months from the date of sale (or knowledge of the sale) to attach the assets transferred to the buyer. Once notice is provided, creditors' claims against the goods sold to the buyer terminate if no legal action to stop the sale is taken within the 10-day period.

The only instances where a buyer should consider not complying with the Bulk Sales Act is when:

1.   The buyer is assuming all the seller's liabilities, or

2. When the creditors' claims are for a small amount; the seller agrees to pay them at the time of sale and the buyer had adequate indemnification and recourse should claims arise later.

You would not comply with the Bulk Sales Act when you acquire the shares in a corporation, since the same corporation still owns its assets subject to existing liabilities. Another exception is when a buyer acquires business assets from a secured party (mortgage holder) foreclosing on the assets, or upon purchase from a Receiver, Assignee for the Benefit of Creditors, or Trustee in Bankruptcy, as these individuals are appointed to safeguard the interests of creditors.

13.Q: After looking at a small restaurant for several weeks, I asked the seller to show me his tax returns and financial records. The seller refuses me access to these records, suggesting I take his word on what the business grosses. I believe the business grosses the $180,000 he represents, but I'd be more confident if he showed me the books. Should I pursue the sale?

  A: Not unless he delivers the books. Some sellers play "cloak and dagger" games in providing buyers vital operating information. But sometimes sellers have their reasons. The most common is that the seller doesn't believe the buyer is serious or qualified to buy. Your best approach is to work through your accountant and have him call the seller's accountant. The fact that you have an accountant shows you are serious. Further, the seller may be inclined to show the books to your accountant if he's concerned about confidentiality.

14.Q: A high-volume paint and wallpaper supply firm is for sale at an excellent price and, since I have several years experience in this type of business, I'm interested in buying it. The problem is that the business is owned by two partners. One wants to sell and the other refuses, but also refuses to buy his partner out. Can the business be sold if only one partner choses to sell?

  A: No. A business owned by two partners requires the agreement of both to sell. If the business is incorporated, it requires the approval of stockholders holding at least 67% of the voting shares, although this may vary under state law.

  I wouldn't waste time actively pursuing this business, as in most cases a buy-out is arranged between the partners. However, you should constantly let him know you're still interested, in case the dissenting partner changes his mind.

15.Q: I am negotiating to buy a large Italian-style restaurant. The financial statements show the book value of the furniture to be worth $12,000. The seller places the value on these items at $30,000. Why should I pay more than the seller's own books say they're worth?

A: Book value only reflects the depreciated value for tax purposes. Seldom does book value reflect what these assets are truly worth. For example, real estate may be acquired for $200,000, but after 20 years' depreciation the real estate would have no book value. In reality, the real estate may now be worth $600,000. Would you expect to obtain it free? Conversely, equipment may have a book value well in excess of its true value. For example, your seller may have recently acquired the business and allocated a high portion of the purchase price to equipment so he would have the benefit of an equally high depreciation expense.

You should ignore book value in valuing fixtures and equipment. The proper valuation method is to estimate their replacement cost if you had to buy the items in their present used condition on the open market. A restaurant supply firm can give you a reasonably good idea of what it would cost to duplicate the equipment.

16.Q: The sale terms on a greeting card and gift shop I plan to buy are acceptable, but it's the rent that troubles me. The landlord wants $12 per square foot on the 200 sq ft store, or an annual rent of $24,000. Most greeting card shops pay $5–6 a sq ft in rent. How would this excess rent affect the value of the business?

A: It wouldn't necessarily have any adverse effect because the rent may be very reasonable. With retail businesses you should look at rent as a percentage of sales and not worry about it on a rent per square foot basis. The reason should be obvious. Another store may pay $4 per sq ft but only generate sales of $50 per sq. ft. Your store may generate sales of $150 per sq. ft. So although you are paying the higher rental, it's compensated by the proportionately higher sales, as both stores will pay rent equal to 8% of sales. Since most expenses are fixed, your store may be considerably more profitable than the store with the lower rent and sales.

Consider also the gross profit obtainable in one location versus another. For example, a tobacco and sundry shop grossing $200,000 and located in a hotel lobby may work on a 45% gross profit, considering lack of competition. The same size and volume tobacco shop in a competitive downtown location may operate on a 32% gross. Therefore the store situated in the hotel can afford to pay a higher percentile rent.

All factors being equal, look at rent only as a percentile of sales and compare it to industry averages. If it's in excess of what other businesses pay within the same industry, it will cut into profits and does detract from the value of the business.

17.Q: I am at a standstill with the seller of a liquor store I hope to buy. The liquor license has a $3,000 annual fee paid on January 1 of each year. We plan to close the sale on March 1 and the seller wants me to adjust for the license fee by having me pay $2,500 for the remainder of the year. Isn't he unreasonable?

A: No demand in the negotiating process is unreasonable. However, I think the seller has the better argument. Prepaid licenses, as with utilities or insurance, commonly are adjusted at the time of sale, so convention is on his side. Why not try to split the difference?

18.Q: Three weeks after acquiring a supermarket the refrigeration compressor broke down and it will cost $6000 to replace. Wouldn't the seller have to make good on it?

A: The seller would be liable only if he expressly warranted the condition of the equipment at the time of sale, or agreed to an extended warranty beyond the date of sale.

Most sellers refuse to warrant the working order of equipment beyond the date of sale, and to avoid legal problems knowledgeable sellers expressly state that they shall have no liability for defects once the buyer takes title.

Disputes more commonly arise when equipment breaks down between the date of contract and the date of closing. The contract certainly should provide that the seller will deliver the equipment in the same working order as existed at the time of agreement. This should be followed up by an actual inspection of equipment before you sign the contract, verifying the working condition of the equipment.

19.Q: I recently discovered that the seller is being sued for $3,000,000 by an elderly customer who slipped on an empty can on the store floor and suffered a broken leg. Can this customer make claim against the assets I acquired?

A: Not if you are an "arms-length" buyer who paid fair value for the business.

Had you acquired the stock ownership in the seller's corporation, then the claim would be against your corporation and would present a very different problem. The undisclosed contingent liability possibility is one good reason why it's best to buy assets rather than to take over the seller's corporation. In a corporate take-over situation the buyer should always ascertain the existence of insurance to protect the acquired business from this or any other type of claim.

20.Q: How important is it to conduct an actual physical inventory at the time of closing? The seller represents his clothing store as having $60,000 in merchandise and his books reflect the same.

A: An actual inventory is very necessary. You don't really know inventory value unless an inventory is conducted. Estimates are rarely accurate and certainly the seller has good reason to estimate on the high side. His books may reflect either a prior inventory level or be based on estimate. I have seen many cases where a seller estimated inventory, but actual inventory was 20–30% lower. The price of the business should be adjusted based on actual versus estimated inventory on which the sales price was estimated. The contract should also specify whether the adjustment shall be added to or subtracted from the down payment or financed portion of the purchase price.

Make certain the inventory is tabulated by an independent inventory appraiser who can be impartial and who will take into consideration shopworn or merchandise of questionable value. Typically, the buyer and seller agree to share the inventory tabulation cost.

You also want an inventory conducted so you can accurately determine beginning inventory to measure your year-end profitability. A final reason deals with insurance. Unless you have proof of inventory levels, the insurance company can challenge the stated inventory value in the event of casualty.

21.Q: What form of organization do you recommend I choose for operating the stereo shop I plan to buy. My accountant suggests I operate as a sole proprietorship to save the accounting fees on filing corporate tax returns.

A: It may be a matter of professional judgment, but I strongly disagree with your accountant. In my opinion the advantages of a corporation far outweigh its disadvantages.

The primary advantage of the corporation is in the limited liability it affords you. If your business becomes insolvent, the corporate creditors cannot hold you personally liable. Under a sole proprietorship you and the business are considered one entity, and therefore business creditors have full claim to your personal assets. Don't plan just for success. Protect yourself in case of failure.

There are considerable tax benefits also with a corporation. For example, a corporation can provide tax-deductible medical insurance, health and life insurance, and many other fringe benefits.

The corporation can be treated for tax purposes as a sole proprietorship by electing to be taxed as a Subchapter S corporation under the Internal Revenue Code. This eliminates the double taxation or tax on corporate profits, and instead profits (and losses) are taken directly on your own personal return. So for a corporation qualifying as a Subchapter S, even the tax consequences remain the same as with a sole proprietorship.

Certainly these advantages exceed in value the few dollars a year you'll pay in extra accounting fees.

22.Q: I am embroiled in a dispute with my business broker who is claiming a commission on a business he sold for me. I found out he is not licensed as a real estate broker and therefore I say he cannot enforce his claim for a commission. Am I right?

A: Most states do not require a license for business brokers. However, if a business broker sells property including real estate he must be licensed as a real estate broker, at least to the extent that he or she expects a commission for the real estate portion of the sale. The same is true when the broker earns a commission from the rental or lease of real estate.

Check with your state licensing agency for real estate to see if business brokers require licensure in your state.

23.Q: Is it a selling point to a bank considering the financing of my business that I'll use them as my depository bank?

A: Of course. Banks are in the business of attracting depositors. Your money is their inventory. Your average bank balance allows your bank to borrow several times that amount from the Federal Reserve Bank, so the bank really obtains a substantial benefit from each dollar on account.

In one case a bank was induced to lend $80,000 to a buyer of a tobacco and novelty shop in anticipation of an average account balance of $100,000, representing lottery ticket sales sold by the store.

Prospective buyers offering high cash balances in the bank's account always have a valuable bargaining tool.

24.Q: Do you suggest I use an expert appraiser to place a value on the clothing store I'm interested in and, if so, where can I locate a qualified appraiser?

A: A business appraiser can be valuable if you can find the right one. The problem is that unlike real estate appraisers, business appraisers are not a recognized or certified professional group. Therefore, it's difficult to evaluate competency.

Your best bet is to find someone with years of experience in the retail clothing field, and particularly one who has actively acquired stores similar to the one you're considering. He is probably best qualified to approximate a reasonable price.

Some buyers rely on business professors, but they generally use too theoretical an approach based on the capitalization method, but this has the limitation of ignoring the market conditions and potential that a person within the industry would consider.

Don't rely on your accountant and attorney. Appraisals of value is not their field.

25.Q: I'm planning to sell my bookstore within the next few months. Should I remodel to get a better price?

A: No. The buyer will have his own ideas on remodeling the store and isn't likely to increase the price enough to repay you for your investment. The best investment you can make is to make certain you have sufficient lighting and perhaps a fresh coat of paint.

Remember, to some buyers the "run down" business is even more interesting, since they look at it as one with potential.

26.Q: There's a terrific opportunity to acquire a variety store in a high-crime area on the outskirts of my city. I'm not sure whether I can handle the problems of operating a business in this area. Should I consider it?

A: Probably not. If you aren't sure you can put up with the ever-present problems of this type, you probably can't.

You may ask the seller if you can work in the business for a week or two to test it out. You'll have a much better perspective on whether you are able or want to tackle the headaches.

Businesses in high-crime areas oftentimes show the best profits considering the low rents and lack of chain competition allowing for higher prices. But don't let that influence you if you're not comfortable with it.

27.Q: How large a deposit is customary when signing a contract. I'm about to buy a motel for $300,000 and the seller wants me to place a $30,000 deposit in escrow pending the closing.

A: The deposit should be sufficiently large to give the seller assurance that the buyer won't abandon the deal, and adequate compensation if he does. A forfeited deposit is usually divided between the broker and the seller.

The deposited amount will depend on negotiations, the total price, and the down payment under the contract. Another factor is the contemplated length of time between contract and closing date.

I don't think $30,000 is unreasonable, although $15,000 or 5% of the total price would be more realistic.

28.Q: I gave a broker a listing to sell my trailer park for $480,000. The broker found a buyer who is willing to buy for $480,000, but wants me to finance $300,000 of the price. I've changed my mind about selling but want to know if I'll be liable for a brokers commission.

A: No. A broker is only entitled to a commission if he finds you a buyer ready, willing, and able to buy on the terms you required when listing the property. Since your listing was for all cash, the broker didn't find you your qualified buyer.

You should call the broker and cancel the listing before the buyer changes his mind and offers the $480,000 cash. If the broker still had an active listing when the buyer offered $480,000 cash, you would be liable for the commission.

29.Q: How much working capital do you think I'd need to start after I take over a health and beauty aid store grossing $400,000 annually?

A: The answer depends on two factors: 1) the inventory level, and 2) available credit.

For example, if you only need $40,000 in inventory to operate the business effectively, but you have $60,000 in stock on the shelves, you can "sell down" $20,000 in merchandise and turn it into working capital.

On the other hand, if you have $40,000 in stock, and take over the business with no liabilities and good credit, you can quickly build up $20,000 in working capital through a corresponding build-up of one month's purchases on credit.

If either of these possibilities represents your situation, you won't need working capital to start.

Working capital becomes important when you have too low an inventory and no credit available to increase inventory to profitable levels. That's when undercapitalization can cause a rapid bankruptcy.

30.Q: To what extent can I rely on the accuracy of financial statements to evaluate a small firm?

A: It depends of course on the business and how accurate the owner and his accountant wanted the statements to be.

Frankly, I don't consider them sufficiently accurate to rely upon. In most cases sales are understated, expenses overstated, and inventory levels distorted to create the lowest taxable profits. In other cases the inaccuracies result from faulty bookkeeping or estimates for key entries. In still others a seller will overstate income and profits for the year or two prior to sale for the specific purpose of obtaining the best price.

I use financial statements only as an approximation, but never the precise reality, of what the financial picture is all about. You'll need your accountant to audit and verify the seller's statements and, more importantly, to reconstruct the financial statements to portray your operation of the business.

31.Q: How can I determine the credit rating of the sundry wholesale firm I am interested in buying?

A: You have three methods. The quickest and easiest is simply to review its accounts payable file to see whether it's being shipped on open account and how current his payments are to all vendors. A high percentage of vendors shipping on C.O.D. terms mean a poor credit rating.

A second method is to pull the credit report from commercial credit reporting services such as *TRW* and *Dun and Bradstreet*. A subscriber to their services can order the report for you.

A third method is to check with any credit agency within the industry. Many industries have their own centralized credit or collection bureau.

32.Q: I am planning to acquire a large machine shop that employs 26 employees. Since the sale will occur about June 1, I don't know whether the seller or I should be responsible for paying the two week's vacations due the employees. What's customary?

A: Accrued vacation or sick leave time should be apportioned between the seller and buyer. If the vacation time accrued under the seller's owner-ship, it should be treated as his liability. The most common procedure is to deduct such adjustments from the purchase price, and specifically from the down payment portion.

33.Q: A failing furniture store is for sale in my area. The business has sales of $640,000 with losses of $70,000. I think the business has some turnaround potential, but it will take a new merchandising and pricing strategy. How would you value the business?

A: I would be more concerned with the terms than with the price. The business may head into bankruptcy under your management or perhaps you will turn it around and achieve spectacular sales and profits.

You should bargain to take over the shares of stock with a very small down payment, and any further payment on the purchase price should be tied to future profits.

Essentially you want to ask yourself these questions:

1. What is the stock worth (net worth) based on the actual value of inventory and fixtures (there is no good will) less existing liabilities? If assets are $200,000, but liabilities equal $100,000, the net worth is $100,000.

2. You may agree to pay the $100,000 for ownership interest based perhaps on a $10,000–15,000 down payment. The balance may be payable over 5–10 years. Your obligation for the balance of the purchase price should be paid only from profits, and if the business fails, or doesn't achieve profitability, you'd have no further liability on the purchase price.

Risk assessment is the important item. What do you have to lose if the business doesn't make it? Aside from your hard work, you may lose your down payment and any capital you invested in the company. Measure those dollars from a risk viewpoint.

34.Q: I have a chance to buy a large ice cream shop in a high-traffic mall. The business is incorporated and has a very favorable 15-year lease at a $500 monthly rental. The landlord will only give me a lease on the space for $1,200 a month, insisting that rental values in the mall have skyrocketed. Can the seller compel the landlord to allow me to take over his $500 a month lease?

A: If the lease provides that "assignment or sublet must have lessor approval," then the landlord can refuse. However, there have been several court cases holding that a landlord cannot arbitrarily refuse an assignment of lease. So you may want to consider a legal challenge.

A more practical solution would be to buy the shares in the seller corporation. Since it would be the same tenant in possession of the premises, the landlord could do nothing about it and you would have the continued benefits of the long-term, low-rental lease.

35.Q: We operate a six-store supermarket chain under the name King's Supermarkets. We want to sell one of our locations and the buyer wants the rights to the name "King's" for that location. How can we safeguard both his rights and ours to the name.

A: Your contract should provide that the buyer only has rights to the name at that location and agrees not to use it in any other location. The contract should also resolve whether or not the buyer can transfer the name to a successor buyer. It would be reasonable to grant him that right since the buyer paid for the rights to the name as part of the good will.

Conversely, the buyer should acknowledge your exclusive rights to the name at all existing and subsequent locations. You should be willing to define a radius in proximity to the buyer's location wherein he will have exclusive rights to the name.

Circular promotions must also be considered. Can the buyer send circulars into your trading area? Can you mail circulars into his area?

If your name is trademarked, you will have to grant him the limited rights to the name under a trademark license agreement spelling out the terms.

36.Q: What financing is available for a service business? I have an opportunity to buy a large real estate brokerage firm for $150,000; however, I only have a $40,000 down payment.

A: The difficulty in financing a service business is the lack of collateral (inventory, furniture, and fixtures) to pledge. Many banks resist lending to service businesses for the additional reason that their future sales and profitability are more dependent upon management performance than is a retail business that creates sales largely by reason of location alone.

You will have problems with bank or SBA financing unless you agree to pledge personal assets to secure the loan.

This type business lends itself best to seller financing, with the loan agreement specifying strict performance standards to assure the seller that sales and profits are being maintained during the loan period.

37.Q: How can I be certain that the seller of the convenience store I am about to buy owns all the fixtures and equipment he intends to sell?

A: It's impossible to be certain. In many businesses certain types of equipment are oftentimes loaned to the business, and as the seller has no title to these items, he can't give you good title.

Your contract should have the seller warrant that he has good title to all the fixtures and equipment and will indemnify you against any adverse claim. This language would also be in your bill of sale. Make certain you have a practical way of obtaining recourse against the seller if a claim of title is made. You can accomplish this either by setting aside a part of the purchase price in escrow for several months, or by set-off on any notes owed to the seller. A seller should expressly list the goods or equipment he does not have good title to, but that are on the premises on a loan or lease basis.

In your type of business the items most commonly leased or loaned include: refrigerated units for milk, ice cream, and soda, and burglar alarms.

38.Q: In acquiring a small department store, I am uncertain how we should handle goods orders by the seller prior to the sale, but shipped and received after the sale.

A: The agreement should provide that the buyer can either accept the goods and assume the obligation to pay, or reject the goods and return them to the supplier.

This is based on the assumption that the goods were not tabulated as part of the closing inventory, so they were not included in the price. Further, no liability yet existed prior to sale since the goods had not arrived.

A supplier may claim breach of contract by the seller upon rejection of the goods. However, very few actually do once they understand that the business changed hands, unless the goods were made to specification or special order.

A buyer and seller should work closely together between the date of contract and take-over to agree on ordered goods. This is the most effective way to solve the problem of a seller ordering goods that do not meet the buyer's approval.

39.Q: A retail pharmacy is for sale in a nearby town and I have been interested in it for several months. The business grosses $450,000 annually and the seller now wants to sell for $100,000, which I believe is a fair price considering its $70,000 inventory and profitable history. I hesitate to buy because a larger discount pharmacy chain is planning to open shortly within two miles of this pharmacy. Should I forget the acquisition?

A: I wouldn't forget it, but I wouldn't buy it quite yet either. You can't accurately measure the impact of the new competition until it's been in business awhile. You should defer the decision and review the sales of the pharmacy 3–4 months after the chain store opens. You will then be able to determine the new sales figures and the impact on profits and value of the business.

40.Q: A young man has shown an interest in buying my mattress and bedding store for the past several months. I want $140,000 for the business and estimate a buyer will need about $50,000 of his own money to close. The buyer is agreeable to my price and terms but wants three months to find financing and a clause if the contract canceling the agreement and return of deposit if he can't obtain the financing. I don't want to take the business off the market if the buyer can't raise the money, but I do want to give him a reasonable opportunity to obtain financing. How should I handle it?

A: Many buyers do and should demand a "financing contingency" clause in the agreement calling for contract cancellation and deposit return if they can't line up the financing. But it can hold up a seller, particularly if the buyer has no reasonable chance of finding the financing.

The best way to handle it is to have the contract describe the needed financing. For example, is it conditional upon the buyer obtaining a bank loan for $80,000 with interest not in excess of 20%, payable in or within five years; or is the financing condition unspecified? Find out just what financing the buyer needs and assess his chances of obtaining it. The buyer should be willing to provide you with personal financial information to help you make the decision.

Another approach is to insert in the agreement a provision stating that if the buyer does not obtain the specified financing you have the right to self-finance on the same terms and bind the buyer. Of course, this should only be considered if you are willing to self-finance as a final alternative.

Still another method is to transfer some of the risk to the buyer by insisting he forfeit a part of his deposit if he fails to obtain the financing. This will scare away the lookers, who only want to tie up your business while being protected by their own financing loophole.

If you do agree to a financing contingency clause, provide that the buyer must either obtain the financing within 30 days or the contract is canceled. It shouldn't take the buyer longer to see if he can obtain financing unless he is applying to the SBA. If it is to be SBA financed, you should probably not sign the contract, but still encourage the buyer to apply with the possibility that the business may still be available if and when SBA approval comes through.

41.Q: What do you consider the most important factor in evaluating a business?

A: Potential. It far outweighs any other consideration. Few businesses under new ownership continue to operate at the same level of sales and profits as under the seller's management. You may find two businesses for sale, each grossing $400,000. The first may be operating at its greatest potential with excellent management and you may be lucky to even maintain the sales. The second business may have been operated inefficiently and then may be quickly built to $700,000–800,000 in sales. That's why the evaluation process should be based on the important question—what can you do with the business?

42.Q: We want to buy a beauty parlor, however, the landlord claims the sinks, mirrors and counters are his property, since they are now attached to the real estate. He's willing to allow our use of these items during the tenancy but insists we will not be allowed to remove and take them should we leave. The seller wants to charge us $5,500 for these fixtures. What should we do?

A: Either require the seller to obtain a waiver or release of claim to these items signed by the landlord so he can give you good title, or deduct their value from the price of the beauty parlor.

The landlord probably has a poor claim to these fixtures as they are for a specific business and remain personal property even though they may be attached to the property, but why should you argue the seller's case? Let him resolve it with the landlord so you get title for what you're buying.

43.Q: We recently acquired a landscaping service and found out that the seller transferred the telephone numbers of the business to his home. We, of course, expected the telephone numbers to be transferred to our account in order to receive calls from existing and prospective customers. To whom should the telephone numbers be assigned?

A: Your contract will have to provide the answer, and every contract should provide that the seller will notify the telephone company to assign the telephone numbers to the buyer, if that's the buyer's intention.

If the contract is silent on telephone numbers, it probably would be implied under good will. If the telephone numbers have an important value, legal action would be necessary to order the seller to transfer the account. As a practical matter you may find it easier and less expensive to obtain a new number and notify your existing accounts. What you would then lose is the benefit of inquiries from new customers responding to prior ads or yellow page telephone listings.

44.Q: Many books suggest borrowing needed capital from relatives. My mother and brother are each willing to lend me $20,000 to buy an auto body shop. Do you recommend borrowing from relatives?

A: Not usually. I have seen too many cases where buyers borrowed from friends and relatives only to lose the business and the ability to repay the loans. It can certainly cause a loss of friendship, and even a family relationship can become strained over money. Many of these failed buyers tell me borrowing from relatives was their biggest mistake in the venture, as the hard feelings continued long after the business disappeared.

45.Q: I'm afraid to go into business considering all the failures. How good (or bad) are the odds?

A: Failure rates are highest in start-ups rather than in established businesses. The *Harvard Business Review* reports that 85% of all small businesses show a profit. Bankruptcy statistics prove that only 20% of the established businesses are headed for failure. Of course success or failure will depend on many individual factors relating to you and the business, but if you're the average buyer, you have an 80% chance of succeeding.

APPENDIX 1

LETTER OFFER

MEYERS, GOLDSTEIN & CHYTEN

ATTORNEYS AT LAW
850 BOYLSTON STREET
CHESTNUT HILL, MASSACHUSETTS 02167

(617) 277-4100

IRVING S. MEYERS
ARNOLD S. GOLDSTEIN, P.C.
EDWIN R. CHYTEN
STANLEY N. FREEDMAN
BARRY R. LEVINE
JAMES J. LARKIN

CABLE: MEYGOLD

OF COUNSEL:
LOUIS K. NATHANSON

Apex Business Brokers
10 Elm Street
Anytown, Massachusetts

Attention: Robert Smith

Dear Mr. Smith:

Please be advised that we represent John Doe relative to his interest in acquiring the business known as Surfside Shoes, Inc. ("Surfside"). We understand that Mr. Doe has been introduced to this business through your office.

My client is interested in acquiring the business on the following terms:

1. The transfer shall be through a sale of assets (not shares in the seller corporation). The assets would consist of all inventory, fixtures, furniture, equipment and the name and good will of the business.

2. The seller would retain all cash on hand, accounts and notes receivable, prepaid expenses, motor vehicles, tax rebates and any pending claims owed by the corporation.

3. The offered purchase price for the business is $55,000 based on an inventory level of $35,000 wholesale cost at the time of transfer. In the event the inventory is less or more than $35,000 the difference shall be added or subtracted from the purchase price.

4. We would expect the final documents to reflect that the purchase price shall for tax purposes be allocated:

   $35,000 for inventory (or as adjusted)
    15,000 for fixtures and equipment
     5,000 for good will

   $55,000 total purchase price

5. The proposed purchase price would be paid in the following manner:

218

$ 1,000   cash down payment (tendered as a deposit
             herein)
  4,000   Deposit upon signing formal agreement
15,000   by the assumption of seller's existing
             liabilities at the time of closing
35,000   to be financed by seller, payable over
             5 years with 12% interest. The note
             would be guaranteed by Mr. Doe, and
             secured by a first mortgage on assets,
             and an assignment of lease if assented
             to by the landlord

6. Any adjustment based on any increase or decrease in
either inventory or liabilities shall be added or
subtracted from the note balance, and not the down
payment.

7. Except for liabilities expressly to be assumed, the
assets shall be sold free and clear of all claims,
debts, liens or other liabilities with Mr. Doe
receiving good and marketable title.

8. We shall expect the seller, and Mr. Sam Seller, its
owner to agree to a non-compete agreement preventing
them from engaging in the retail shoe business for
5 years, within 5 miles of the present business
address.

9. This offer is expressly conditional upon:

   a) The buyer obtaining a lease on the premises
   on such terms, rents and conditions as he deems
   acceptable.

   b) The buyer's accountant verifying further
   additional information and his satisfaction
   of same.

   In the event these two conditions are not fully
   satisfied, this offer, or any subsequent formal
   agreement, may be terminated by the buyer and all
   deposits shall be promptly refunded.

10. We enclose the buyer's certified check for $1,000 to
be held in escrow by your firm pending the closing
and transfer.

If this offer is acceptable to the seller, please have
him signify by signing where indicated and return a signed
copy to our office within 10 days of above date. In the event
we do not receive a signed copy by that date, you should consider
the offer withdrawn. Upon acceptance, we propose to immediately
enter into a formal purchase and sales agreement on these
terms.

We understand that all brokerage fees shall be paid
by the seller and that an acceptable date of closing would
be on or about July 15, 1982.

I appreciate your cooperation in bringing this offer
to the attention of the seller.

Very truly yours,

John Doe
By his attorney,
Arnold S. Goldstein

The foregoing offer is accepted
on its terms:

Surfside Shoes, Inc.

By: _____
    President

_____
Sam Seller, as an individual

APPENDIX 2

AGREEMENT FOR SALE OF ASSETS

AGREEMENT

AGREEMENT made and entered into by and between SELLER SUPER-MARKET, INC., a Massachusetts corporation with a usual place of business at Main Street, Anytown, Massachusetts (hereinafter referred to as "SELLER"), and BUYER COMPANY, INC., another Massachusetts corporation (hereinafter referred to as "BUYER"), with a usual place of business at the same location, all as their respective interests exist and are herein represented.

WHEREAS, SELLER operates a supermarket business at said aforementioned address and is desirous of selling certain assets of the same to BUYER as a going business concern; and

WHEREAS, BUYER is desirous of purchasing said assets and continuing the operation of the supermarket business on terms as herein contained;

NOW THEREFORE, it is for good and valuable consideration and in consideration of the covenants, agreements, terms, and provisions as herein contained mutually agreed by and between the parties as follows:

ARTICLE I

Sale of Assets

SELLER agrees to sell, and BUYER agrees to purchase and acquire all of the following assets, chattels, and items as owned by, located on, and

221

used in connection with the business of the SELLER known as SELLER SUPERMARKET, Main Street, Anytown, Massachusetts.

a) All of the inventory, merchandise, and goods for resale existing as of the date of closing.

b) All of the furniture, fixtures, equipment, and supplies, furnishings, leasehold improvements and without limiting the generality of the foregoing to include all office equipment, counters, shelves, check-out units, cash registers, heating equipment, air conditioners, wall cases, refrigerated units, lighting fixtures, signs, display units, freezers (walk-in or otherwise), compressors, decorative accessories and tools of the trade, accessories, appurtenances, provided and only to the extent the same are located within the inside walls, ceiling, and floor of the presently existing ground-floor store.

c) All of the good will of the SELLER, including such exclusive rights to the name "SELLER SUPERMARKET"; together with all policy manuals, price lists, supplier lists, customer lists, secret formula, recipes, or trade secrets to the extent they exist.

d) Transfer of SELLER'S right of an existing beer and wine license to BUYER or its nominee as more fully set forth herein; together with such rights to an all-alcoholic license as may exist, if any, at time of closing; or thereafter as hereinafter provided.

ARTICLE II

Assets to be Retained by Seller

SELLER shall retain all right, title, and interest in and to the following items:

a) All cash on hand or on deposit.

b) All notes receivable, accounts receivable, prepaid expenses, utility deposits, tax rebates, insurance claims, choses in action; credits due from suppliers and other allowances.

c) Motor vehicles and automobiles, excepting for a certain compactor truck now owned which shall be subject to sale hereunder.

d) Any equities in SELLER or any other incorporated or nonincorporated entity.

Specifically excluded also from any sale are any fixtures, plumbing, wiring and/or equipment contained within the walls and/or attached to or upon the exterior walls or roof whether or not said fixtures, plumbing, wiring and/or equipment passes through or is connected to the interior walls, ceiling and/or floor of the presently existing ground-floor store or are fastened or connected to any item being sold to BUYER under this Agreement.

ARTICLE III

Purchase Price

BUYER agrees to pay to SELLER, and SELLER agrees to accept as the full purchase price for all the singular the assets to be sold under Article I, supra; the total purchase price of FIFTY THOUSAND ($50,000.00) DOLLARS plus the cost value of the inventory at the time of closing as hereinafter defined and to be evaluated. At the time of closing a physical inventory shall be conducted and tabulated by XYZ Inventory Tabulators located at Elm Street, Boston, Massachusetts (hereinafter referred to as the "Tabulators"). The cost values shall be defined as retail price less twenty (20%) percent. For illustration only, if an item has a retail price of ONE ($1.00) DOLLAR its cost value shall be EIGHTY (80¢) CENTS. SELLER and BUYER shall mutually agree in the rejection or assignment of other partial values to any inventory for reason of questionable salability, marketability, retail value, or it being deteriorated, shopworn, or otherwise not suitable for sale at full retail price; however, it is agreed that any item of inventory which can be returned to the distributor or manufacturer for full credit to BUYER shall not be rejected, but rather accepted at cost value, thereby giving BUYER the option of making any return. SELLER may retain title to any goods agreed upon as having no value. SELLER and BUYER each pay one-half (½) of the Tabulator's fee.

For illustration only, if the cost value of the inventory is determined to be FIFTY THOUSAND ($50,000.00) DOLLARS the total purchase price shall be ONE HUNDRED THOUSAND ($100,000.00) DOLLARS.

ARTICLE IV

Allocation of Purchase Price

The purchase price shall be allocated in the manner following:

$ Cost value as may be determined   — For Article Ia) assets.
$ 45,000.00   — For Article Ib) assets.

$ 2,500.00   — For Article Ic) assets.
$ 2,500.00   — For Article Id) assets.

ARTICLE V

Payment of Purchase Price

The purchase price as hereinabove to be determined in accordance with Article III, supra; shall be paid in the manner following:

$ 10,000.00   deposit upon execution hereof by certified check to be held in escrow jointly by SELLER and BUYER.

$ 90,000.00   at time of closing by certified check or bank check; provided that said amount shall be decreased pro-rata if the total purchase price shall not equal $100,000.00. Any balance due thereafter, and in the event the sales price shall exceed $100,000.00, shall be paid timely twenty-one (21) days from date of closing.

ARTICLE VI

Sale Free and Clear

SELLER agrees that it shall sell said assets free and clear of all liens, encumbrances, liabilities, and claims of all parties adverse thereto. SELLER agrees that it shall:

1. Waive all the conditions and requirements of the Bulk Sales Act, M.G.L. Chapter 106 §6; but SELLER shall complete and execute affidavit as annexed as Exhibit A.

2. At time of closing, SELLER shall provide BUYER with a tax waiver from the Department of Revenue, Commonwealth of Massachusetts.

3. That any and all liens, encumbrances, security agreements, tax liens, or attachments of record shall be fully discharged at time of closing.

4. SELLER shall provide BUYER with an indemnity agreement as annexed as Exhibit B, indemnifying BUYER from any asserted claims against assets sold to BUYER.

ARTICLE VII

Seller's Warranties

The SELLER warrants and represents to BUYER with knowledge the BUYER shall rely on same to enter into this transaction, each and all of the foregoing:

a) That the SELLER owns all and singular the assets being sold hereunder, and has full marketable title to same excepting only for items set forth on Exhibit C., "non-owned assets."

b) That the SELLER has full right and authority to enter into this agreement and right to perform and sell hereunder.

c) That there are no known eminent domain or condemnation proceedings affecting the ground store area containing the supermarket business or any of its common areas.

d) That at the time of the sale, all fixtures, equipment, air conditioners, heating equipment, and other apparatus shall be in good working order at the time of passing except those items which, upon the date of this Agreement, not functioning. Acceptance of the bill of sale by BUYER shall be conclusive evidence of satisfaction of this warranty. The parties agree that the amount of consideration paid for the above fixtures, equipment, air conditioners, heating equipment, and other apparatus is based upon the fact that these items above being bought and sold "as is" and SELLER disclaims any warranty of merchantability for periods beyond the closing, and BUYER accepts the same "as is" and hereby waives forever any rights he may have had otherwise.

e) That there are no known governmental or administrative proceedings against SELLER, including but not limited to, the Board of Health or Building Inspector, which have arisen due to, or in connection with, its conduct of the supermarket business.

ARTICLE VIII

Covenant Not To Compete

SELLER agrees and covenants that it shall not compete with the supermarket business being transferred herein; pursuant to the terms of the covenant not to compete agreement as annexed as Exhibit D.

ARTICLE IX

Seller's Obligation Pending Closing

SELLER agrees, warrants, and covenants that during the pendency of this agreement, that:

1. SELLER shall maintain customary store hours.
2. SELLER shall maintain its customary and usual pricing and promotional programs.
3. SELLER shall maintain an adequate stock necessary to maintain the good will of the business.
4. SELLER shall not conduct any liquidation or so-called close-out sales.
5. SELLER shall maintain the current employees for the benefit of BUYER; however, nothing herein shall prevent a discharge for cause, or require BUYER to employ any present employee.

Acceptance of the bill of sale shall be conclusive evidence of satisfaction of this Article IX. In the event of any asserted breach, BUYER shall give SELLER written notice thereto and SELLER shall cure within three (3) days thereafter. In the event SELLER shall not so cure, then BUYER shall have the option to terminate this Agreement without further recourse to either party hereto.

ARTICLE X

Casualty

It is further provided that if there is any casualty, destruction, or loss to the assets described in Article I b) in an amount equal to or in excess of ten (10%) percent of the total value; then in such instance this Agreement may be terminated at the election of BUYER, unless said assets or premises shall, before the date of closing be restored or replaced to their former condition.

ARTICLE XI

Conditions Precedent—Concurrent—and Subsequent

This Agreeement and all of BUYER'S obligations hereunder shall be fully conditioned upon the occurrence of the following:

BUYER obtaining a lease for the present premises of SELLER, together with certain land purchase options as included therein (hereinafter "Lease") and as annexed hereto as Exhibit E. It is expressly agreed and understood that this Agreement and the Lease shall be mutually dependent; and BUYER shall not be obligated to perform under this Agreement without benefit of said Lease and reciprocally BUYER shall have no rights under said Lease unless the sale is concluded under this Agreement. The purchase options are attached as Exhibits F, G, and H.

ARTICLE XII

Brokers

The parties warrant and represent to each other that there are no brokers to this transaction and none entitled to commission.

ARTICLE XIII

Adjustments

The parties agree that at the time of closing they shall prorate and adjust for allocable and other expenses subject to adjustment in the manner following:

1. Merchandise ordered by SELLER prior to closing but received by BUYER subsequent to closing and therefore not tabulated in the inventory shall either be (a) paid for by BUYER or (b) rejected by BUYER and returned to shipper for credit to SELLER. BUYER agrees to indemnify and hold harmless SELLER for BUYER'S failure to comply with this provision. This paragraph shall survive the closing date.

2. There shall be no adjustment for yellow page advertising, electric, telephone, or gas as BUYER shall simultaneously with closing establish its own accounts.

3. There shall be no adjustment for insurance premiums as BUYER shall obtain its own insurance.

4. Payroll (excepting for accrued wages, benefits) shall be adjusted. There shall be an adjustment for fuel oil, rent, burglar alarm rentals, service contracts, and alcoholic licensing fees (provided that noth-

ing herein shall obligate BUYER to assume any executory contracts of SELLER).

ARTICLE XIV

Miscellaneous

1. All Exhibits are hereby incorporated by reference.
2. This constitutes the entire agreement and there are no other terms, conditions, warranties, representations, or inducements except as are expressly set forth herein.
3. Headings are for convenience only and are not an integral part of this Agreement.
4. This Agreement, executed in duplicate, shall be binding upon and shall inure to the benefit of the parties, their successors, assigns, and personal representatives.
5. The parties shall do, undertake, execute, and perform all acts and documents reasonably required to carry out the tenor and provisions of this Agreement.

ARTICLE XV

Closing

The closing shall be on October 1, 1981 at 2 o'clock P.M. at office of SELLER.
Time is of the essence.
Signed under seal this   day of   , 1981.

SELLER SUPERMARKET, INC.
By:_____'_____
    President
BUYER COMPANY
By:_____
    President

APPENDIX 3

STOCK SALE/REDEMPTION AGREEMENT

AGREEMENT

Agreement made and entered into by and between CAPITAL CORPORA-TION, a Massachusetts corporation with a usual place of business at 100 Main Street, Anytown, Massachusetts (hereinafter referred to as "CORPO-RATION"), SAM SELLER of Boston, Massachusetts (hereinafter referred to as "SELLER") and BEN BUYER, of Boston, Massachusetts, (hereinafter referred to as "BUYER").

WHEREAS, SELLER is the owner of all the issued and outstanding shares of stock of the corporation and is desirous of selling and transferring said shares to the CORPORATION under a redemption, all in accordance with the terms as herein contained, and

WHEREAS, the CORPORATION is desirous of purchasing and acquiring all of the SELLER'S shares, redeeming same, and retiring said shares as nonvoting treasury stock, and otherwise fulfilling the terms and obligations as herein contained, and

WHEREAS, the CORPORATION is desirous of issuing new shares to the BUYER, and the BUYER is desirous of acquiring said shares from the CORPORATION, with the intent that upon the consummation of this agreement, the BUYER shall be the sole stockholder of the issued and outstanding shares of the CORPORATION.

WITNESSETH

That for one dollar, and other good and valuable consideration, and in consideration of the agreements, conditions, terms, provisions, covenants,

229

representations, and inducements as herein contained, it is mutually and reciprocally agreed by and between the parties as follows:

ARTICLE I

Sale of Corporate Shares by Seller

SELLER agrees to sell, and the CORPORATION agrees to purchase and acquire all of the shares of stock in and to the CORPORATION as held and owned by SELLER, it being further described as 100 shares of common stock, evidenced by stock certificate nos. 1; and being further referred to herein as "SELLER SHARES".

ARTICLE II

Seller's Representation as to Seller's Shares

The SELLER expressly represents and warrants to each the CORPORATION and the BUYER, each of the following:

- **a)** That the SELLER has good and marketable title to the SELLER'S SHARES.
- **b)** That said SELLER'S SHARES are free from lien, encumbrance, pledge, or sequestration and are free from any adverse claim thereto.
- **c)** That there are no outstanding proxies, assignments of rights, or any other form of stock power issued and arising from SELLER'S SHARES.
- **d)** That SELLER'S SHARES represent all of the issued and outstanding shares of the CORPORATION, of all classes, and there are no outstanding subscriptions.
- **e)** The SELLER has full right and authority to sell and transfer said shares, pursuant to the terms of this agreement.

ARTICLE III

Purchase Price

The CORPORATION agrees to pay to the SELLER for the purchase and redemption of the SELLER'S SHARES, a price to be determined as follows:

The agreed base price shall be SEVENTY-FIVE THOUSAND ($75,000.00) DOLLARS, subject to adjustments as follows:

a) *Inventory.* The base price shall be based on an inventory owned by the CORPORATION in the amount of FIFTY-NINE THOUSAND ($59,000.00) DOLLARS. If the inventory is more, the difference shall be added to the base price; however, if the inventory is less, the difference shall be deducted. For the purposes of establishing the inventory value, the following definitions and procedures shall govern: Immediately prior to the passing, an actual physical inventory shall be conducted by XYZ (hereinafter referred to as "INVENTORY TABULATORS"). The INVENTORY TABULATORS shall value the inventory at cost, inclusive of generally prevailing trade, cash or quantity discounts. The INVENTORY TABULATORS shall reject from tabulation any inventory that in their discretion is deemed unmerchantable or unsalable or having an expired date. Items of questionable value shall have a partial value assigned. The determination by the INVENTORY TABULATORS shall be binding upon all parties.

b) *Liabilities.* The base shall be further adjusted based on total liabilities of FIFTY-SIX THOUSAND ($56,000.00) DOLLARS. In the event the liabilities at the time of passing are less, the difference shall be added to the base price. If the liabilities are in excess of FIFTY-SIX THOUSAND ($56,000.00) DOLLARS, the excess shall be deducted from the base price. The term liabilities as used herein shall mean all debts, obligations, and liabilities of the CORPORATION, including but not limited to: accounts payable, expenses payable, taxes accrued to date, accrued rent expenses and charges, loans due officers, directors, or any other party, notes whether secured or unsecured, accrued wages, and any other debt or obligation, whether disputed or undisputed liquidated or unliquidated, contingent or not contingent, and notwithstanding whether now due, past due, or due at some future time, and notwithstanding whether known or unknown. The SELLER shall prepare a schedule of liabilities as above defined, and existing at the time of passing, and annex same as Exhibit A. In the event there shall be any debts or liabilities not scheduled, or for an amount in excess of that scheduled, then in such instance,

    i) The CORPORATION and BUYER shall have full rights to indemnity as against the SELLER, pursuant to Indemnity Agreement as set forth as Exhibit B, and/or

ii) The CORPORATION may pay said unscheduled liability and deduct same from the next due installment(s) due under the Redemption Promissory Note due the SELLER as further described, infra.

ARTICLE IV

Payment of Purchase Price

The purchase price of SEVENTY-FIVE THOUSAND ($75,000.00) DOLLARS (subject to adjustment) shall be paid to the SELLER by the CORPORA-TION, in the manner following.

$ 5,000 in cash, said sum representing all of the CORPORATION'S cash on hand and on deposit as of the date of passing.

$10,000 by a transfer to the SELLER of existing accounts receivable, having a face value equal to said amount. Said receivables shall be selected by the SELLER, but shall be acquired on a nonre-course basis as against the CORPORATION. The SELLER may at his option, have the CORPORATION bill for and collect said receivables, and any sums paid thereon shall be rendered to the SELLER on a weekly basis, with an adequate accounting thereto. The CORPORATION shall impose no collection charge. All payments on any receivable shall be credited first to the oldest balance.

$60,000 evidenced by a Promissory Note to be executed by the CORPORATION; all as set forth on Exhibit C, said sum payable in thirty-six (36) equal, consecutive, and successive monthly installments, bearing interest at ten (10%) percent on the unpaid balance. Said Note shall be secured by a security interest in and to the assets of the CORPORATION, as annexed as Exhibit D. Any adjustments in price to be added to Note Principal.

ARTICLE V

Redemption by Corporations

The CORPORATION agrees that upon acquiring all the SELLER'S SHARES, it shall undertake all acts necessary to hold same as nonvoting treasury stock.

ARTICLE VI

Warranties by Seller and Corporation

The SELLER and the CORPORATION, represent to each other to the extent consistent, and jointly and severally to the BUYER, each of all of the following:

1.   That the CORPORATION is in good standing as a Massachusetts corporation.

2.   That the only liabilities of the CORPORATION are those set forth in Exhibit A, and that said amounts are accurate, and there are no others.

3.   That all of the assets of the CORPORATION or on its premises are owned by the CORPORATION, excepting as may be set forth on Exhibit E, and all of said assets are free of security interests, liens or encumbrances.

4.   That there are no known lawsuits against the CORPORATION.

5.   That there are no known proceedings commenced by any governmental body or agency as against the CORPORATION, and that all licenses and permits are in effect and in good standing.

6.   That the present lease held by the CORPORATION is set forth as Exhibit F, and that said lease is without modification, is in full force and effect, in good standing, and there are no known breaches thereto by the CORPORATION, and there are no known proceedings to evict, terminate said lease, or otherwise curtail or impair the tenancy or the CORPORATION'S rights thereunder.

7.   That the financial statements annexed as Exhibit G, are materially true and accurate, as of the date set forth.

8.   That the CORPORATION has full authority to enter into this agreement, acquire SELLER'S SHARES and enter into all of CORPORATION'S undertakings hereto.

9.   That all tax returns or filing due any taxing authority, have been filed and paid.

ARTICLE VII

Covenant Not to Compete

The SELLER agrees to execute and deliver to the CORPORATION a covenant not to compete as set forth as Exhibit H. It is understood that the consideration for this covenant shall be ONE ($1.00) DOLLAR and not the redemption payment, in whole or in part.

ARTICLE VIII

Adjustments

Other than adjustments to the redemption price as above defined, the parties further agree that they shall adjust as between SELLER and BUYER, at the time of passing for the following:

1. Wages accrued, including vacation pay.
2. Fuel oil.
3. Insurance premiums.
4. Merchandise received by the CORPORATION, subsequent to the inventory taking, but prior to the passing, unless said liability is listed on Exhibit A.
5. The fee for the INVENTORY TABULATORS shall be paid on an equal basis as between BUYER and SELLER.
6. Rents, including any accrued but unbilled and/or unpaid taxes or other lease charges.
7. Utility bills.

ARTICLE IX

Miscellaneous

1. The parties agree to execute all documents and undertake all acts consistent with the terms of this agreement.

2. All Exhibits are incorporated into this agreement by specific reference.

3. This constitutes the entire agreement, and there are no other terms, conditions, inducements, warranties or representations except as provided for herein.

4. This agreement shall be binding upon and inure to the benefit of the parties, their successors, assigns, and personal representatives.

5. The SELLER shall at the time of passing deliver and other-

wise make available to the CORPORATION and the BUYER, all books and records of the CORPORATION including:

a) All financial books and records.

b) Invoices for scheduled liabilities.

c) Tax returns for the prior three years.

d) Insurance policies.

e) Resignations of all existing corporate officers and directors.

ARTICLE X

Date for Passing

The date for passing shall be on August 9, 1981, at 8:30 o'clock, A.M. at the office of Capital Corporation, Anytown, Massachusetts.

Signed under seal this 9th day of August, 1981

CAPITAL CORPORATION

By_____
President

_____
Sam Seller

_____
Ben Buyer

APPENDIX 4

FRANCHISE AGREEMENT

FRANCHISE AGREEMENT

THIS AGREEMENT, made and entered into at   , this   day of   , 19   , by and between   , doing business under the name of   , a Massachusetts corporation, hereinafter referred to as Company, and hereinafter referred to as Franchisee.

PREAMBLE

WHEREAS, Company is the owner of certain trademarks, including Universal Fitness Centers, which have been registered with the Patent Office of the United States of America under Registry Nos. and   ; and with the Secretary of the Commonwealth of Massachusetts Office of Corporations Trademark Division; and

WHEREAS, Company is engaged in the business of franchising health and fitness centers throughout the United States; and, in connection therewith, licensing the use of trademarks, which said health and fitness centers are herein referred to as Universal Fitness Centers; and

WHEREAS, Company has established a high reputation with the public as to the quality of products and services available at Franchised Health and Fitness Centers, which said high reputation and good will has been and continues to be a unique benefit to Company and its franchisees; and

WHEREAS, Franchisee recognizes the benefits to be derived from being identified with and licensed by Company, and being able to utilize the system, names and marks which Company makes available to its franchisees; and

WHEREAS, Franchisee desires to be franchised to operate a Franchised Health and Fitness Center pursuant to the provisions hereof and at the location specified herein, and Franchisee has had a full and adequate opportunity to be thoroughly advised of the terms and conditions of this Franchise Agreement by counsel of its own choosing.

NOW, THEREFORE, in consideration of the mutual covenants herein contained, the parties agree as follows:

I. FRANCHISE PAYMENT; SERVICES BY COMPANY

    A. *Franchise Payment.*   The Company acknowledges payment to it by Franchisee of the total sum of $ consisting of $ as and for a franchise fee; $ for initial assistance essential to the Franchisee consisting of the training and the services detailed at Paragraph B, subparagraphs 2, 3, and 4 below; and $ for a grand opening advertising fund. Franchisee acknowledges that the grant of the franchise constitutes the sole consideration for the payment of the franchise fee and that said sum shall be fully earned by the Company upon execution and delivery hereof. No further franchise fee shall be payable during the term hereof. In the event a promissory note or other evidence of indebtedness is accepted by Company as partial payment, then the prompt and faithful discharge of such obligation shall be a material consideration. Failure of Franchisee to pay such obligaticn on its due date shall constitute a material default of this Franchise Agreement and Company shall not be obligated to give notice of such default, anything in Article XII hereof to the contrary notwithstanding.

    B. *Services by Company.*   Company agrees during the term of this Franchise Agreement to use its best efforts to maintain the high reputation of Franchised Health and Fitness Centers and in connection therewith to make available to Franchisee:

        1. Initial standard specifications and plans for the building, equipment, furnishings, decor, layout, and signs identified with Franchised Health and Fitness Centers, together with advice and consultation concerning them.

        2. A pre-opening training program conducted at Company's training school and at a Franchised Health and Fitness Center.

        3. Opening supervision and assistance from employees of

Company at Franchisee's premises.

4. Opening promotion programs conducted under the direction of Company's Market Department.

5. The Company's confidential standard business policies and operations data instruction manuals (hereinafter collectively called "Manual"), a copy of which is (or will be) delivered and loaned to Franchisee for the term hereof.

6. Such merchandising, marketing and advertising research data and advice as may be from time to time developed by the Company and deemed by it to be helpful in the operation of Franchised Health and Fitness Centers.

7. Consultation and advice by Company's field supervisors, either by personal visit, telephone, mail, or otherwise, as may from time to time be reasonably required by Franchisee.

8. Such special techniques, instructions, services, and other operational developments as may be from time to time developed by the Company and deemed by it to be helpful in the operation of Franchised Health and Fitness Centers.

II. FRANCHISE GRANT: AREA: TERM

A. *Franchise Grant.*   Subject to the terms and conditions of this Franchise Agreement and the continuing good faith performance thereof by Franchisee, Company grants to Franchisee the franchise to operate a Franchised Health and Fitness Center at the location of the premises; and in consideration of the payment by Franchisee of the royalties and advertising and sales promotion contribution hereinafter specified, Company's licenses to Franchisee for the term hereof the Company's right to use at the premises and in the operation of such health and fitness centers, the name Universal Fitness Centers together with such other insignia, symbols and trademarks which may be approved and authorized by Company from time to time in connection with Franchised Health and Fitness Centers, and the good will derived from such previous use by Company. .

B. *Area.*   This franchise shall be exclusive within a radius of   mile(s) from the boundary of the premises.

C. *Term.*   The term of this Franchise Agreement shall commence on the date Franchisee's health and fitness center opens for business and shall expire at midnight on the day preceding the tenth

(10th) anniversary of said opening, unless sooner terminated in accordance with the terms and conditions hereof.

III. PREMISES

A. The premises at which Franchisee shall operate a franchised health and fitness center are fully described in Exhibit "A" attached hereto. It shall be the obligation of the Franchisee to procure, on its own terms, a suitable location for the operation of a franchised health and fitness center and submit same to Company for approval. The Company shall make the final decision as to the desirability and viability of any proposed health and fitness center location.

B. Franchisee shall conduct business from said location only if and when the premises have been improved with a health and fitness center building and decorated, furnished, and equipped with health and fitness center equipment, furnishing and supplies which meet Company's specifications.

C. During the term of this agreement, the premises shall be used only by the franchised health and fitness center pursuant to the terms of this agreement.

IV. TRAINING

Franchisee will designate itself or another person approved by the Company as a trainee to attend Company's training school. Company approval of trainee shall be based upon results of reasonable testing procedures. All expenses of travel, room, board and wages of trainee shall be paid by Franchisee. A portion of trainee's schooling will consist of in-store training at a Franchised Health and Fitness Center approved by Company. If at any time trainee shall voluntarily withdraw from training, or shall be unable to complete training, or shall fail to demonstrate to the satisfaction of Company an aptitude, spirit, or ability to comprehend and carry out the course of study, methods and procedures being taught, then in such event Company shall have the right to require Franchisee to appoint another trainee to undertake and successfully complete the training course.

V. ROYALTIES AND ADVERTISING CONTRIBUTION

A. *Royalties.* Franchisee agrees in consideration of Company's licensing its use of the name Universal Fitness Centers, together with such other trademarks and service marks as may be authorized for use by Company, to pay a weekly royalty in the amount of ten percent (10%) of Franchisee's gross sales. Royalties shall be paid on or before the Monday of each week and shall be based upon gross sales for the preceding calendar week.

B. *Advertising and Sales Promotion.* The Franchisee agrees, as partial consideration for the grant of this franchise, to pay to Company a weekly advertising and sales promotion contribution. This sum shall be equal to two percent (2%) of Franchisee's gross sales. The advertising and sales promotion contribution shall be paid on or before the Monday of each week and shall be based upon Franchisee's gross sales for the preceding calendar week. The advertising and sales promotion contribution shall be expended by Company at its discretion for advertising and sales promotion both in Franchisee's market area and on a national basis, except for that portion used for creative and production costs of advertising and sales promotion elements, and for those market research expenditures which are directly related to the development and evaluation of the effectiveness of advertising and sales promotion.

C. *Gross Sales Defined.* The term "gross sales" as used in this agreement shall include the sale of all memberships, health and fitness programs, health and fitness equipment, attendant merchandise or services. In the event of the use of vending machines for the sale of food and drink items is ever approved by Company, sales from such vending machines will be included in gross sales. The term "gross sales" shall exclude the amount of any federal, state, county or city sales taxes, excise taxes, or other similar taxes which may now or hereafter be imposed upon or be required to be paid by Franchisee as against its sales on the premises, and it shall also exclude cash received as payment in credit transactions where the extension of credit itself has already been included in the figure upon which the royalty and maximum advertising cost percentage is computed.

D. *Accounting Procedures: Right of Audit.*

1. *Accounting.* Franchise agrees to keep complete records of its business. Franchisee shall furnish monthly profit and loss statements for the preceding month and a profit and loss statement from the beginning of Franchisee's fiscal year to the end of the preceding month. Franchisee shall also submit to Company quarterly balance sheets, the first of which shall be for the period ending three (3) months after the beginning of Franchisee's first fiscal year. All profit and loss statements and balance sheets shall be in accordance with generally accepted

principles of accounting, and shall be submitted to Company not later than the   (   ) day of the month following the period for which the written statement shall be submitted.

2. *Certified Statements.*

   (a) A Franchisee shall submit an annual financial statement as to gross sales, which statement shall be certified to by a certified public accountant within ninety (90) days after the close of its fiscal year.

   (b) In the event Franchisee wishes to apply for an additional franchise, or in the event Franchisee applies to the Company for financial assistance or relief, or seeks a financial arrangement with the Company that differs substantially from existing Company policies, then, in any such event, Franchisee shall be required to submit a complete financial statement which shall be certified by a certified public accountant. The extent of certification shall be determined by the Treasury Department of the Company.

3. *Audits.*   Franchisee agrees that Company or its agents shall, at all reasonable times, have the right to examine or audit the books and accounts of Franchisee to verify the gross sales as reported by Franchisee.

VI. STANDARDS AND UNIFORMITY OF OPERATION

Franchisee agrees that Company's special standardized design and decor of buildings and uniformity of equipment and layout, and adherence to the Manual are essential to the image of a Franchised Health and Fitness Center. In recognition of the mutual benefits accruing from maintaining uniformity of appearance, service, products, and marketing procedures, it is mutually covenanted and agreed:

A. *Building and Premises.*   Except as specifically authorized by Company, Franchisee shall not alter the appearance of the improvements or the premises. Franchisee will promptly make all repairs and alterations to the health and fitness center and to the premises as may be determined by Company to be reasonably necessary. Franchisee will paint its health and fitness center when Company, in the exercise of reasonable discretion, determines it advisable, and paint colors will be in accordance with specifications of Company.

B. *Signs.*   Franchisee agrees to display Company's names and trademarks at the premises, in the manner authorized by Company. Franchisee agrees to maintain and display signs reflecting the current image of Company. The color, size, design, and location of said signs shall be as specified by Company. Franchisee shall not place additional signs or posters on the premises without the written consent of Company.

C. *Equipment.* Franchisee is acquiring through Company and other approved sources by purchase or lease, machinery, equipment, furnishings, signs, and other personal property (hereinafter collectively called equipment). Appended hereto as Exhibit B is a list of equipment which must be used by Franchisee in the operation of its business. Franchisee agrees to maintain such equipment in excellent working condition. As items of equipment become obsolete or mechanically impaired to the extent that they require replacement, Franchisee will replace such items with either the same or substantially the same types and kinds of equipment as are being installed in Franchised Health and Fitness Centers at the time replacement becomes necessary. All equipment used in Franchisee's Health and Fitness Center, whether purchased from Company or other approved suppliers pursuant to Paragraph F herein, shall meet Company specifications.

D. *Vending Machines.* Telephone booths, newspaper racks, juke boxes, gum machines, games, rides, or any coin vending machines will not be installed on the premises without the written approval of Company. Company shall not object to the installation of a coin telephone which meets Company specifications, including its location on the premises.

E. *Health and Fitness Programs and Services.* Franchisee agrees to establish, provide and offer health and fitness programs specified by Company, to follow all specifications, methods, and formulae of Company as to standards, procedure, content, and use of the health and fitness programs provided, and to use no other programs, methods or other like devices of any kind without the prior written approval of Company.

Franchisee agrees that it will operate its health and fitness center in accordance with the standards, specifications, and procedures set forth in the Manual. Franchisee agrees further that changes, revisions or modifications is such standards, specifications and procedures may become necessary from time to time and agrees to accept as reasonable such modifications, revisions and additions to the aforementioned which Company believes, in the good faith exercise of its judgment, to be necessary. Franchisee agrees not to deviate from the standards as set and maintained by Company in the operation of Franchised Health and Fitness Center.

Franchise shall remain open for business from   to daily and in conformity of all state "Blue Laws" and/or local ordinances restricting those days of operation, unless Company consents to other hours or days at the request of Franchisee. Company recognizes that considerations peculiar to the location of Franchisee's premises may make it desirable to alter the aforesaid hours of operation, and Company will not unreasonably withhold its consent to modify the aforesaid hours of operation.

F. *Alternate Suppliers.*   Irrespective of any other provision hereof, if Franchisee gives Company notice sufficiently in advance to permit supplier and specification verification and testing, that it wishes to purchase equipment for the health and fitness center from reputable, dependable sources other than Company or its designated or previously approved sources of supply, Company will not unreasonably withhold the prompt approval of such purchases provided said purchases conform to the appearance, quality, size, and uniformity standards and other specifications of Company. Company may require that samples from alternate suppliers be delivered to Company or to a designated independent testing laboratory for testing before approval and use. A charge not to exceed the actual cost of the test may be made by Company or by an independent testing laboratory designated by Company, and shall be paid for by Franchisee.

G. *Right to Entry and Inspection.*   Company or its authorized agent and representative shall have the right to enter and inspect the premises and examine the operation of the franchise for the purpose of ascertaining that Franchisee is operating the health and fitness center in accordance with the terms of this agreement and the Manual. Inspection shall be conducted during normal business hours. Company shall notify Franchisee of any deficiences detected during inspection and Franchisee shall diligently correct any such deficiencies. Upon notification by Company that any equipment or aspect of the operations does not meet the specifications, standards, and requirements of Company, Franchisee shall immediately desist and refrain from the further use thereof.

VII. INSURANCE INDEMNIFICATION

A. Franchisee agrees to secure and pay premiums thereon for the term of this Franchise Agreement, a Comprehensive General Liability Policy, including Products Liability, in the amount of bodily injury liability, and   property damage liability, or in such other amounts as Company may reasonably request, for the operation on the premises. Franchisee agrees to name Company in said policy as additional named insured and such policy shall stipulate that Company shall receive a thirty (30) day written notice of cancellation. Original or duplicate copies of all insurance policies shall be furnished promptly to Company, together with proof of payment therefor. All policies shall be renewed and evidence of renewal mailed to Company prior to expiration date.

B. Franchisee is responsible for all loss or damage and contractual liabilities to third persons originating in or in connection with the operation of the Franchised Health and Fitness Center and for all claims or demands for damages to property or for injury, illness or death of persons directly or indirectly resulting therefrom; and Franchisee agrees to defend, indemnify and save Company harmless of, from, and with respect to any such claims, loss, or damage.

VIII. TAXES

Franchisee shall promptly pay when due all taxes levied or assessed by reason of its operation and performance under this agreement. Franchisee further agrees to secure and pay premiums on a Worker's Compensation policy covering all its employees and, if applicable, to pay state unemployment tax, state sales tax (including any sales or use tax on equipment purchased or leased), and all other taxes and expenses of operating the Franchised Health and Fitness Center on the premises. In the event of any bona fide dispute as to the liability for the taxes assessed against Franchisee, Franchisee may contest the validity or the amount of the tax in accordance with procedures of the taxing authority. In no event, however, shall Franchisee permit a tax sale or seizure by levy of execution or similar writ to warrant to occur against the premises or equipment.

IX. OPTION AT END OF TERM

Provided that Franchisee shall have substantially compiled with all of the terms and conditions of this agreement between Franchisee and Company, and shall have substantially compiled with the operating standards and criteria established for Franchised Health and Fitness Center, then at the expiration of the term hereof, Company will offer Franchisee the opportunity to remain a Franchisee for one additional period of ten (10) years, provided that:

A. Franchisee shall not be in default on any obligation due Company, and if said default shall not be cured sixty (60) days prior to the renewal, Company may elect to refuse a renewal, by giving notice of such intent to Franchisee thirty (30) days prior to renewal date.

B. Franchisee shall agree to make such capital expenditures as may be reasonably required to renovate and modernize the premises, signs, and equipment, so as to reflect the then current image of Company.

C. Franchisee must have the right to remain in possession of the premises, or other premises acceptable to Company, for the new term. If Franchisee elects (or is required) to relocate, then Franchisee shall pay Company's reasonable expenses in relocating, developing or evaluating the new premises. Company shall not be required to extend its credit or resources in obtaining financing for premises or equipment.

D. Franchisee shall execute a new franchise agreement on the form then being used by Company, which may differ as to royalty and advertising contributions.

E. Franchisee shall pay the then current franchise fee as established by Company, and shall reimburse Company for the costs and other expenses incurred incident to the exercise of Franchisee's option.

F. Franchisee shall give Company written notice of its desire to exercise its option to continue as a franchisee not less than twelve (12) months prior to the expiration of the term of this agreement.

X. ASSIGNMENT: CONDITIONS AND LIMITATIONS

A. Franchisee shall neither sell, assign, transfer, nor encumber this agreement or any right or interest therein or thereunder, nor suffer or permit any such assignment, transfer, or encumbrance to occur by operation of law unless the written consent of Company be first had and obtained. The assignment of any interest, other than as provided in this article, shall constitute a material breach of this franchise agreement.

B. In the event of the death or disability of a franchisee, Company shall consent to the transfer of the interest to Franchisee's spouse, heirs, or relatives, by blood or by marriage, whether such a transfer is made by Will or by operation of law if, at the sole discretion and judgment of Company, such person or persons obtaining said interest shall be capable of conducting said business in a manner satisfactory to Company.

C. Franchisee, its heirs or personal representatives, may sell and assign its rights under this agreement to a bona fide purchaser as hereinafter set forth, providing Franchisee shall first offer to sell to Company upon the same terms and conditions as offered to other prospective purchasers. All offers shall be fully set forth in writing and Company shall have ten (10) days within which to accept any offer. If Company has not accepted the offer within ten (10) days, Franchisee may conclude the sale to the prospective purchaser provided that Franchisee is not in default hereunder and further provided that Company may impose reasonable conditions on any assignment permitted hereunder which may include, without limitation, the following:

1. Assignor must satisfy fully all obligations to Company or others arising out of the operation of the Franchised Health and Fitness Center or Assignee must agree to assume and discharge all obligations to Company or others arising out of the operation of the Franchised Health and Fitness Center.

2. Assignee must satisfactorily demonstrate to Company that it meets at least the same financial and managerial criteria required of the Franchisee in qualifying for this agreement.

3. Assignee shall have sufficient equity capital in the business to result in a debt-to-equity ratio of one to one, or such other debt-equity as may be approved by the chief financial officer of Company.

4. Assignee must agree to meet with Company's staff personnel and agree to take the personnel tests to determine his aptitude and ability to own and operate a Franchised Health and Fitness Center.

5. Assignee must agree to avail itself of the training required of new franchisees and pay Company's then current charges therefor.

6. Assignee, prior to effectiveness of the assignment, shall pay to Company the sum of $ as an assignment expense. If more than one health and fitness center is assigned, there is a charge of $150.00 for each additional health and fitness center included in the same transaction.

D. If Franchisee desires to conduct business in a corporate capacity, Company will consent to the assignment of this agreement to a corporation approved by Company provided Franchisee complies with the provisions hereinafter specified and any other condition that Company may require, including a limitation on the number of stockholders of the assignee corporation. Such assignee corporation shall be closely held and shall not engage in any business activity other than those directly related to the operation of franchised health and fitness centers pursuant to the terms and conditions of franchise agreements with Company. There shall be no transfer charge imposed by Company if such assignment is made within ninety (90) days after the execution of this agreement.

If the rights of Franchisee are assigned to a corporation, the Franchisee shall be the legal and beneficial owner of the stock of the assignee corporation and shall act as such corporation's principal officer. Provided Franchisee retains controlling interest of the assignee corporation, it may sell, transfer or assign stock in such assignee corporation to members of its immediate family or to a trustee in trust for same, to its operating managers, or to other franchisees of Company if the franchisee to whom such stock interest is assigned is not then in default of any of the terms of other franchise agreements with Company, Franchisee may sell, assign or transfer the controlling interest of such assignee corporation under the provisions of Paragraph C of this Article. The sale, transfer, or assignment of any stock interest of such assignee corporation, other than as herein provided, without the written consent of Company, shall constitute a material breach of this Franchise Agreement permitting Company, at its sole option, to terminate same forthwith. The Articles of Incorporation and the By-Laws of the assignee corporation shall reflect that the issuance and transfer of shares of stock are restricted, and all stock certificates shall bear the following legend, which shall be printed legibly and conspicuously on the face of each stock certificate:

The transfer of this stock is subject to the terms and conditions of a franchise agreement dated   : Reference is made to said franchise agreement and to restrictive provisions of the charter and by-laws of this corporation.

Franchisee acknowledges that the purpose of the aforesaid restriction is to protect Company's trademarks, service marks, trade and operating procedures as well as Company's general high reputation and image, and is for the mutual benefit of Company,

Franchisee and other franchisees and that violation of this provision shall be cause for cancellation of this Agreement and termination of the Franchise granted herein.

E. The Company may, at any time during the duration of this agreement, assign, transfer or convey its interest in and to the franchise to a party of its choosing. Any such assignment is without limitation. In the event of an assignment of Company's interest, the obligations and duties of the Franchisee shall remain the same.

XI. LIMITATIONS OF FRANCHISE

A. *Trademarks, Trade Names, and Trade Secrets.*

1. The Franchisee acknowledges the Franchisor's sole and exclusive right (except for certain rights granted under existing and future license agreements) to use the Franchisor's Trademarks in connection with the products, accessories and services to which they are or may be applied by the Franchisor, and represents, warrants and agrees that neither during the term of this Agreement nor after the expiration or other termination hereof, shall the Franchisee directly or indirectly contest or aid in contesting the validity or ownership of the Company's Universal Fitness Centers Trademarks and Trade Names and the goodwill now or hereafter associated therewith. Any and all goodwill associated with or identified by the Company's Universal Fitness Centers Trademarks and Trade Names shall inure directly and exclusively to the benefit and is the property of the Franchisor.

3. No Franchisee advertising or other use of the Franchisor's Trademarks and Trade Names shall contain any statement or material which may, in the judgment of the Franchisor, be in bad taste or inconsistent with the Franchisor's public image, or tend to bring disparagement, ridicule or scorn upon the Franchisor, the Trademarks or Trade Names or any advertising material which has been disapproved by the Franchisor for the reasons set forth in this paragraph.

4. The Franchisee shall adopt and use the Company's Universal Fitness Centers Trademarks only in the manner expressly approved by the Franchisor. The Franchisee shall advertise and promote the health and fitness center only under the Company's Universal Fitness Centers Trademarks and Trade Names without any accompanying words or symbols except

as otherwise required by law and approved in writing by the Franchisor.

5. The Franchisee acknowledges and agrees that the Franchisor is the owner of all proprietary rights in and to the health and fitness center programs, systems and methods and all other products, services and materials related there to as described in the Franchisor's Manual, training guides and informational materials, and that the program formulae and health and fitness center systems and methods in their entirety constitute trade secrets of the Franchisor which are revealed to the Franchisee in confidence, and that no right is given to or acquired by the Franchisee to disclose, duplicate, license, sell, or reveal any portion thereof to any person other than an employee of the Franchisee required by his work to be familiar with relevant portions thereof. The Franchisee further acknowledges that the program formulae, Standards and other similar materials furnished to Franchisee hereunder are and will remain the property of the Franchisor, and must be returned to the Franchisor immediately upon the termination of this Agreement.

B. *No Agency.*

1. Nothing contained in this Agreement shall constitute the Franchisee as an agent, legal representative, partner, subsidiary, joint venturer, or employee of Company. Franchisee shall have no right or power to, and shall not bind or obligate Company in any way, manner, or thing whatsoever, nor represent that it has any right to do so.

2. In all public records and in its relationship with other persons, on letterheads and business forms, Franchisee shall indicate its independent ownership of said business, and that it is only a franchisee of Company. Franchisee agrees to exhibit on the premises in a place designated by Company, a notification that it is a franchisee of Company.

XII. DEFAULT: TERMINATION

A. *Default.* The occurrence of any of the following events shall constitute good cause for Company, at its option and without prejudice to any other rights or remedies provided for hereunder or by law or equity, to terminate this agreement.

1. If Franchisee shall be adjudicated a bankrupt, becomes insol-

vent, or if a receiver (permanent or temporary) of its property or any part thereof is appointed by a court of competent authority; if it makes a general assignment for the benefit of creditors, or if a final judgment remains unsatisfied of record for thirty (30) days or longer (unless supersedeas bond is filed) or if execution is levied against Franchisee's business or property, or suit to foreclose any lien or mortgage against the premises or equipment is instituted against Franchisee and not dismissed within thirty (30) days; or if Franchisee defaults in the performance of any term, condition or obligation in payment of any indebtedness to Company, its suppliers or others arising out of the purchase of supplies or purchase or lease of equipment for operation of its said health and fitness center, and if any such default is not cured within thirty (30) days after written notice by Company to Franchisee.

2. If Franchisee defaults in the payment of royalties or advertising due hereunder or fails to submit profit and loss statements or other financial statements or data or reports on gross sales as provided herein, and fails to cure said default within thirty (30) days after notification thereof, or if Franchisee makes any false statement in connection therewith.

3. If Franchisee fails to maintain the standards as set forth in this agreement, and as may be supplemented by the Manual, as to cleanliness, health and sanitation, and uniformity (including without limitation, the quality of the Company's health and fitness program), and said failure or default shall continue after notification; or if Franchisee repeatedly commits violations of such provisions.

4. If Franchisee suffers a violation of any law, ordinance, rule, or regulation of a governmental agency in connection with the operation of the Franchised Health and Fitness Center, and permits the same to go uncorrected after notification thereof, unless there is a bona fide dispute as to the violation or legality of such law, ordinance, rule or regulation, and Franchisee promptly resorts to courts or forums of appropriate jurisdiction to contest such violation or legality.

5. If Franchisee ceases to do business at the premises or defaults under any lease or sublease or loses its right to the possession of the premises. Provided, however, that if the loss of possession is attributed to the proper governmental exercise of eminent domain, or if the premises are damaged or destroyed by a

disaster of such nature that the premises cannot be reasonably restored, then Franchisee may relocate to other premises approved by Company for the balance of the term hereof.

6. If Franchisee violates any other term or condition of this agreement and Franchisee fails to cure such violation within thirty (30) days after written notice from Company to cure same.

7. The Franchisee may not, at any time during the duration of this agreement, terminate this agreement without prior written approval of Company.

B. *Effect of Termination.*

1. Upon termination of this agreement by lapse of time or upon occasion of default, Franchisee's right to use in any manner the trademark Universal Fitness Centers or any other mark registered by Company or insignia or slogan used in connection therewith, or any confusingly similar trademark, service mark, trade name, or insignia shall terminate forthwith. Franchisee shall not thereafter, directly or indirectly, identify itself in any manner as a Universal Fitness Centers franchisee, or publicly identify itself as a former Universal Fitness Centers franchisee or use any of Company's trade secrets, signs, symbols, devices, equipment, programs, procedures, or other materials constituting part of the health and fitness system. Franchisee grants to Company the option to purchase all equipment and any and all insignia bearing Company's trade name or marks thereon at the lower of cost or fair market value at the time of termination.

2. Franchisee agrees that, upon termination of this agreement by lapse of time or default, it will immediately make such removals or changes in signs and colors of buildings and structures as Company shall reasonably request so as to distinguish effectively said premises from their former appearance and from any other Franchised Health and Fitness Center. If Franchisee shall fail to make such changes forthwith, then Company may peaceably or by use of legal process enter upon Franchisee's premises and make such changes at Franchisee's expense.

3. In the event of termination for any default of Franchisee, the extent of all damage which Company has suffered by virtue of such default shall be and remain a lien in favor of Company against any and all of the personal property, machinery, fixtures, and equipment owned by Franchisee on the premises at the time of such default.

XIII. ARBITRATION

A. If this agreement shall be terminated by Company and Franchisee shall dispute Company's right of termination or the reasonableness thereof, the parties shall submit said dispute for binding arbitration as hereinafter set forth:

    1. Each party shall select one arbitrator and the two shall select a third, and, failing selection of an arbitrator by either or by the two selected by the parties, the third arbitrator shall be selected by the American Arbitration Association or any successor thereof. The arbitration proceeding shall be conducted in accordance with the rules of the American Arbitration Association or any successor thereof. Judgment upon an award of the majority of arbitrators filed in a court of competent jurisdiction shall be binding.

    2. If Company or Franchisee shall operate the health and fitness center pending the adjudication of the matter in dispute, said party shall be considered the trustee of the prevailing party and shall be required to make a full and complete accounting of such trusteeship.

B. In the event that any other dispute arises between the parties hereto in connection with the terms or provisions of this agreement, either party, by written notice to the other party, may elect to submit the dispute to binding arbitration in accordance with the foregoing procedure. Such right shall not be exclusive of any other rights which a party may have to pursue a course of legal action in an appropriate forum.

XIV. MISCELLANEOUS: GENERAL CONDITIONS

A. *Interpretation.* The preamble recitals are incorporated in and made a part of this agreement. Titles of articles and paragraphs are used for convenience only and are not a part of the text. All terms used in any one number or gender shall be construed to include any other number or gender as the context may require. All exhibits attached hereto are specifically incorporated into this agreement by reference and are made an integral part hereof.

B. *Entire Agreement.* This agreement constitutes the entire agreement of the parties and supersedes all prior negotiations, commitments, representations and undertakings of the parties with respect to the subject matter hereof. Franchisee agrees that Company has made no representations including execution of this agreement which are not included herein.

C. *Non-Waiver.* The failure of Company to exercise any right, power, or option given to it hereunder, or to insist upon strict compliance with the terms hereof by Franchisee, shall not constitute a waiver of the terms and conditions of this agreement with respect to any other or subsequent breach thereof, nor a waiver by Company of its rights at any time thereafter to require exact and strict compliance with all terms hereof. The rights or remedies hereunder are cumulative to any other rights or remedies which may be granted by law.

D. *Governing Law.*

   1. This agreement shall become valid when executed and accepted by Company at   , Massachusetts, and it shall be governed and construed under and in accordance with the laws of the Commonwealth of Massachusetts.

   2. Anything herein to the contrary notwithstanding, Franchisee shall conduct its business in a lawful manner; and it will faithfully comply with all applicable laws or regulations of the state, city or other political subdivisions in which it conducts its said business.

E. *Severability.* If any provision of this agreement is held invalid by arbitration or court decree, such finding shall not invalidate the remainder of this agreement.

F. *Notices.*

   1. All notices to the Company shall be in writing and shall be delivered or sent by registered or certified mail, postage fully prepaid, addressed to its offices at
   Massachusetts, or at such other address as Company shall from time to time designate in writing.

   2. All notices to Franchisee shall be in writing and shall be sent by registered or certified mail, addressed to Franchisee at the premises or at such other address as Franchisee may from time to time designate in writing.

G. *Employees.* Company shall have no control over employees of Franchisee, including the terms and conditions of their employment.

H. *Competition with Company.* Franchisee agrees that during the term of this agreement it shall not engage in any health and fitness business which is the same or similar to Company's business. Franchisee further agrees that, for a period of twenty-four (24) months after termination of this agreement, it will not engage in any business the same or similar to Company's business within an area of five (5) miles from the premises without the prior written consent of the Company. In applying for Company's consent, Francise has the burden of establishing that any such activity by it will not involve the use of benefits provided hereby or constitute unfair competition with Company or other franchisees.

I. *Interference with Employment Relations of Others.* Franchisee shall not attempt to attain an unfair advantage over other Company franchisees or Company by soliciting for employment any person who is, at the time of such solicitation, employed by other Company franchisees or Company, nor shall Franchisee directly or indirectly induce any such person to leave his or her employment as aforesaid.

J. *Liability of Multiple Franchisees.* If the Franchisee consists of more than one natural person, their liability under this contract shall be deemed to be joint and several.

K. *Modification.* This agreement may only be modified or amended by a document of equal dignity. The Company shall undertake no modifications of this agreement without the prior written approval of Franchisee, and Franchisee shall undertake no modifications of this agreement without the prior written approval of Company.

L. *Execution.* This agreement is executed in triplicate originals, any one of which may be introduced into evidence as conclusive proof of the context thereof. The agreement shall be binding upon the parties, their heirs, executors, personal representatives, successors, or assigns.

IN WITNESS WHEREOF, Company has caused these presents to be executed in its name and on its behalf by its proper corporate officers, and Franchisee has hereunto affixed its hand and seal all on the day and year first above written.

FRANCHISOR   FRANCHISEE

By _____   By _____

GLOSSARY OF TERMS

ACTUARIAL METHOD. The method of determining loan repayment amounts based on the principles of compound interest; used by financial institutions.

ALLOCATION. The process of distributing an expense to a number of items or areas.

AMORTIZATION. A reduction in a debt or fund by periodic payments covering interest and part of the principal.

AMORTIZATION SCHEDULE. A tabular presentation of reduction of a debt.

ANNUITY. A series of equal payments over a period of time.

ASSESSED VALUATION. The taxable value of a property.

ASSET, CURRENT. An asset that is either currently in the form of cash or is expected to be converted into cash within a short period, usually one year.

ASSET, FIXED. Tangible property of relatively long life that generally is used in the production of goods and services.

ASSET, FIXED, GAIN (OR LOSS) ON THE DISPOSITION OF. Difference between net book value and amount actually realized from sale.

ASSET, NET BOOK VALUE OF. Cost less accumulated depreciation.

ASSETS. Everything a company owns or is due to it: *current assets*, such as cash, investments, money due, materials, and inventories; *fixed assets*, such as buildings and machinery; and *intangible assets*, such as patents and good will. Property or property right owned by the business which is valuable either because it will be converted into cash or because it is expected to benefit future operations and which was acquired at a measurable cost.

AUTHORIZED STOCK. The maximum number of shares allowed by a corporation's charter.

BALANCE SHEET. A statement showing the nature and amount of a company's assets, liabilities, and capital *on a given date*. In dollar amounts, the balance sheet shows what the company owned, what it owed, and the ownership interest in the company of its stockholders. A *consolidated balance sheet* is one showing the financial condition of a corporation and its subsidiaries.

BASE YEAR.   A year chosen for comparison of prices as the 100%, or normal, year from which index numbers are computed.

BOND.   A written promise to pay the holder a sum of money at a certain time (more than one year after issue) at a stated rate of interest. Generally issued in multiples of $1,000. A debt due in less than one year from date of issue is usually called a *note*.

BOOK VALUE.   Book value of a stock is determined from a company's records, by adding all assets (generally excluding such intangibles as good will), then deducting all debts and other liabilities, plus the liquidation price of any preferred issues. The sum arrived at is divided by the number of common shares outstanding and the result is book value per common share. Book value of the assets of a company or a security may have little or no significant relationship to market value.

CAPITAL.   The amount that an individual, partner, or stockholder has invested in his business; net worth of a business; the owner's (owners') claim to his (their) assets.

CAPITAL STOCK.   All shares representing ownership of a business, including preferred and common.

CAPITALIZATION.   Total amount of the various securities issued by a corporation. Capitalization may include bonds, debentures, and preferred and common stock. Bonds are usually carried on the books of the issuing company in terms of their par or face value. Preferred and common shares may be carried in terms of par or stated value. Stated value may be an arbitrary figure decided upon by the directors, or may represent the amount received by the company from the sale of the securities at the time of issuance.

CASH DISCOUNT.   A reduction of 1–3% in the amount due the seller on a purchase, granted for early payment.

CASH FLOW.   Reported net income of a corporation plus amounts charged off, such as depreciation and charges to reserves (which are bookkeeping deductions and not paid out in actual dollars), plus the decrease in accounts receivable or less the increase in accounts receivable for the period.

CHARTER.   A formal document, issued by the state, permitting the establishment of a corporation.

COLLATERAL.   Securities or other property pledged by a borrower to secure repayment of a loan.

COMMON STOCK. Securities that represent an ownership interest in a corporation. If the company has also issued preferred stock, both common and preferred have ownership rights. However, the preferred normally has prior claim on dividends and, in the event of liquidation, on assets as well. Claims of both common and preferred stockholders are junior to claims of bondholders or other creditors of the company. Common stockholders assume the greater risk, but generally exercise the greater control and may gain the greater regard· in the form of dividends and capital appreciation.

CONVERTIBLE. A bond, debenture, or preferred share that may be exchanged by the owner for common stock or another security, usually of the same company, in accordance with the terms of the issue.

CORPORATION. Entity or organization created by operation of law with rights of doing business essentially the same as those of an individual. The entity has continuous existence regardless of that of its owners, and limits liability of owners to the amount invested in the organization. The entity ceases to exist only if dissolved according to proper legal process.

COST OF GOODS SOLD. The price paid for the merchandise that has been sold by a trading business; beginning inventory + net purchases − ending inventory = cost of goods sold.

CREDIT ENTRY. An entry on the right-hand side of an account. The record of a decrease in any asset account. The record of an increase in an equity account.

CURRENT ASSETS. Those assets of a company that are reasonably expected to be realized in cash, or sold, or consumed during the normal operating cycle of the business. These include cash, U. S. Government bonds, receivables, inventories, and money due usually within one year.

CURRENT LIABILITIES. Money owed and payable by a company, usually within one year.

CURRENT RATIO. The comparison of current assets to current liabilities; standard is 2:1. Total current assets divided by total current liabilities.

DEPRECIATION. Charges against earnings to write off the cost, less salvage value, of an asset over its estimated useful life. It is a bookkeeping entry and does not represent any cash outlay, nor are any funds earmarked for the purpose.

DIVIDEND. The payment designated by the board of directors to be distributed pro rata among the shares outstanding. On preferred shares, it is generally a fixed amount. On common shares, the dividend varies with the fortunes of the company and the amount of cash on hand, and may be omitted at the discretion of the directors if business is poor or if they determine to withhold earnings to invest in plant and equipment, research and development, and so on. Sometimes a company will pay a dividend out of past earnings even if it is not currently operating at a profit.

EARNINGS PER SHARE. Net earnings divided by the number of shares outstanding.

EARNINGS, RETAINED. Cumulative increase in the stockholder's equity as a result of company operations.

EQUITY. The ownership interest of common and preferred stockholders in a company.

EXPENSE. A decrease in owners' equity resulting from the operation of the business.

EXPENSE, ACCRUED. A liability account arising from expenses that are incurred prior to the related expenditure; example, accrued wages.

EXPENSE, NONOPERATING. Expense not related to company's business operations.

EXPENSE, OPERATING. The costs associated with sales and administrative activities as distinct from those associated with production.

EXPENSE, PREPAID. An expense recognized after a relevant expenditure; an expense for future benefits.

FICA TAX. (Federal Insurance Contributions Act Tax) A required payroll deduction, the amount of which must be matched by the employer, that provides for old-age pensions, survivors' benefits, disability payments, and Medicare.

FIFO: The first-in-first-out method of inventory valuation, which assumes that the goods that enter inventory first are the first to be sold.

FINANCIAL STATEMENT. A formal document stating the results of business activity.

FIXED ASSET. An asset whose life will extend beyond the next business activity.

FIXED CHARGES. A company's expenses, such as bond interest, that it has agreed to pay whether or not earned.

INVESTED FUNDS, RETURN ON. Net income divided by either (1) funds invested by stockholder or (2) funds invested by stockholders and long-term creditors.

ISSUED STOCK. Stock that has been sold by the corporation for whom the stock was authorized.

JOURNAL. Preliminary records of transactions, kept in chronological order.

LIABILITIES. All the claims against a corporation. Liabilities include accounts and wages and salaries payable, dividends declared payable, accrued taxes payable, and fixed or long-term liabilities, such as mortgage bonds, debentures, and bank loans.

LIABILITY, CURRENT.   Obligation that becomes due within a short time, usually one year.

LIFO.   The last-in-first-out method of inventory valuation which assumes that the goods that enter inventory last are the first to be sold.

LIQUID ASSETS.   Those assets easily convertible into cash; marketable securities, receivables, and cash itself.

LIQUIDITY.   Is a measure of the quality and adequacy of current assets to meet current obligations as they come due.

LONG-TERM LIABILITY.   A liability due at a time after the next business year.

LOSS, NET.   Excess of total expenses over total revenues in a given period.

MAKER.   The person signing a promissory note; the giver of the note.

MARKET VALUE OF STOCK.   The price at which stock is sold by a stockholder to a third party.

MARKUP.   That amount added to cost to arrive at the original retail price; expenses + desired profit.

NET ASSET VALUE.   The worth of a share of stock, determined by dividing the net worth of the corporation by the number of outstanding shares.

NET PROFIT (LOSS).   Profit remaining after deducting all operating expenses; gross profit − operating expenses.

NET WORTH.   Total assets less amounts due creditors. It includes both capital stock and surplus.

NOTE.   A written promise to repay a loan.

NOTE RECEIVABLE.   A debt that is evidenced by a note or other written acknowledgment.

OBSOLESCENCE.   Loss of value of a fixed asset arising because improved assets become available.

OUTSTANDING STOCK.   Stock in the hands of stockholders; stock that is issued but not reacquired by the issuing corporation.

OVERHEAD RATE.   Method of allocating overhead to the various products manufactured.

OWNERS, MAJORITY.   Owners of a majority of the stock in a corporation.

OWNERS, MINORITY.   Owners of a minority of the stock in a corporation.

OWNERS, RESIDUAL.   Owners of instruments with junior claim in participation in dividends and against assets in the event of liquidation.

PAR.   In the case of a common share, par means a dollar amount assigned to the share by the company's charter. Par value may also be used to compute the dollar amount of the common shares or the balance sheet. Par value has little significance so far as market value of common stock is concerned. Many companies today issue no-par stock, but give a stated per-share value on the balance sheet. Par at one time was supposed to represent the value of the original investment behind each share in cash, goods, or services. In the case of preferred shares and bonds, however, par is important. It often signifies the dollar value upon which dividends on preferred stocks, and interest on bonds, are figured. The issuer of a 3% bond promises to pay that percentage of the bond's par value annually (see: Capitalization).

PARTNER.   One of the owners of an unincorporated business.

PARTNERSHIP.   An association of two or more persons co-owning a business for profit.

PATENT.   A right to a process or a product granted to its inventor or his assignee for his exclusive use.

PHYSICAL INVENTORY, TAKING OF.   Counting all merchandise on hand, usually at the end of an accounting period.

PREFERRED STOCK.   A class of stock with a claim on the company's earnings, at a specified rate, before payment may be made on the common stock. Also usually entitled to priority over common stock if the company liquidates. *Cumulative preferred stock* has a provision that if one or more dividends are omitted, the omitted dividends must be paid before dividends may be paid on the company's common stock.

PRESENT VALUE.   The value in current dollars of a future sum.

PRICE-EARNINGS RATIO.   Average market price of a company's stock divided by earnings per share.

PROFIT AND LOSS STATEMENT OR INCOME STATEMENT.   A statement summarizing the income and expenses of a company to show net profit or loss for the period involved.

PROFIT, GROSS.   Sales minus cost of goods sold.

PROMISSORY NOTE.   A written promise to pay a sum of money at a specified future date.

PROPRIETOR.   The owner of an unincorporated business.

PRORATE.   To spread equally over a period of time; allocate.

REDEMPTION.   The process of repaying the stockholders (or bondholders) of a corporation for their investments (or loans).

RESIDUAL VALUE.   Estimated scrap value of a tangible asset.

RETAINED EARNINGS.   Those profits kept in a corporation and not distributed as dividends.

RETURN ON STOCKHOLDERS' INVESTMENT. Net income divided by average owners' equity for the period.

REVENUE. An increase in owners' equity arising from operations.

SERVICE BUSINESS. A firm dealing in nonmerchandising activities.

SIMPLE INTEREST. Interest on principal only, as compared to compound interest which is interest on both principal and accumulated interest.

SINKING FUND. Money regularly set aside by a company to redeem its bonds or preferred stock from time to time as specified in the indenture or charter.

SOCIAL SECURITY TAX. See FICA tax.

SOLE PROPRIETORSHIP. A business owned by one person.

SOLVENCY. Ability to meet interest costs and repayment schedules associated with long-term obligations.

STOCK, AUTHORIZED. The number of shares authorized by directors, for issuance to investors.

STOCK, COMMON. A residual share in the ownership of a corporation after liabilities and other property claims have been satisfied, and entitling the owner to dividends and a vote in certain matters.

STOCK DIVIDEND. A dividend paid in securities rather than in cash. The dividend may be in additional shares of the issuing company, or in shares of another company (usually a subsidiary) held by the company.

STOCK, PREFERRED. A class of stock entitled to preferential treatment with regard to dividends or with regard to the distribution of assets in the event of liquidation.

STOCKHOLDER. An owner of an incorporated business, the ownership being evidenced by stock certificates.

SURPLUS. The excess of assets over creditor liabilities and capital stocks. When accumulated from profits, it is called retained earnings. If from other sources, it is called *capital surplus*, which is sometimes broken down into categories, such as paid-in surplus, recapitalization surplus, and so on. The sale of stock at prices above the par value results in *paid-in-surplus* equal to the excess of sale price over par value.

SURPLUS, CAPITAL. An increase in owners' equity not generated through the company's earnings.

SURPLUS, EARNED. Obsolete name for retained earnings.

TANGIBLE ASSET. A physical asset; a plant asset.

TAXABLE INCOME. Income on which income tax is computed; gross income − both exemptions and personal deductions.

TRADEMARK. A right given for a name or symbol, granting its creator exclusive use.

TRADING BUSINESS. A firm whose primary activity is the purchase and sale of merchandise.

TREASURY STOCK. Stock issued by a company but later reacquired. It may be held in the company's treasury indefinitely, reissued to the public, or retired. Treasury stock receives no dividends, and has no vote while held by the company.

TURNOVER. The rate at which an asset is replaced within a given time period; usually refers to annual rate of replacement of stock (inventory turnover) or payment of accounts (accounts receivable turnover).

U. S. RULE. In debt reduction, all payments are applied first to interest on the unpaid balance, and second, to reduction of principal.

WITHHOLDING TAX. Income tax deducted from gross wages; "pay-as-you-go" income tax.

WORKING CAPITAL. The readily convertible capital required in a business to permit the regular carrying forward of operations free from financial embarrassment. In accounting, the excess of current assets over current liabilities as of any date.

WRITE DOWN. To reduce the value of an asset to its current market value.

YIELD. Also known as *return*. The dividends or interest paid by a company expressed as a percentage of the current price, or, if you own the security, of the price you paid originally. Also, the return on one's investment, expressed as an annual rate of earnings based on your cost.

INDEX

Abandonment, and broker's commission,
200–201
Accountants:
  and closing, 169, 173
  in investigation process, 62
  in negotiation process, 163–164
  role of, 203
  selecting, 60–61
Accounting procedures, in franchise
    agreement, 241–242
Accounts receivable:
  in contract, 175
  valuation of, 199
Acquisition, business, competition for,
    101. See also Competition
Advertising:
  of brokers, 47
  in buyer's search, 42–43
  in franchise agreement, 91, 240–241
  of franchises, 78
  newspaper, 49–51
  on Projected Income Statement, 107
  in yellow pages, 177
Advisors:
  "from afar," 166
  selecting, 60–61
Agreement for sale of assets:
  adjustments in, 227–228
  assets retained by seller in, 222–223
  and brokers, 227
  casualty in, 226
  closing in, 228
  conditions in, 226–227
  covenant not to compete in, 225

  miscellaneous in, 228
  purchase price in, 223–224
  sale of assets in, 221–222
  seller's obligation pending closing in,
    226
  seller's warranties in, 225
American Arbitration Association, 181
Appraisers:
  business, 207
  certified real estate, 197
Appreciation factor, in business valuation,
    112
Arbitration, of franchise agreement, 253
Asking price, in investigation process,
    59
Assets:
  in agreement for sale of, 221–223
  cash value from, 143
  in closing of sale, 170
  described in contract, 174–175
  and potential business liabilities, 12
  and price determination, 100
  see also Agreement for sale of assets
Attorney General, 89
Attorneys:
  and closing, 169, 174, 185
  franchise, 89
  in negotiation process, 163–164
  role of, 181
  role in investigation process, 62
  selecting, 61
Auctioneers, 54
Audit, right of, in franchise agreement,
    241–242

265

Balance sheet, in investigation process,
     67–69
Bankruptcy:
  due to excess rent, 64
  statistics, 215
  trustees, 54
Bankruptcy code, Chapter 11 of, 16
Bakruptcy courts, 14
Banks:
  choosing among, 124–125
  loan proposal for, 122–124
  negotiating terms with, 125–127
  prime lending rate of, 117
  and purchase price, 118
  refusal of, 128–129
  selling points for, 207
Barron, Kenneth, 103
Better Business Bureau, 89
Bogey offer, 156–157
Book value, limitations of, 204
Borrowing:
  advantages of, 116–117
  from relatives, 215
  see also Financing
Brokers:
  abandonment of, 200–201
  business vs. real estate, 207
  checking, 44–45
  commissions of, 48
  dealing with, 45–47
  liability for commissions of, 208–209
  and negotiations, 159, 161, 162
  seller's viewpoint of, 47–49
  as source of cash, 141–142
  using, 43–44
Buildings, in franchise agreement, 242
Bulk Sales Act, 173, 202, 203
Bulk Transfers Act, 202
Business:
  determining value of, 197. See also
     Valuation
  qualifying, 58–60
  retail vs. service, 211–212
  testing, 74–75
Business appraiser, finding, 207
Business Development Corporation (BDC),
     130
Buyers:
  advertising of, 41–42
  competition measured by, 213
  and customer relations, 195

goals of, 169
and inventory valuation, 176
and myths about price, 97–100
negotiations of, 153
overcapitalized vs. undercapitalized, 6
perspective of, 95
between signing and closing, 183–184
Buyers/Business Profile, 20
Buying:
  advantages of, 33
  decision making about, 2–3
  reasons for, 16–17
  time for, 17–18
Buy-out option, in partnership, 146
Buy price, in negotiations, 157–158
Bye-bye price, in negotiations, 158

Canvassing, for leads, 39–42
Capital:
  and loan proposal, 122, 123
  requirements for, 4–5
  working, 209
  see also Down payment; Financing
Capital finders, 133
Capital gains tax, 169
Capitalization method, of pricing profits,
     108–110
Capitulation, 164
Cash, hidden assets for, 144. See also Down
     payment
Cash availability, in matching process, 20,
     30
Cash flow:
  and credit, 192–193
  and down payment, 143–144
  and leverage, 148
  and loan proposal, 122, 123
Casualty, in agreement for sale of assets,
     222
Chains, 77. See also Franchises
Character, and loan proposal, 122
Checklist, for analyzing product-oriented
     firm, 70–71
Choosing business, pitfalls of, 19–20. See
     also Matching process
Circular promotions, 211
Closing:
  in agreement for sale of assets, 228
  books and records on, 180–181
  casualty to business prior to, 179
  contract terms for, 174–182

and coping with last-minute problems,
    184–185
and customer relations, 195
existing contracts and leases and, 172
and financing, 172–173, 180
and goods orders, 212
inspection of equipment before, 205
and inventory, 205–206
lease in, 180
liability considerations in, 171
restrictions placed on seller prior to, 179
and sale of shares of stock, 170–171
selecting time for, 181–182
seller's obligation pending, 224
between signing and, 183–184
and size of deposit, 208
and transfer of assets, 170
Collateral:
  for finance companies, 132
  and loan proposal, 122, 123
  and retail vs. service business, 211
  and SBA, 129
  and seller financing, 121
Commission, broker's, 48
  liability for, 208–209
  see also Brokers
Commitment:
  need for, 6
  testing, 18
Comparison game, 98
Competition:
  determining impact of, 213
  protection from, 198
  of seller, 179
  see also Covenant not to compete
Concessional space, cash value from, 145
Consultant, selecting, 61
Contingency fund, 7
Contract:
  accounts receivable in, 175
  adjustments in, 176–177
  assets in, 174–175
  in closing of sale, 169
  conditions attached to, 180
  disputes and, 181
  "financing contingency" clause in,
    213–214
  franchise, 89–93
  inventory adjustments in, 176–177
  protection of seller in, 178
  purchase price in, 175–176

rights to name in, 211
seller's liabilities in, 177–178
seller's warranties in, 178
and size of deposit, 208
telephone numbers in, 214–215
Contract rights, transfer of, 180
Control:
  in franchise contract, 90–92
  in franchising, 79–80
Corporation:
  advantages of, 206
  sale of, 170
  Subchapter S, 206
Cost of goods, on Projected Income
    Statement, 105
Costs, and matching process, 30
Counter-offer, interpreting, 160–161
Covenant not to compete:
  in agreement for sale of assets, 225
  in stock sale/redemption agreement,
    233–234
Credit, and new management, 192–193
Credit rating:
  and closing of sale, 173
  determining, 209–210
Creditworthiness, in negotiations, 163
Customer lists, cash value of, 143
Customers:
  losing, 73
  and new management, 195

Death, in franchise contract, 91
Debt, as financing tool, 138
Debt/equity ratio, 146
Debt financing, and partnership, 145
Debt-ridden companies, acquiring, 138
Decision making:
  about buying, 2–3
  security in, 7–8
Default, in franchise agreement, 250–252
Demand, and value of business, 99
Deposit, size of, 208. See also Down
    payment
Depreciation, on Projected Income
    Statement, 107
Direct mail inquiry, in buyer's search,
    39–40
Disclosure statement, of franchisor, 84–86
Disposable fixtures, cash value of, 144
Disputes, over broker's commissions, 184
Do-or-die session, 164

Down payment:
  associated with franchises, 79
  cash from cash flow for, 143–144
  determining, 30
  leverage in, 147
  liabilities in, 138–140
  "low cash down," 149–150
  and negotiations, 158–159
  partner in, 145–146
  problems of, 135–136
  pyramiding seller loan for, 137–138
  raising, 5–6
  role of broker in, 141–142
  selling suppliers in, 140–141
  tapping inventory for, 142–143
  and value of business, 102
Dun and Bradstreet, 193, 210

Earnings, and matching process, 20–23
Earn-out, 199
Economy, of franchises, 79
Efficiency, of franchises, 79
Emotions, and negotiations, 165–166, 168
Employers, as sellers, 54
Employment contract, as condition of sale,
  200
Enjoyment, and matching process, 27–28
Enterpreneur, 51
Enthusiasm, 12–13
Equipment:
  book value of, 203
  in contract, 172
  in franchise agreement, 243
  seller's warranty for, 205
  title to, 212
Equity, and partnership, 146
Escape clause, for avoiding liability, 183
Escrow account:
  accounts receivable in, 199
  and seller's liabilities, 177
Evaluation, of franchises, 84–86
Expectations, testing of, 15–17
Expense, on income statement, 66
Experience:
  importance of, 9
  in matching process, 25

Failure rates, 215
Family affair, business as, 13–14
Fear-of-failure, problems of, 1–13
Federal Trade Commission, 84, 201

Fees, associated with franchises, 79, 92
Finance companies, 132–133
Financial pyramid, 150–151
Financial statements, reliance on, 209
Financing, 4–6
  and advantages of borrowing, 116
  bank, 122–129
  and brokers, 43–45
  building blocks for, 150–152
  and closing of sale, 170, 179
  creative, 30, 115
  down payment in, 5–6. See also Down
    payment
  in franchise contract, 91
  and franchising, 72
  in investigation process, 59
  key points of, 133
  and matching process, 29
  and negotiations, 157–158
  and partnership, 146
  SBA, 129–131
  seller, 117–121
  of service business, 212
  sources for, 132–133
  supplier, 133, 136
  two layers of, 115–116
  and value of business, 103
"Financing contingency" clause, 213–214
Firm, product-oriented, analyzing, 69–70
Fixtures:
  book value of, 204
  cash value of, 144
  in contract, 173
  title to, 212, 214
Franchise agreement:
  accounting procedures in, 241–242
  advertising in, 241
  alternate suppliers, 244
  arbitration and, 253
  building and premises in, 242
  conditions and limitations of assignment
    in, 246–249
  default in, 250–252
  equipment in, 243
  franchise grant in, 239–240
  "gross sales" in, 241
  health and fitness programs in, 243–244
  insurance indemnification in, 245
  miscellaneous in, 253–255
  no agency in, 250
  option at end of term in, 245–246

payment in, 238
preamble to, 237–238
premises in, 240
right to entry and inspection in, 244
royalties in, 240–241
sales promotion in, 241
signs in, 242–243
taxes in, 245
termination of, 250–252
trademarks, trade names, and trade
    secrets in, 249 250
training in, 240
vending machines in, 243
Franchisees, information from, 86–88
Franchises:
advantages of, 78–79
to be avoided, 93
checklist for, 94
and conditions of transfer, 201
disadvantages of, 79–80
evaluation of, 83
failure with, 80–81
how they work, 77–78
looking for, 52–53
return-on-investment view of, 83
selection of, 81–83
sources of information on, 89
success with, 81
termination of, 93–95
Franchising, 10
contract negotiations in, 89–93
and matching process, 29
Franchisor, information from, 84–86,
    87–88
Furniture:
book value of, 204
in contract, 174

Galahow, Eliot, 25
Geneen, Harold, 109
Goldstein, Arnold S., 13
Goods orders, and closing, 212
Good will:
assignment of telephone numbers under,
    215
and competition, 194
paying for, 33, 35
protection of, 119
in purchase price, 173
value of, 113
Government, doing business with, 73–74.

See also Small Business
    Administration
"Gross sales," in franchise agreement, 241

Hall, Prentice, 31
Harvard Business Review, 215
Health and fitness programs, 243–244
High-crime areas, business in, 208
Hobbies and outside interests, in matching
    process, 20
Housewives, and matching process, 25
How to Buy a Country Business
    (Kirkpatrick), 29
Human element, and value of business,
    103, 109

Inc., 52
Income:
gross rental, 194
and matching process, 20–23
Income statement, in investigation process,
    65–67
Indemnification:
and closing of sale, 169
seller, 176
Information, in investigation process,
    62–63
Insolvent companies, acquiring, 139
Institute of Certified Business Brokers, 108
Insurance:
in business acquisition, 205
in franchise agreement, 244–245
and inventory value, 206
and loan proposal, 123
on Projected Income Statement, 107
Interest payments, on borrowed funds, 116
Interest rates:
of finance companies, 131
negotiating, 126
seller's vs. bank's, 117
International Franchise Association, 89, 93
Internal Revenue code, Subchapter S
    corporation under, 206
Internal Revenue Service, and buyer's
    liability, 200
Inventory:
and closing, 205–206
in contract, 172
adjustments, 176–177
in down payment, 142–143
and seller financing, 120–121

Investigation process:
  asking price in, 59
  avoiding pitfalls in, 73–74
  and competition, 72–73
  financing in, 59
  income statement in, 65–67
  information in, 62–63
  lease in, 59
  object of, 57
  sales in, 58–59
  and team selection, 60–61

Jones, Don, 94
Journals, trade, 41

Kirkpatrick, Frank, 29

Lawsuits, involving franchisors, 83–86
Lawyers, insolvency, 54. *See also*
        Attorneys
Leads, looking for, 52–53
Leases:
  checking, 63–65
  in closing of sale, 172, 180
  evaluation of, 64
  in investigation process, 59
  last-minute problems with, 185
  requirements for, 201–202
  restrictions on, 211
  and right of first refusal, 202
Letter offer, 217
Leverage, 147, 148
Liabilities:
  as asset, 138
  avoiding, 182–183
  in closing of sale, 171
  potential business, 12
License, negotiating cost of, 205
License transfers, in contract, 180
Licensure, of business brokers, 207
Lilly Digest, 24
Liquidated damage clause, for avoiding
        liability, 182
Liquidation, and protection for seller, 121
Loanmanship, 5 Cs of, 122
Loans:
  bank, 125–127
  from broker, 141–142
  proposal for, 122–124
  SBA, 129–131
  structuring, 127

Location:
  in franchise contract, 90–91
  paying for, 35
  and seller financing, 121

Magic multiplier fallacy, 98–99
Management, and franchising, 78
Management, new, 187
  and credit, 192–193
  customers and, 195–196
  and employees, 189–191
  guidelines for, 194
  and new name, 188–189
  and suppliers, 191–192
Management mentality, measuring, 25–26
Marriage, and business acquisition, 13–14
Matching process, 19
  beginning, 20–23
  earning in, 23–25
  financing in, 30
  finding business, 31–32
  management mentality in, 25–27
  motivation in, 27–30
  starting from scratch, 32–35
  see also Search, buyer's
Minority Enterprise Small Business
        Investment Corporation (MESBIC),
        132
Money brokers, 133
Motivation:
  and matching process, 27–31
  sufficient, 5
  testing of, 15–17
Motor vehicles, excess, 145

Name:
  changing, 187–188
  right, 211
Negotiations:
  for bank loans, 125–127
  beginning of, 154
  for best buy, 153
  bluffing seller in, 162–163
  bogey offer in, 156–157
  bye-bye price in, 165–166
  ending of, 169
  first offer in, 158–159
  of franchising contract, 89–93
  and hold-out seller, 163
  importance of communication in, 166
  interpreting counter-offer in, 160–161

phantom offer in, 161–162
pointers for, 167–168
price in, 96–97
proposing offer in, 159–160
saving collapsed negotiations, 164–165
seller's ploys in, 155–156
setting limits for, 157–158
and three-for-one rule, 161
walk-away artist in, 167
Neighborhoods, declining, 74
Newsletters, trade, 42
Newspapers, advertising in, 49–52
New York Times, 53
Nicholas, Burt, 19
No agency, in franchise agreement, 250
Northeastern University study, 104–105

Offer:
conditions for, 158
letter, 217
phantom, 161–162
Offer forms, brokers', 159
OPM (other people's money), 147
Opportunity, hunting, 37
Owners Draw, on Projected Income
Statement, 106
Ownership:
vs. franchising, 10
and management, 25
nature of, 9
see also Real estate
*Own Your Own/The No Cash Down
Business Guide* (Goldstein), 31, 137

Paper clip net worth theory, 147–148
Parlow, Syd, 15
Partnership:
and agreement to sell, 203
and down payment, 145–146
and earnings, 24–25
and management, 27
nature of, 9–10
possibility of, 8
sale of, 170
Part-time business, 7–8
Patent rights, cash value of, 144–145
Patience, importance of, 168
Payroll, on Projected Income Statement,
106
Performance standard, and seller
financing, 121

Phantom offer, 161–162
Planning, for potential business liabilities,
12
Positioning, in negotiations, 165
Posturing, in negotiations, 165
Potential, estimating, 214
Price:
asking, 99–100
comparisons for determining, 98
considerations, 95–96
contingent on future profitability, 199
developing new perspective on, 100–101
in franchise contract, 90–91
and magic multiplier, 98–99
setting limits on, 157
vs. value, 96–97
see also Purchase price; Valuation,
business
Pricing, dual, 49
Procrastination, problem of, 17
Profits:
and franchising, 78
and growth factor, 112
on income statement, 66
and net worth, 199
potential vs. in motion, 113
projecting, 104–108
purchase price attached to, 210
putting price tag on, 108–110
and reality of figures, 110–111
Projected Income Statement, 104–106
Promotion:
in franchise contract, 91
of franchises, 79
Prospectus, of franchisor, 84
Purchase price:
in agreement for sale of assets, 223–224
allocation of, 223–224
in contract, 175–176
financing of, 118
paying, 176, 224
in stock sale/redemption agreement, 230

Questionnaire, in buyer's search, 40

Real estate:
determining value of, 197
lease requirements for, 201
ownership of, 197–198
Reality, looking at, 15
Receivers, court-appointed, 54

Records, in closing of sale, 180–181
Relatives, borrowing from, 215
Remodeling, need for, 208
Rent:
    and business valuation, 204
    on Projected Income Statement, 107
Retail business:
    and real estate ownership, 197, 198
    vs. service business, 211
Retirees, and matching process, 25
Return on investment method, of pricing
        profits, 108–110
Rice, James, 99
Right, of first refusal, 201
Risk:
    associated with franchising, 81
    and value of business, 102
Risk assessment, 211
Rosen, Marlene, 96
Royalties, associated with franchises, 77,
        240–241

Sales:
    free and clear, 224
    on income statement, 66
    in investigation process, 58
    on Projected Income Statement, 105
    rent as percentile of, 204
    and seller financing, 121
Sales forecasts, faulty, 74
Sales promotion, in franchise agreement,
        241
Search, buyer's, 32–33
    canvassing for leads, 39–42
    developing experienced eye, 37–38
    direct mail inquiry in, 39–40
    for franchise, 82
    importance of follow-up in, 43
    pointers for, 54–55
    and sources of information, 53
    and supplier's leads, 42
    telephoning in, 41–42
    see also Matching process
Securities and Exchange Commission, 87
Security, 6
    and small down payment, 148
    see also Collateral
Self-confidence, problems of, 8–11
Sellers:
    balance sheet of, 65–67
    bluffing of, 162–163

competition rights of, 179
and customer relations, 195
employers as, 52
financing with, 117–119
goals of, 168
hold-out, 161
information needed from, 60
and inventory valuation, 174
investigating, 167–168
liabilities of, 177–178
management ability of, 168
and myths about price, 99–100
perspective of, 95
ploys of, 155–156
profit and loss statement of, 104
restrictions placed on, 179
between signing and closing, 183–184
warranties of, 178
Selling, for "low cash down," 148–150
Service business, financing, 211–212
Shares of stock, in closing of sale, 170–171
Sick leave time, responsibility for, 210
Signs:
    in contract, 173
    in franchise agreement, 242–243
Silver, A. David, 132
Skills, management, 25–26
Small Business Administration (SBA):
    benefits offered by, 130
    limitations of, 129
    loan arrangements of, 130
    loan qualifications of, 130–131
    and purchase price, 118
Small Business Investment Corporation
        (SBIC), 132
Small Business Reporter, 23
Sole proprietorship:
    disadvantages of, 206
    sale of, 170
Solo ownership, 9
Starting business, see Management, new
Start-up, advantages of, 33–35
State taxes:
    continuing tax claim, 200
    waiver for buyer, 177–178
Stock sale/redemption agreement, 229
    adjustments in, 234
    covenant not to compete in, 233–234
    date for passing in, 235
    miscellaneous in, 234–235
    purchase price in, 230–232

INDEX

corporations in, 232
shares by seller in, 230
on as to seller's

Trade-offs, 5
Transfer, in franchise contract, 91
TRW Credit Service, 193, 210
Turnaround consultants, 54

Undercapitalization, 147, 209
Unemployment, and business acquisition, 16, 101, 103
Upfront Financing (Silver), 132
Utilities, on Projected Income Statement, 107

Vacation time, responsibility for, 210
Valuation, business:
  appreciation factor in, 112
  capitalization method of, 108–1...
  financial statements, 209
  will in, 113
  process ... 104
  projecting profi...
  questions to be a...
  reality of, 110–111

Supp...

Take-over period, customer ...
    during, 196
Taxes:
  and closing of sale, 173–174
  establishing cost "basis" for, 197
  in franchise agreement, 245
  state, 177, 200
Team approach, 10
Telephone numbers, assignment of,
    214–215
Termination, in franchise contract, 89, 252
Termination clause, in employment
    contract, 200
Testers, sellers as, 154
Theater, managing, 28
Three-for-one rule, applying, 161
Total scan, 38–39
Trademark:
  cash value of, 144–145
  and limitations of franchisee, 249
Trademark license agreement, 211
Trade name, 78

Valuation formula, in contract, 176
Value:
  factors controlling, 101–104
  perception of, 95
  vs. price, 96–97
Vending machines, in franchise agreement,
    242
Venture, 51
Venture capital, attracting, 132
Von Buskirk, Bill, 37

Walk-away artist, 167
Wall Street Journal, The, 51, 94
Working capital, need for, 209

Yerardi, Mike, 93

10

04

108
red in, 114

redemption by corporations in, 232
sale of corporate shares by seller in, 230
seller's representation as to seller's
    shares in, 230
warranties in, 233
"Straw transferee," 200
Subchapter S corporation, 206
Subletting, cash value from, 145
Suppliers:
    and down payment, 140
    financing by, 132
    franchising information from, 88
    information from, 86–88
    leads of, 42
    losing, 73
    and new management, 191–192
Supply, and value of business, 101

Take-over period, customer relations
    during, 196
Taxes:
    and closing of sale, 173–174
    establishing cost "basis" for, 197
    in franchise agreement, 245
    state, 177, 200
Team approach, 10
Telephone numbers, assignment of,
    214–215
Termination, in franchise contract, 89, 252
Termination clause, in employment
    contract, 200
Testers, sellers as, 154
Theater, managing, 28
Three-for-one rule, applying, 161
Total scan, 38–39
Trademark:
    cash value of, 144–145
    and limitations of franchisee, 249
Trademark license agreement, 211
Trade name, 78

Trade-offs, 5
Transfer, in franchise contract, 91
TRW Credit Service, 193, 210
Turnaround consultants, 54

Undercapitalization, 147, 209
Unemployment, and business acquisition,
    16, 101, 103
Upfront Financing (Silver), 132
Utilities, on Projected Income Statement,
    107

Vacation time, responsibility for, 210
Valuation, business:
    appreciation factor in, 112
    capitalization method of, 108–110
    and financial statements, 209
    good will in, 113
    myths about, 97–100
    limitation of book value, 204
    process of, 104
    projecting profits, 104–108
    questions to be answered in, 114
    reality of, 110–111
Valuation formula, in contract, 176
Value:
    factors controlling, 101–104
    perception of, 95
    vs. price, 96–97
Vending machines, in franchise agreement,
    242
Venture, 51
Venture capital, attracting, 132
Von Buskirk, Bill, 37

Walk-away artist, 167
Wall Street Journal, The, 51, 94
Working capital, need for, 209

Yerardi, Mike, 93

HD1393.25 .G64 198   GEN
Goldstein, Arnold S.
The complete guide to buying and selling   SCC
Wiley, c1983.
3 3666 00316 7573

Somerset County College LRC

3 3666 00316 7573

HD 1393.25 .G64 1983
Goldstein, Arnold S.
The complete guide to buying
   and selling a business /
   376

Raritan Valley Community College Library
Route 28 & Lamington Road
North Branch NJ 08876-1265